Art Inspired by Nature

Hilary Ansell

Acknowledgements

I would like to say a big 'Thank you' to all the staff and students at Woodlands Primary, Askern Moss Road Infants, Mallard Primary and Park School for their hard work and enthusiasm whilst working on the various projects. It was a joy working with you all.

Thank you to staff at Doncaster council for your co-operation over the 'Doncaster in Bloom' project and to the schools whose work features in this book.

Thank you also to the staff and service users at the Oaks Centre, all the children and adults in and around Rotherham who worked on the Dream Tree, the staff at the Sandall Wood Visitor Centre, my friends Gail and Wendy who showed such interest and enthusiasm for my projects, once again all my friends at St. John's Hospice for their unfailing support in everything that I do and, last but not least, my long-suffering husband who puts up with a lot! Thanks to you all.

'Lake Wall Hanging' (pages 29–31)

Published by Collins, An imprint of HarperCollins*Publishers*
77 – 85 Fulham Palace Road, Hammersmith, London, W6 8JB

Browse the complete Collins catalogue at
www.collinseducation.com

© HarperCollins*Publishers* Limited 2011
Previously published in 2008 by Folens as Environmental Art
First published in 2008 by Belair Publications

10 9 8 7 6 5 4 3 2 1

ISBN-13 978-0-00-743955-3

Hilary Ansell asserts her moral rights to be identified as the author of this work

All rights reserved. No part of this publication may be reproduced, stored in a retrieval system, or transmitted in any form or by any means, electronic, mechanical, photocopying, recording or otherwise, without the prior written permission of the Publisher or a licence permitting restricted copying in the United Kingdom issued by the Copyright Licensing Agency Ltd., 90 Tottenham Court Road, London W1T 4LP.

British Library Cataloguing in Publication Data
A Catalogue record for this publication is available from the British Library

Every effort has been made to trace copyright holders and to obtain their permission for the use of copyright material. The authors and publishers will gladly receive any information enabling them to rectify any error or omission in subsequent editions.

Commissioning Editor: Zoë Nichols   Editor: Daniel Bottom
Cover design: Mount Deluxe   Page layout: Barbara Linton
Photography: Hilary Ansell and Roger Brown; Page 6: Spring Grass – © Andy Goldsworthy, Leaf Stalk Room – © Jonty Wilde; Page 20: A La Ronde – © NTPL/Geoffrey Frosh; Page 24: Pebbles – © iStockphoto/Sandra Gasser; Page 33: Blossom – © iStockphoto; Page 36: Rousseau painting – © National Gallery, London, UK/The Bridgeman Art Gallery; Page 40: Barking up the Right Tree photos – © Sheffield Galleries and Museums Trust; Page 62: CowParade – with thanks to Jurrian van Hall and 'THE GALLERY' Donkersloot; Page 64: Gaudi Lizard – © iStockphoto/Carri Keill; Page 66: Entorn-Contorn – © DACS 2007

Printed and bound by Printing Express Limited, Hong Kong

Contents

Introduction   4

Using Found Materials
The Artist and the Environment   6
Working with Leaves   10
Funky Fungi   12
Gardens in Winter   14
Flotsam and Jetsam   16
Working with Shells   20
Pebbles   24

Inspired by the Environment
The Sea   26
Ponds and Lakes   28
Spring   32
Inspired by Flowers   34
A trip to the Garden Centre   36
The Rainforest   38

Recycle Recycle Recycle
Constructing with Everyday Objects   40
Fun with Plastic Bottles   44
Underwater World   46
Painting on Packaging Plastic   52
Beads and Buttons   54
Make It with Magazines   58
Cut It from Card   60

Art in a Public Place
Inspired by Holiday Photos   62
Your Town in Bloom   68
The Dream Tree   70

Introduction

In the seven years since the publication of my first book in the Belair series, *Art Inspired by Recycling*, the awareness of environmental issues has grown astronomically. Hardly a day goes by without one subject of environmental importance being reported in the press or discussed on radio or television. Globally, people are now more aware of the necessity of conserving world resources and the need to look after the environment. This book looks at the environment as a starting point for artwork in a primary school and, by doing so, hopes to stimulate children's interest in their local environment and promote recycling and a general awareness of environmental issues.

On a recent weekend break to Amsterdam, I was delighted to see that it's not only humans that have started to recycle; the local bird life had also joined in! The enterprising coot shown opposite had put to good use some of the city's litter that, unfortunately, had not been recycled elsewhere.

Collecting Materials

The book starts by looking at artwork that can be created from naturally found objects, be it twigs and fallen leaves in autumn or pebbles and driftwood gathered from the beach in summer. Whether living in the country, a town or a city, it is still possible to collect leaves, seeds, twigs, pebbles, grass and other natural materials with which to work. When gathering natural materials, health and safety issues must be observed. Children must be told clearly what to gather and what not to gather. Clear plastic sandwich bags are very useful as collecting bags. They fit easily into most pockets and also restrict the amount that can be collected.

Apart from the section working with found objects, most of the artwork in the book uses recycled materials wherever possible. Most of my friends and family now have great difficulty in throwing anything away! They have started to look at mundane everyday objects in a new light. If they can't find an original use for them they are quite sure that I can! This can become a problem. Storage space is often limited in school and forward planning, especially when starting large-scale projects such as the 'Underwater World' (see page 46), is essential. Send letters to parents listing the things to be collected, stressing that all containers should be thoroughly washed before being sent to school. Have plastic crates or large cartons ready to sort the things into. This can be done by older children at breaks or lunchtime.

Once parents know the theme of the work in hand, it is often surprising what they are able to bring in either for the school to keep or to borrow, and a sense of co-ownership can build up between parents and children.

This feeling of community can be fostered even more by taking projects out to different community groups. The project 'The Dream Tree' (see page 70) is an example of this. Are there parents in your school who have contacts with care homes, youth clubs or church groups and so on? If so, why not make links with these groups and work out a project together.

Using Photographs

Sometimes it is not possible to take the children out as a class into the environment but it is possible to stimulate their imaginations by showing them photographs taken in the local environment. For instance, close-up photographs of plants taken at the local garden centre could be used as a starting point for work about rainforests and jungles. Photographs of trays of fruit and vegetables in the local market could stimulate work on colour and pattern. Use the photographs in the book to generate conversations about shape, line, colour, pattern and texture.

Looking to the wider environment, encourage the children to make a note of interesting public sculptures and architecture in their home towns and cities or when on holiday. Encourage them to bring back postcards and photographs of interesting public art that they have seen. These could be used as starting points for large-scale work in school. Forge links with the local council departments such as Neighbourhood and Community Services and see if there are any local projects that the school could become involved with. The ideas in this book are merely starting points. They are there to be adapted to your needs and situation. Some ideas are presented as whole-school projects but could easily be scaled down for classroom use or small-group activities. On the other hand, some of the individual or small-group activities could be developed into large-scale work. Everything is open to adaptation.

Enjoy!

Hilary Ansell

Using Found Materials

The Artist and the Environment

The Yorkshire Sculpture Park, established in 1977, has developed during the last 30 years into a leading international centre for modern and contemporary art. Andy Goldsworthy (1956–present), one of Britain's leading contemporary artists, returned to the park in 2007 to celebrate its anniversary. He first worked at the park in 1983 and then again in 1987, when he was the park's artist in residence. During that period, working closely with the seasons, he used the natural materials found in the park to explore themes such as holes, cracks, lines and pathways. In winter he used evergreen leaves, ice and snow to explore his ideas; in spring he used flowers and grasses; in summer he used strong green leaves as construction material and in autumn the many coloured leaves became his palette.

Spring Grass, by Andy Goldsworthy (1956–present), Yorkshire Sculpture Park © Andy Goldsworthy

In order to mark the Yorkshire Sculpture Park's 30th anniversary, he created three specially commissioned permanent outdoor works. Both outdoor and indoor works explore themes that have fascinated Goldsworthy throughout his artistic career; themes such as holes, lines, pathways and journeying. His work provides a good starting point for the creation of artwork in the outside environment.

Leaf Stalk Room, by Andy Goldsworthy (1956–present), Yorkshire Sculpture Park © Jonty Wilde

Using Found Materials

Sculptures from Found Materials

The following work was created by children at the Yorkshire Sculpture Park after seeing the Goldsworthy exhibition but the same activities can be re-created in any open woodland or park land that offers an abundance of natural materials. Obviously, autumn would be a very good time to carry out these activities because of the many coloured leaves and seeds to be found on the woodland floor. **Always warn children about the dangers of poisonous berries and plants. Insist that they keep an adult in view at all times.** The activities could also be carried out in the school grounds if you have a field surrounded by trees or hedges.

Resources

- Leaves and twigs
- Lengths of larger branches
- Stones
- Cards with words relating to Goldsworthy's work – for example, pathway, journey, flowing, permanent, temporary, crack, fissure, high, low

Approach

1. Show the children pictures of Goldsworthy's work, such as pieces from the Yorkshire Sculpture Park (shown on the opposite page). For more ideas, use the Internet for research. www.ysp.co.uk shows examples of Goldsworthy's work. Explain to the children how Goldsworthy is fascinated by human interaction with the environment, the difference between farmed and natural landscape and how humans have shaped, and continue to shape, our environment.

2. In the outside area, show the children the words on the cards and ask them to explain what they think each word means. Divide the children into small groups, let each group choose a word and then encourage them to express this word in the manner of Goldsworthy, using the materials provided.

3. Some groups will be focussed but others will need a lot of support as some of the concepts are very difficult.

4. Discuss the fact that an artwork made of leaves is very temporary, as it will soon blow away in the wind. One made of wood is more permanent but will eventually rot away given sufficient time. A stone construction is permanent – until someone knocks it down!

Paving Slab Patterns

This small-scale activity is ideal for schools without access to a park or woodland. A paved path would be an ideal venue, as the children could each be given their own slab on which to work.

Resources
- Leaves of as many shapes and sizes as possible
- Twigs, stones, pebbles and gravel
- Dead grass and plant heads from the school grounds

Approach

1. Ask the children what they understand by the word 'pattern'. Talk about lines, shapes and repeated patterns. Discuss the various materials available and how they might be used.

2. Restricting them to the designated area, ask the children to make patterns with their collections.

Woodland Floor Pictures

This is a simple, enjoyable activity for children of all ages. The pictures they make are entirely dependent upon materials they find as they explore an area of woodland.

Resources
- Twigs, stones, pebbles, leaves, ferns and gravel
- Lengths of rope or a clothes line
- Photographs of woodland creatures, birds and insects

Approach

1. Ask the children to list the creatures they might expect to find in an area of woodland. You could use photographs of woodland creatures to stimulate the discussion.

2. Divide the children into threes or fours and ask them to choose the creature they are going to create with the materials they find. Ask them to be thinking about the materials they are going to use as they are walking through the woodland. If they see anything particularly interesting they might like to take it with them.

3. Give each group a length of rope to mark out their plot. Let them scavenge around the area looking for suitable materials. At this point they may be inspired to make something entirely different because of something they have found.

4. Some groups will start to build their creature straight away, while others will find it easier if it is drawn out on the floor with a stick. They could outline shapes with small stones to start with and use other materials they find to fill in the detail.

Using Found Materials

Lines and Holes

Two recurring themes in Goldsworthy's works are holes and lines. The lines might take the form of cracks and fissures, scrapings on the woodland floor or twisting pathways through the countryside. The holes might be dark and mysterious or light and airy as shown in his work the 'Leaf Stalk Room' (page 6).

Approach

1. Show the children the images from **'Parkland'**, the Yorkshire Sculpture Park catalogue of the 1987 exhibition, which is still in print (reprinted by Yorkshire Sculpture Park in 2007, ISBN: 1-871480-58-2). Discuss how Goldsworthy created holes and lines.
2. Divide the children into groups. Ask them to choose either the word 'hole' or 'line' as a starting point and express this in some form of pattern using the materials on the woodland floor.
3. The photographs show some ideas that one group created.

Resources
- Any materials from the woodland floor

Stone Circles

This started from a circular scraping on the floor. One child put a stone in the circle, another ringed this with small stones, and the idea was born. Concentric stone circles were then added.

Line Pattern

A linear scraping was used as the starting point for this pattern. Note the repeated pattern of twig, large stone and then small stone around the edge of the scraping. Along the centre of the scraping, the pattern is a large green leaf followed by a small yellow leaf. Someone said that the pattern looked like a caterpillar!

Large Flower

It was interesting to watch the development of this design. It started quite simply around a scraped ring on the floor. The group decided to outline the ring with twigs in order to define it. Then someone started to lay out a circle of stones on the inside of the scraping. Suddenly someone else shouted that they had found a hole! This turned out to be a lump of concrete with a circular hole in the middle. It had obviously been used to secure a post in the ground at some time. Now it was half buried in leaves under a tree. It was decided to set the 'hole' in the centre of the stone circle. At this point one child had an overview of the whole pattern and arrived with a long piece of tree branch, set it in place and announced that the whole thing was a flower!

Lightning Strike

The group responsible for this design took the idea of a line, turned it into a zigzag and came up with a bolt of lightning streaking to earth, which they then marked out in twigs.

Working with Leaves

Obviously, the best time of year to work with leaves is autumn but, with a little planning, the following activities may be carried out in any season. The easiest way to preserve leaves is by pressing them. This can be accomplished quite simply by placing the leaves between sheets of absorbent kitchen paper and placing the sheets between heavy books. However, flower presses are not difficult to make and the children could make their own.

Make a Flower Press

Approach

1. Thread the four bolts up through the base piece of plywood.
2. Cut pieces of carton card slightly smaller than the piece of plywood and then cut the corners off the cards so that they fit between the bolts.
3. Cut sheets of kitchen paper to the same size as the pieces of card.
4. Place a piece of card on the plywood base, followed by two sheets of kitchen paper, followed by a sheet of card. Continue in this way until almost at the top of the bolt, before slipping on the top piece of plywood and the wing nuts.

Resources

- Two rectangles of plywood cut to size, with holes drilled at each corner
- Four bolts and wing nuts
- Carton card
- Kitchen paper

Leaf Window Screen

Approach

1. Cut pieces of tissue to fit inside the clear cellophane bags.
2. Using a smear from a glue stick, attach leaves to the tissue pieces and slip each one inside a cellophane bag.
3. When enough bags have been prepared, join them together with the clear adhesive tape, making sure that all bags are sealed and that the leaves cannot drop out.
4. Tape the panel to a window or suspend it from a garden cane.

Resources

- A selection of pressed leaves
- Clear cellophane wrappers used to protect greeting cards
- Clear adhesive tape
- Coloured tissue paper
- Glue sticks

Using Found Materials

Window Pendants

Approach

1. Draw a circle on a piece of paper (making sure that the leaf will fit inside the circle). This should be used as a template to draw a circle in outliner paste on a piece of clear packaging plastic.
2. Outline another circle about 1cm outside the first and divide the border into sections.
3. When the outliner paste is dry, cut out the circle. Next, cut out another circle of plastic the same size as the first.
4. Stick small pieces of double-sided tape around the edge of one of the circles and sandwich the leaf between the two.

Resources
- Pressed leaves
- Clear packaging plastic
- Glass outliner paste
- Double-sided adhesive tape
- White paper

Skeleton Leaf Cards

Although in winter you may be lucky enough to find skeleton leaves, it is possible to make your own skeleton leaves at any time of the year.

Approach

1. Put a cupful of washing detergent into a pan of water and add the leaves.
2. Bring the pan to the boil and let it simmer for about 20 to 30 minutes.
3. Next, rinse the leaves in cold water and then carefully brush away the soft tissue to reveal the filigree leaf shapes.
4. The leaves should be placed in a flower press between sheets of absorbent paper and left to dry.
5. Fold the card to A5 size. Cut an aperture in the front of the card large enough to display the leaf.
6. Cut a piece of packaging plastic slightly larger than the aperture and fix it to the underside of the card with double-sided tape.
7. Then cut another piece of clear plastic the same size as the first. After positioning the leaf centrally on it using double-sided tape, fix this piece of plastic behind the first.
8. Draw a border around the aperture using a felt-tipped pen.
9. Finally, fold a sheet of A4 paper and glue it into the card.

Resources
- A large pan
- Leaves
- Washing detergent
- A soft toothbrush
- Kitchen paper
- A sheet of A4 card and matching A4 paper
- Clear packaging plastic
- Fine felt-tipped pens
- Double-sided adhesive tape

Variations
- Instead of cutting an aperture in the front of the card, simply glue the leaf to the front of the card and draw a border in felt-tipped pen.
- Handmade paper could be made from scrap paper and then used to create a border for the card.

Funky Fungi

A walk around gardens, parks and woods in autumn will reveal a wealth of interesting forms of fungi. From the poisonous fly agaric and bracket fungus, to the common field mushroom, all can be used as starting points for 2-D and 3-D artwork.

DO NOT ATTEMPT TO PICK ANY WILD FUNGI BUT RECORD THEIR SHAPES BY DRAWING THEM OR TAKING PHOTOGRAPHS.

If it is not possible to take the children out to look at these forms in the wild, show them photographs, magazine pictures and colourful wall charts. Ask the children to see how many types of mushroom they can find in the supermarket. Bring edible mushrooms into the classroom and let the children draw and paint them – both as whole mushrooms and as cross sections.

Using Found Materials

Ceramic Toadstools

Approach

1. Firstly, produce detailed drawings of a fungus using photographs such as the ones opposite for further inspiration as to form and colour.
2. Roll a palm-sized amount of clay into a ball.
3. Form a thumb pot by pushing a thumb into the centre of the ball and gently squeezing the clay between thumb and fingers. Turn the ball of clay after each squeeze and gradually work around the pot, squeezing and shaping.
4. With frequent reference to the original drawing or photograph, the pot should be formed to look like the top of the fungus.
5. Roll a smaller amount of clay into a long sausage shape to form the stalk of the fungus. Remind the children that the stalk has to be long enough to push into the soil.
6. Next the toadstools need to be fired and glazed.
7. The stalks should be pushed into the soil and the tops balanced on the stalks.
8. Indoor toadstools for plant pots may be made with self-hardening clay and painted with acrylic paints.

Resources
- Clay
- Clay boards
- Glazes
- Access to kiln

Furry Fungi

This is a fun way of introducing knitting to children. Any mistakes in the knitting add to the overall effect of the toadstools.

Approach

1. Measure the length of the card tube and with a smooth yarn, cast on sufficient stitches to produce a piece of knitting that will wrap around the tube. This may be worked in garter stitch or stocking stitch.
2. For the top of the toadstool, measure the circumference of the card disc and cast on sufficient stitches to produce a piece of knitting the same width. Experiment with different types of yarn to give a variety of textures. When the knitting is long enough, break off the wool, leaving a long end. Thread the long end of wool through a large-eyed needle and, one by one, transfer all the stitches from the knitting needle onto the length of wool. Pull the wool to gather up all the stitches, thus forming a circle with the knitting. Fasten off securely in the centre and sew up the two short edges, then repeat this for the underside of the toadstool top.
3. Sew the two circles of knitting together around the edges, slipping in the card disc when you have sewn halfway around. Before closing up the circle entirely, push a small amount of toy filler into the top half of the toadstool. Sew up the gap and then secure it.
4. Sew the top of the toadstool to the covered stalk and then glue the finished toadstool to a felt-covered card base to stop it falling over.

Resources
- Oddments of smooth and bobbly yarn
- A range of knitting needles
- Small pieces of cardboard tube for the stalks
- Wool needles
- Tape measures
- Discs cut from card to keep the tops in shape
- Toy filler
- Glue
- Felt
- Card

13

Gardens in Winter

If we are lucky enough to have snow or a heavy frost, parks and gardens are inspirational in winter, especially if they haven't been tidied too carefully in the autumn. The shapes of plants and trees stand out against the white background and present a starting point for design. The dead heads of the plants themselves can be collected and used to create wintry panels.

Take photographs of your own garden (if you have one) and those of neighbours. Concentrate on the different shapes and lines. If you have time, go to a local park and take photographs there. Use the photographs as inspiration for winter paintings.

Using Found Materials

Plaster Panels

These plaster panels were inspired by the photographs on the opposite page. In the photographs you can see the dead, snow-covered seed heads sticking out of the deep snow in the garden.

Approach

1. Lightly paint the grasses and seed heads to give the effect of snow.
2. Trim the grass stalks and seed heads and then practise arranging them.
3. Make up the casting plaster according to the manufacturer's instructions and pour it into the shallow trays.
4. Press the grasses and seed heads into the plaster.
5. If the plaster doesn't dry perfectly white, paint the lower half of the panel with white paint.

Resources

- A selection of grasses, sedges and seed heads
- Casting plaster
- Shallow card lids or trays
- A bucket and water
- White acrylic paint or household emulsion

Winter Garden Collage

The wintry scenes captured in the photographs on the opposite page inspired this piece of work.

Approach

1. Paint a wintry sky across the top half of the canvas or card.
2. Spread PVA glue across the bottom half and cover it with perlite.
3. Glue perlite granules to a twig that branches out and use it as a small tree. If available, glue a small model animal to the twig.
4. Complete the scene using sprigs of evergreens as bushes.

Resources

- A large piece of carton card or cheap art canvas
- Twigs and sprigs of evergreen
- Perlite (available from garden suppliers)
- PVA glue
- Paints
- A miniature model animal

Flotsam and Jetsam

Flotsam and jetsam; or beach treasures? One of the most enjoyable aspects of working with found materials is actually collecting them in the first place and what could be more enjoyable or inspiring than a walk along the beach looking at the many different things the tide has washed in. Always carry a camera and take photographs of the larger inspiring things that cannot be taken home. The colours of these tangled nets in the sunshine are quite inspirational and could be the starting point for a piece of embroidery or a painting. Pieces of plastic and bits of metal become worn by the sea until they take on the appearance of natural objects. Compare the scrap of pitted tin in the work opposite to the inside of the mussel shell, and the worn grey piece of plastic to the stone next to it.

Using Found Materials

Display Board

Approach

1. Paint the background randomly in sea and beach colours. While the paint is still wet, sprinkle it with sand and leave it to dry before tapping off the surplus sand.
2. Arrange the beach treasures carefully on the board and then glue them in position with PVA glue.

Resources

- A selection of small objects found on the beach such as driftwood, plastic, coloured net, seaweed, empty crab shells, stones, rope, sea-worn china, polystyrene float – the list is endless
- Strong carton card or cheap artist's canvas
- Acrylic paints or school paints mixed with some PVA glue
- Sand

Beach Scenes

The children will find it fun to try and recreate beach scenes with their collections of flotsam and jetsam, shells, pebbles and driftwood. Make sure that there are plenty of photographs of the day the children collected the materials, to jog the memory. Was the beach sandy or pebbly? Was the sea calm or were the waves crashing against the rocks? Was the sky grey or was it a beautiful sunny day? Encourage the children to relive the experience.

Resources
- Strong carton card
- Paints
- Sand, pebbles, stones, shells, driftwood, seaweed, bits of net and other small objects from the beach

Approach

1. Before starting the beach collage, make pencil drawings of the objects collected from the beach. Let the children arrange their own collections into pleasing still-life subjects.

2. Refer to the photographs taken on the day and paint in the sea and sky accordingly. Then spread the lower part of the card with glue and sprinkle this liberally with sand. After leaving it to dry, tap off any excess sand.

3. Create a beach scene using the found objects. Consider the scale of the objects and try not to use anything too large. A very large crab claw would look out of place next to a small piece of driftwood that was supposed to be a washed up tree trunk!

Pebble and Driftwood Sculptures

Little pieces of bent, sea-washed driftwood are quite beautiful and make simple sculptures on their own without doing anything to them. It is simply a question of chancing upon the right shape. An easy way of displaying small pieces of driftwood is to push them into holes in beach stones.

Resources
- Large pebbles with holes
- Small pieces of interesting driftwood
- PVA glue
- Clear acrylic spray

Approach

1. Simply glue the driftwood into the holes in the stones.

2. Spray the sculpture with clear acrylic for a shiny finish, if desired.

Using Found Materials

Driftwood Trees

Approach

1. Discuss the fact that small pieces of driftwood were possibly once part of a great tree. Talk about using them to recreate a picture of that tree.
2. Paint a simple background of sky and the ground.
3. When the background is dry, arrange the pieces of driftwood into a tree shape and glue them down.
4. Glue stones below the tree and along the bottom edge of the picture so that it looks as if the tree is growing out of them.

Resources

- Strong carton card
- Paints
- PVA glue
- Small pieces of driftwood and beach stones

Driftwood Display

This activity is not as simple as it would first appear. Without consciously thinking about it, the children have to make comparisons of size and shape and assess what would fit where in the tray. They will probably need quite a few tries before a satisfactory arrangement is achieved.

Approach

1. Paint the base and sides of the lid with dark paint and then leave it to dry.
2. Arrange the wood in the lid to make vertical and horizontal patterns with the pieces. When satisfied with the arrangement, glue everything down carefully.
3. Fill in any awkward spaces with pebbles or shells.

Resources

- A strong, shallow, card lid
- PVA glue
- Black or dark brown paint
- A collection of driftwood, a few pebbles, stones and shells

19

Working with Shells

Shell work became very popular in the 18th and 19th centuries when it was taken up as a leisure pursuit by the genteel ladies of the time. It became fashionable to have intricate shell displays in the drawing room. Some form of shell grotto or folly was often to be found in the grounds of the large country houses. A fine example of shell work can be seen at 'A La Ronde', Exmouth, the unique house designed by the cousins Jane and Mary Parminter in the late 18th century.

The interest in shell work continued through the Victorian era into the 20th century but then began to wane, only to be taken up again in the 70s when craftwork once again became popular. Shell-covered mirror and photograph frames remain popular to this day and shell kits can be purchased from craft suppliers.

A La Ronde © NTPL/Geoffrey Frosh

Sourcing Shells

A mass collection of shells should be discouraged but if the children each bring a few shells back from their excursions to the seaside during the holidays, a varied collection can soon be gathered. It should be pointed out that it is illegal to collect shells on some foreign beaches and some countries will impose heavy fines on anyone trying to take shells through customs.

It is possible to source shells without even going to the beach. Try asking local restaurants to save you their oyster, scallop and mussel shells. Clean them thoroughly in a strong solution of washing-up liquid. Look in charity shops and at car boot sales for shell necklaces that can be taken apart. Add variety to your collection with nets of shells bought from 'pound shops'. These should carry labels saying that they are ecologically sourced.

Using Found Materials

Shell Pictures

Approach

Fish

1. Paint the carton card in sea colours.
2. While this dries, draw a simple fish outline on paper and cut it out.
3. Draw around this template on the painted background.
4. Spread a thick coat of PVA glue over the tail area and arrange some razor shells in a fan shape. Add other razor shells on top of these to fill in any gaps.
5. Working from the tail towards the head, glue down row after row of mussel shells, starting with rows of smaller shells and gradually increasing in size.
6. Fill in the head area with small shells such as tellin valves or small cockles. Use a winkle for the eye.

Shell Woman

1. Paint the sky and sea and then spread PVA glue on the bottom part of the picture. Sprinkle this with sand and leave it to dry.
2. Glue down a large scallop shell for the skirt, a cockle shell for the upper part of the body, razor shells for the arms and legs and perhaps large tellin valves for the head and hat. Bits of broken shell could be used for the feet.

Flowers

1. Cover the carton card with fabric.
2. Practise making different sorts of flower heads on a table before attempting to glue anything down. Limpets make good flower middles. The other shells should fit snugly around them. The shells used for the flower heads shown here were mussels, slipper limpets and tellin valves. Razor shells were used for the stalks and leaves.

Resources

- Rectangles of strong, carton card
- Paints
- PVA glue
- Sand
- Green Hessian or similar fabric
- An assortment of shells

Shell Jewellery

If you are lucky enough to find shells with holes, either on the beach or pre-drilled shells from old necklaces, you can begin to make your own jewellery.

Limpet Shell Necklace

Approach

1. Gather about 20 limpet shell rings of different sizes.
2. Make jump rings by winding a length of craft wire along the length of a smooth-sided pencil. Then slip the coil off the pencil and snip each ring using the wire cutters.
3. The jump rings can then be used to join the limpet rings into a chain. Make sure the wire rings are firmly closed.
4. Thread cord onto the end shells to tie the necklace up.

Shell and Pearl Pendants

Approach

The pendants above were made from pieces of worn saddle oyster.

1. Thread a pearl bead onto a length of silver-coloured craft wire and twist the two ends of wire at the top of the bead so that the bead won't fall off.
2. Pass the wire through the hole in the shell and twist the ends to create a loop. The shell will hang from the bead but putting a dab of glue behind the bead should secure the shell. Then thread a length of cord through the wire loop.

Resources

- Limpet shells and worn saddle oyster shells with holes
- Thin craft wire
- An old pearl bead necklace
- A jewellery cord
- Wire cutters
- PVA glue

Limpet Ladies

Approach

1. Starting with the larger limpets and gradually using smaller ones, stack up about 12 shells, putting a dab of glue on the crown of each one.
2. For the body, glue a large wooden bead to the top of the stack of shells. Glue a smaller bead into another limpet shell to be used later for the head and hat. Leave it to dry.
3. Then glue the dry head with a hat to the body bead.
4. Glue on a length of pipe cleaner for the arms.
5. Glue a short length of pipe cleaner into an upturned shell to create a basket.
6. Make the limpet-children in the same way as the ladies, but use fewer limpets for the skirt and a smaller bead for the body.

Resources

- Limpets of various sizes
- Large wooden beads
- Pipe cleaners
- PVA glue

Using Found Materials

Desk Tidy

Approach

1. Cut a circle from the card large enough to support the cockleshells, probably about eight to ten centimetres in diameter.
2. Glue four of the upturned shells onto the card and cover any exposed card with the small shells.
3. Glue the remaining cockleshell in the centre, on top of the other four shells.

Resources
- Five large cockleshells
- A small piece of strong carton card
- A few small shells
- PVA glue

Shell Storage Box

Resources
- Shells of all shapes and sizes
- A washing tab box with a hinged lid
- Plain fabrics
- Braid
- PVA glue

Approach

1. Completely cover the box (inside and out) with the fabric, making sure that the lid will open and close.
2. Glue braid around the bottom edge of the box.
3. Completely cover the sides and top of the box lid with shells. You will have to glue one side at a time and leave it to dry overnight before going on to the next side.
4. Glue a flower motif on the front of the box. Use the treasure box to store your favourite shells!

Shell Display Box

Approach

1. Tape the lid of the cereal box down so that it is closed.
2. Measure the depth of the box, then draw a margin the same size all the way around the front of the box.
3. Carefully cut out the centre rectangle. Cut diagonally from the corners of the margin to the outside corners of the box. Fold these flaps back against the sides of the box to reinforce it. Glue them down securely.
4. Cut out some shelves from the carton card and glue them into position. Cut smaller pieces of card to slot between the shelves in order to create individual display boxes.
5. Paint the box in a suitable colour and leave it to dry. Display your favourite shells in the box.

Resources
- A cereal box
- Scraps of strong carton card
- PVA glue
- Paints

Pebbles

There is something about pebbles; the round shape, smoothness and the way that they sit comfortably in the hand. Most children love pebbles, whether it's to send them skimming across water, to put them in a jar with water in order to bring out their colours or to simply carry them around in a pocket and look at them occasionally. Handling smooth, round pebbles is a pleasure, so creating pictures and patterns with them should prove a very satisfying activity.

Pebble Pictures

The pictures above were created using white beach pebbles but any pebbles could be used. Bags of pebbles may be bought quite cheaply from local garden suppliers.

© iStockphoto/Sandra Gasser

Resources

- Rectangles of strong carton card
- Plain Hessians or furnishing fabrics in colours which contrast well with the pebbles
- Adhesive tape
- PVA glue
- Pebbles of assorted shapes and sizes

Approach

1. Cover the rectangle of card with fabric.
2. Arrange and rearrange the pebbles until a satisfactory result is obtained.
3. Carefully glue the pebbles onto the background using PVA glue. Leave it overnight before standing the picture upright.

Using Found Materials

Pebble Mosaics

These panels were inspired by cobbled patterns in public parks and garden centres and were made with garden pebbles and a few white beach pebbles. Look at the children's pebble patterns in the photograph below or find your own examples from magazines to inspire the children. Better still, take photographs of pebbles in the local area.

Resources
- Shallow card lids or trays
- Assorted pebbles
- Sand
- PVA glue

Approach

1. Cut a piece of paper the same size as the base of the tray and arrange the pattern on this.
2. Pour PVA glue into the tray and spread it across the entire base.
3. Carefully transfer the pebbles into the tray until the pattern is complete.
4. Sprinkle sand over the PVA that is still visible. It doesn't matter if you cover the pebbles as the excess sand can be blown away when everything is dry. It may take a few days for the panel to dry completely.

Pebble Jewellery

Approach

1. Show the children examples of the black and white patterns that were popular in the 1960s.
2. Choose a pebble and design a pattern for it. Draw the pattern on the pebble using black marker pen.
3. Thread a length of cord or ribbon through the hole. Jewellery fasteners could be fixed to the cord ends or it could simply be tied at the back of the neck.

Resources
- Small white beach pebbles with holes
- Black ribbon, thin cord or shoe laces
- Black marker pens

25

Inspired by the Environment

The Sea

Ask children to paint a picture of the sea and they will probably paint it using one shade of blue – but it is not like that. Ask the children about their experiences of the sea. Have they seen it in the winter with the waves crashing onto the shore, grey in the driving rain or sparkling and dancing in the summer sun? Provide photographs of the sea in all its moods for the children to look at. Ask them to identify the colours that they can see. Try colour mixing exercises to see how many shades of blue, turquoise or grey they can make.

Seascape with Found Objects

This project may be adapted to suit any sized group as the pieces are worked individually and sewn together afterwards. Alternatively, the individual pieces may be displayed separately and the long strips of stick weaving, French knitting and pompoms omitted.

Approach

Making the Loom and Warping

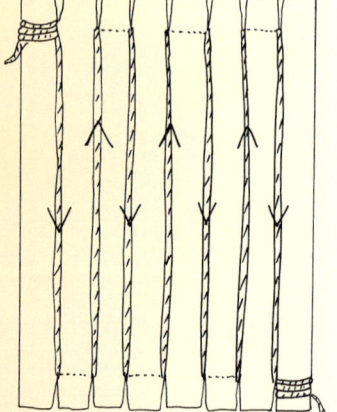

1. To make a card loom, cut the carton card to the required size, allowing an extra two centimetres on the width and length.
2. Mark the top and bottom edges of the card at one centimetre intervals.
3. Cut slits in the card at these marks to a depth of one centimetre.
4. Attach the warp thread to the card loom by winding it around the first 'tooth' several times. Then bring the wool to the front of the card through the first slit.
5. Take it down to the bottom of the card, through the first slit, behind the 'tooth' and out through the second slit.
6. Now take the wool up to the top of the card and into the second slit, behind the 'tooth' and out through the third slit.
7. Continue in this way until the loom is warped.
8. Finish by winding the wool several times around the last 'tooth'.

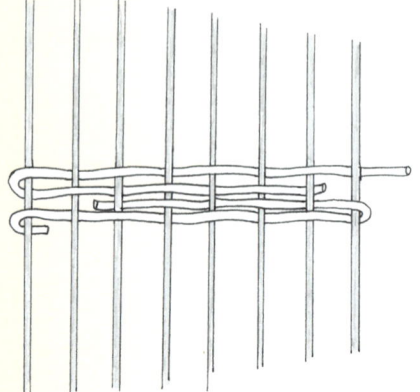

Resources

- Carton card
- Wools and yarns in sea and pebble colours
- Shells
- Small pieces of driftwood
- Net vegetable bags
- Scraps of sacking or Hessian
- Scraps of white nylon or chiffon fabric
- Oddments of thick string and binder twine
- Large-eyed needles
- A long length of dowel
- French knitting bobbins
- Weaving sticks

Inspired by the Environment

Weaving

1. Weave several rows in one colour before changing to the next shade.
2. Always join new lengths of wool at a point near the middle of the line of weaving – never at the end of a row. Joining at the end makes the edges weak and untidy. Push the end of the used wool to the back of the work, count back three or four warp threads and join the new length at this point, repeating the under/over pattern of the previous row. Once past the join, the pattern will be correct.
3. Take care not to pull the wool tightly at the edges of the work or the weaving will start to narrow and get a 'waist'. Always leave a little loop at the edge so that the wool is not pulling against the last warp thread.
4. As the work progresses, weave in strips of orange and green vegetable bags to represent the washed-up nets on the beach.
5. Weave in thin pieces of driftwood and lengths of string.
6. Strips of white nylon or chiffon fabric can be woven through and pulled up slightly to represent white-topped waves.
7. Shells with holes can be threaded onto the wool as you weave or can be sewn on afterwards.  
8. Pebbles can be attached in little net bags.

Making up

1. When the weavings are complete, slip them off the card by bending the 'teeth' forwards and slipping the wool from behind.
2. Ease each weaving out a little to fill the loops at the top and the bottom.
3. Sew the weavings together in long strips.
4. Make lengths of French knitting and stick weaving (see page 28) to hang in between the long strips of weaving.
5. For added texture, make pompoms and sew them onto the ends of the French knitting and lengths of stick weaving.
6. Fold the ends of the lengths of sea weaving over and sew to create slots for the length of dowel.
7. Slip the lengths of weaving onto the dowel and tie the French knitting and stick weaving onto the dowel between the weavings.

27

Ponds and Lakes

The local ornamental lake or the school pond in the environmental area could provide inspiration for a group or whole school project. Observe the area in the different seasons and note the variety of wildlife that visit. How many different types of flowers grow in the area? What kinds of trees are there? Produce pencil drawings and paintings of the pond or lake. Take photographs so that they can be referred to in the classroom. Make individual paper or fabric collages of the pond.

Lake Wall Hanging

The pieces of textile work for the wall hanging on the following pages were worked on by separate groups of children and then joined together at the end.

Approach

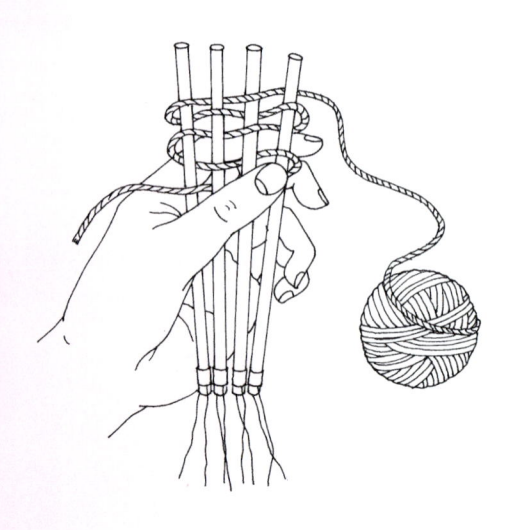

Tree Trunks

1. Use hand-held weaving sticks to produce lengths of stick weaving. Thread up the weaving sticks with the desired length of wool.

2. Hold the sticks about halfway up and fan them out slightly. Hold the end of the weft thread in the same hand until you have got started. Weave in and out of the sticks, working from one side to the other and back again.

3. When the sticks are full, draw the warp thread up through the weaving by pulling the sticks upwards. Continue in this way until the warp threads are full. Pull the sticks up through the weaving and then knot the warp threads at each end of the weaving.

Inspired by the Environment

Resources

- An assortment of green fabrics (old T-shirts, cotton sheets, curtain fabric or fabric of any kind)
- Green plastic carrier bags or bin liners
- Plastic-coated garden mesh with holes one centimetre square
- Small pieces of loose weave Hessian for pegging
- A large piece of backing fabric such as an old sheet
- A length of blue fabric for sky and backing for lake collages
- Green velvet curtain, or similar material, for areas of the background
- Selection of fabrics in the colour of buildings
- Chunky wools in the colour of tree bark and thinner wools for threading the weaving sticks
- A selection of satins and taffetas in blues and greens for the lake
- Bright yellow fabric for daffodils
- Scraps of white net for the fountain
- Peg looms (available from school suppliers)
- Weaving sticks
- French knitting bobbins
- Latex fabric glue

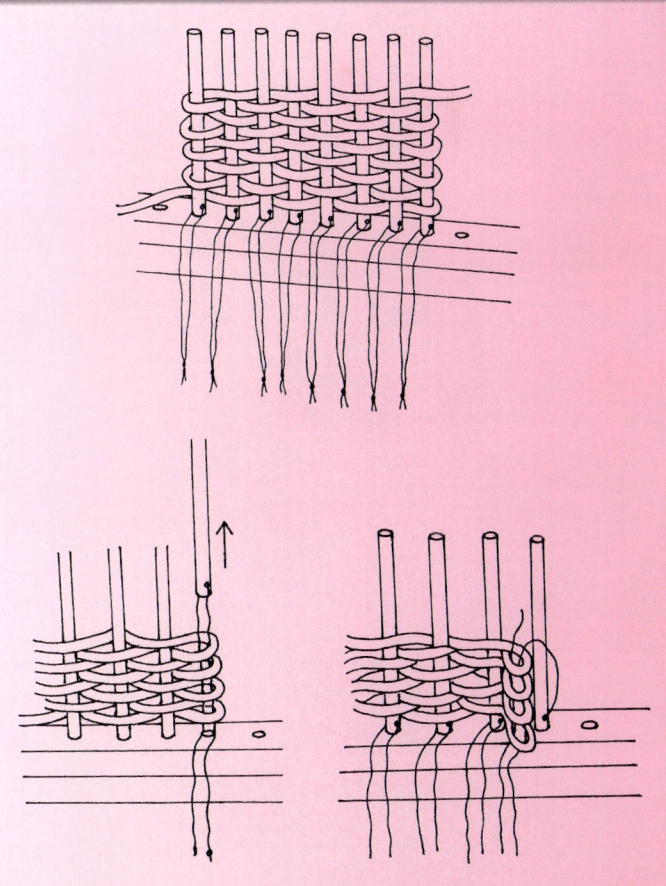

4. Younger children could use peg looms to produce lengths of weaving. Thread up the sticks and place five sticks in each base. Then, bring all the warp threads to the front.

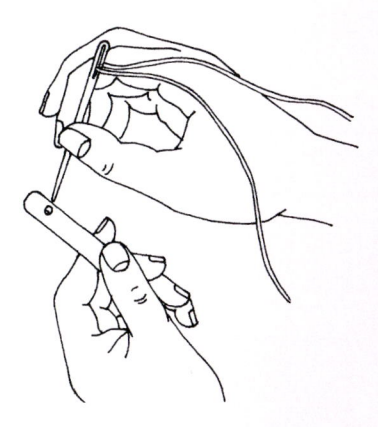

5. To weave, wind in and out of the sticks from side to side. When the pegs are nearly full, lift the first stick out of the base and pull the warp thread up through the weaving until it is visible at the top of the weaving.

6. Then put the stick back into the hole in the base. Repeat this with each stick. The weaving will now be on the warp threads at the front of the loom. Continue and repeat the process until the warp threads are full.

7. To finish off, remove all the sticks and lay the weaving flat. Gently pull the warp threads through the weaving until there is enough thread at each end to knot all the warp threads together.

29

Tree Tops

1. Prepare double-leaf shapes cut from plastic carrier bags. Poke a hole in the centre of a small square of Hessian and push one end of the leaf shape through this hole using a pencil. Make another hole very close to the first and push the other end of the leaf shape through that hole. Continue to poke the leaves through the Hessian, working round and out from the centre, to produce a clump of leaves.

2. Younger children could poke leaves through squares of plastic-coated garden mesh. Cut the mesh into ten-centimetre squares and thread the leaves through the holes, making sure that all the pieces are poked through to the same side.

Grass

1. Use the squares of garden mesh in the same way as for the leaves but use thin strips of fabric instead.
2. Cut the ends of the fabric diagonally to give a spiky effect to the grass.

The Lake and Islands

1. For the lakes, cut thin strips of shiny fabrics. Let the children cut them into shorter lengths and glue them to pieces of blue background fabric, overlapping them and mixing shades of blue and green.
2. For the islands, follow the instructions for creating the lake but glue green strips, already prepared in making the grass, vertically onto a dark green background fabric.

Houses and Shops

1. Cut out rectangles and roof shapes and glue them onto small squares of background fabric. Add doors and windows, curtains, people, trees and so on.
2. When the collages are dry, trim off the excess background fabric.

Daffodils

1. Cut squares of garden mesh six centimetres square and then trim them into a circular shape.
2. Poke short lengths of bright yellow fabric through the mesh (as you did for the grass) and add one or two green strips at the edges.

Inspired by the Environment

Blossom

1. Some of the older children picked up the technique of finger knitting very quickly and white and pink lengths of this were used for the blossom. To finger knit, tie a loop in the end of the wool several centimetres from the end.
2. Then, put the loop on the index finger and hold the short end of wool with the little finger. With the other hand, pass the long length of wool over the index finger, towards the front.
3. Hold this new strand of wool with the thumb whilst passing the first loop over the end of the index finger. Pull on the long end to reduce the size of the stitch.
4. Repeat this until long chains of knitting have been produced. To create thicker chains, finger knit the lengths of finger knitting.

Assembling the Wall Hanging

1. Spread out the children's work on the floor to gauge how large to cut the backing fabric. In this instance, the work filled a panel 3m by 1.4m. Cut a strip of blue fabric and using fabric glue, fix this along the top of the panel for the sky.
2. Cut a curved piece of green velvet for the hill and glue in place, overlapping the blue fabric.
3. Arrange the houses and glue them down.
4. Glue the pieces of collaged lake together and trim them to the desired shape. Glue the lake in place.
5. Fill in any gaps in the picture with more pieces of green velvet.
6. At each side of the picture, arrange the lengths of stick and peg loom weavings to represent trees. Glue these down carefully and add the clumps of plastic leaves.
7. Glue the squares of pegged grass along the bottom edge of the picture.
8. Cut the island shapes from the pieces of green collage, position and then glue them down. Trim the remaining pieces of collage to use as long grass and glue the pieces just above the pegged squares.
9. Create trees on the islands using finger knitting.
10. Glue the daffodil heads into position and cut stems and leaves from the green fabric.
11. Finally, gather up some nylon net and fix it in the centre of the lake to represent the fountain.

Spring

Mention spring and often the first image that comes to mind is the daffodil. Suddenly daffodils appear on roadside verges, on roundabouts, in window boxes, in parks and gardens throughout the land. Spring has arrived. Soon towns and urban areas are transformed as trees burst into blossom. The yellow of forsythia and the pinks of cherry and almond blossoms transform the previously grey streets. In the countryside, you see banks of celandines and primroses. In towns, brightly coloured primulas are on sale once again.

In late spring there are the bulb festivals, the most famous being those of the Netherlands. Here in Britain, we have the Lincolnshire bulb festival with its wonderful parade of colourful floats, each covered with thousands of flower heads.

Spring Collage

This is an activity that must be planned well in advance, as the flowers have to be collected and dried in silica gel. Drying is to be carried out by adults, who should follow the manufacturer's instructions. **DO NOT ALLOW THE CHILDREN TO HANDLE THE SILICA GEL.**

Resources

- A large piece of carton card or cheap artist's canvas
- Preserved or artificial heads of small, spring-garden flowers
- Sand, gravel, small white pebbles and bits of wood, twigs or natural cork
- Small sprigs of pussy willow and garden shrubs
- Paints
- PVA glue
- Miniature models of butterflies, birds, and frogs
- A miniature plastic plant pot

Approach

1. Paint a spring sky on the top half of the canvas or card.
2. Divide the bottom half into a gravel patio area and a flower bed. Glue small white pebbles along the divide line.
3. Spread a layer of PVA glue across the patio area and sprinkle it well with sand and/or gravel.
4. Glue a line of shrub sprigs along the horizon. Create a cherry tree by gluing tiny pink flowers to a twig. Glue small pieces of willow at the corner of the canvas to create an overhanging tree.
5. Glue the preserved or artificial flower heads to the canvas to create the flower bed. A cocktail stick is very useful for applying small amounts of glue. Glue bits of natural cork or wood onto the gravel area for logs. Add miniature models and plant pots.

Inspired by the Environment

Spring Embroideries

'Flowers' have been a favourite subject of embroiderers through the centuries. Show the children pictures of many different styles of flower embroideries: from Jacobean and earlier, to the stunning work of the Australian textile artist, Annemieke Mein, and those of British artist, Richard Box.

Blossoms in Spring

Approach

1. If possible, look at actual trees covered in blossom; otherwise, look at photographs such as the one shown here. How much branch can be seen between the clusters of blossom? How much sky?

2. Using a pencil, lightly mark the tree branch on the fabric. Thread up a length of chunky brown wool and stitch along the lines with long stitches. Do not pull the wool tightly. Let it lie slackly on the surface of the fabric. Pass another length of wool under these stitches to make a continuous brown line. Remember to fasten off all ends at the back of the fabric.

3. Cut irregular-shaped snippets of fabric about four centimetres across. Fold each scrap of fabric into four and stitch it onto the background fabric, through the folded point, using embroidery thread or sewing cotton and a fine needle. Sew the scraps of fabric on in clusters, mixing textures such as chiffon, lace, silk, taffeta and fine cotton. Use several shades of the blossom colour to give depth.

4. Add stitching in similar shades of embroidery thread.

5. Mount the finished embroidery on stiff card, turning all the raw edges to the back of the card and securing it with double-sided adhesive tape. Alternatively, cut a card mount to disguise the raw edges on the front of the card.

© iStockphoto

Resources

- Loose-weave background fabric in sky blue that is easy to stitch through. Alternatively, use white fabric and paint it with diluted school paint or fabric paints
- Scraps of thin fabrics in white, pink and yellow
- Brown chunky wools, embroidery needles and thread

33

Inspired by Flowers

Flowers remain one of the favourite design motifs in the history of art and design. From the exquisite *'Mille-fleurs'* tapestries of the Middle Ages (a fine example of which are the *'Lady and the Unicorn'* tapestries in the Cluny Museum, Paris) to the designs of William Morris and the Arts and Crafts movement, the sinuous flowers of Art Nouveau and the huge flower canvases of Georgia O'Keefe, makers and artists throughout the history of art have been inspired by flowers. Flowers have been re-created in just about any medium you can think of: paint, paper, ceramics, wood, metal and fabrics to name only a few. They appear on everything from clothing to furniture and exist as motifs in the design history of just about every culture.

Salt Dough Flower Plaques

Approach

1. Make up a quantity of salt dough by mixing up three cups of plain flour with one cup of salt and one cup of water.

2. Roll out the dough to a thickness of about half a centimetre on a floured surface. Cut the desired background shape for the plaque: oval, circle, square or rectangle.

3. Experiment by making different flower shapes with the dough before starting to assemble the motif for the plaque. For the foxglove flowers, roll up a small ball of dough, pinch the back of the ball to elongate it and then push the end of a paint brush into the front of the ball to create the opening. Move the paintbrush around to shape the flower. For roses or similar flowers, cut out little circles from rolled dough, trim off the bottom edge of the circle so that it is more crescent shaped, roll up one shape for the centre and then add more shapes to build up the flower. Daisies and flatter flowers can be made from flat circles cut into shape or fringed with scissors. Several fringed circles can be joined, one on top of the other, to create a more 3-D effect. Remember that when adding the flowers to the background plaque, water must be used as a 'glue' to ensure that the flowers stay attached.

4. The plaque can then be dried out very slowly in a low oven or a microwave. Care must be taken when using the microwave. Cook on low or medium power for very short periods at a time. If the surface of the dough starts to bubble, switch off and remove the dough. Flatten the surface with a spatula and allow it to cool before starting the drying process again.

5. When the plaque is completely dry, paint it with acrylic paints and then varnish.

Resources

- Plain flour
- Salt
- Water
- A cup and a bowl
- A wooden spoon
- A rolling pin
- Cutting and shaping implements
- Acrylic paints
- Brushes
- Varnish

Inspired by the Environment

Fabric Flowers

This idea is a quick and simple way for children to make flower heads, which can then be used on wall hangings (shown below) or turned into fabric flowers to put in vases. Plan ahead and ask parents for unwanted garments such as underslips and blouses in thin, shiny fabrics. Thick fabrics are not suitable for this project, as they will not gather satisfactorily.

Approach

1. Cut out a large circle of fabric. Sew a running stitch around the edge of the circle. Do not fasten off. Draw up the running thread until the edges of the circle are drawn into the centre. Flatten out the now reduced circle. Stitch from front to back through the centre several times and fasten off the thread.

2. Choose a large button and cut out a circle of fabric a little larger than this. Sew around the circle and draw up as before but this time, slip the button into the 'bag' before fastening off. Sew seed beads and other small beads onto the surface of the covered button to create texture. When finished, sew the button onto the centre of the gathered flower. Alternatively, simply sew on an appropriately coloured button.

3. Push a length of wire through a large wooden bead and twist the wire to secure it. Make sure there is still sufficient room to pass the needle through the bead. Then, sew the fabric flower onto the wired bead.

4. To make fuller flowers, sew two or three gathered circles of different sizes together before adding the button.

Resources

- Oddments of fabric such as taffeta, velour, cotton, silk or silk jersey
- Needles and sewing thread
- Buttons of various sizes and colours
- Large wooden beads for the backs of the flowers
- Small seed beads or similar
- Lengths of craft, garden or florist's wire
- A selection of round objects or card templates to draw around, no smaller than 15cm in diameter – a large dinner plate is the ideal size for the larger flower

A Trip to the Garden Centre

A visit to the local garden centre or botanical gardens is an ideal way to start a project about the rainforest. Look at the many different-shaped leaves, their colour and texture. Some of the plants will have exotic blooms. Record their names and research their origins when you return to school. If it isn't possible to organise a visit, make a collection of plants in the classroom for the children to sketch and paint.

Paper Jungles

Approach

1. This could be an individual or small-group activity. Using many shades of green, paint the insides of the tray. This does not have to be a carefully drawn jungle scene, as most of it will be covered up later.
2. While this is drying, paint both sides of the sheets of cartridge paper, some in shades of green and others in the colours of exotic flowers.
3. When these are dry, draw and cut out different-shaped leaves. Fold some along the centre. Curl others around a pencil.
4. Cut out large flower shapes. Create trumpets from different-sized strips of paper and glue them into the centres. Make flowers with several layers of petals, curling each layer around a pencil to create a 3-D effect.
5. Arrange the leaves and flowers in the tray, allowing them to overlap one another to create the impression of a dense forest. Glue them into position.

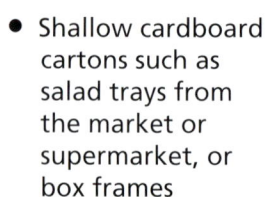

Resources
- Shallow cardboard cartons such as salad trays from the market or supermarket, or box frames
- Good quality cartridge paper or thin card
- Paints
- PVA glue

Inspired by the Environment

Tiger in a Tropical Storm (Surprised!), by Henri Rousseau (1844–1910) © National Gallery, London, UK/The Bridgeman Art Library

Jungle Drawings

Approach

1. Show the children paintings of different artists' representations of the rainforest, such as the one above by Henri Rousseau (1844–1910). Look at the many different shapes of plants, the variety of colour and the direction of lines. This painting is entitled *'Tiger in a Tropical Storm (Surprised!)'*. Do the children think it is a good portrayal of the subject?

2. Let the children produce their own interpretations using oil pastels or paint.

Resources

- Oil pastels or paints
- Suitable paper or card

The Rainforest

This could be a class or a whole school project and the overall size depends upon the amount of work produced by the children. Start planning well in advance by sending out letters to parents and carers requesting the various recyclable materials. Make arrangements for sorting and storage. Show the children pictures of the rainforest and discuss relevant issues such as deforestation and climate change. Outline the project and discuss with the children what kind of images they wish to portray. If time allows, teach skills such as peg loom weaving, pegging and French knitting before the project commences.

Wall Panel

Approach

1. For the leaves, cut double-leaf shapes from plastic carrier bags and peg them through squares of Hessian.
2. Cut circles of thin fabric, tack them around the edges, gather up and then stuff with toy filler to make the fruit.
3. For the creepers, make lengths of French knitting and thick finger knitting (finger knit the lengths of finger knitting to create really thick creepers). Cut leaf shapes from felt or fabric and sew or glue them onto the lengths of knitting. If you have them, sew on the plastic shades from the Christmas tree lights.
4. To make the jungle background, cut narrow strips of green, yellow and brown fabric and collage rectangles of stripy jungle background.
5. For the tree trunks, use chunky wools to produce lengths of stick weaving in all shades of green and brown.
6. For the flowers, glue a brightly-coloured circle into the centre of a square of Hessian. Mark the circle on the back of the Hessian and use the rag-rugging technique to work several rows of petals around the circle.

Resources

- Recycled fabrics in all shades of green and bright colours of flowers and fruits
- Green plastic carrier bags and bin liners
- Loose-weave Hessian
- Toy filler
- Fluted bottle bottoms and yogurt pots
- Chunky brown and green wools
- Coloured and patterned tights
- Weaving sticks, French knitting bobbins
- Coloured shades from broken Christmas tree lights (optional)
- Acrylic paint or household emulsion
- Thick flexible straws and garden wire
- Latex fabric glue and PVA glue

Inspired by the Environment

7. To make plastic bottle flowers, trim the cut-off bottle bottoms to look like flowers. Cut V-shaped sections from the yogurt pot rims and then paint both with acrylic paint or household emulsion. Tape flexible straws to the bottom of the pots so that the flower heads hang down.

8. To make large leaves, cut leaf shapes from the fabric. Cut two of each shape. Spread glue over one leaf, cut a length of wire and place it along the centre of the leaf. Then place the other leaf shape on top, thus sandwiching the wire.

9. To make snakes, cut the legs off tights and stuff them with toy filler. Add felt eyes, a tongue and patterns if necessary.

10. For the grass, use the rag-rugging technique to make squares of grass, which can be glued together later.

Ceiling Panel

Approach

1. Stitch randomly through the opened-out vegetable bags with green and brown wools, criss-crossing the lines of stitching. Use wool to sew the bags together.

2. Make lengths of French knitting and finger knitting and sew on felt and fabric leaves in various colours.

3. To make party-popper flowers, cut circles from coloured carrier bags, snip a hole in the centre of each and slip the circles over the handles of the poppers. Add a blob of glue between each circle. The more layers, the fuller the flower. Tie the flowers onto the French knitting.

4. Sew the lengths of knitting to the net at intervals, leaving loops to dangle down.

5. Make pompoms using strips of plastic bag instead of wool. Tie these to the net for exotic flowers.

6. Stuff tights to create snakes (see 'Wall Panel' section) or make long lengths of knitting, which can be sewn into tubes and then stuffed.

7. Cut butterfly shapes from stiff fabric and cover them with large sequins. Sew these to the net.

8. Hang the finished net from the ceiling by suspending it on cup hooks, or simply by stapling. Make sure it is not too heavy.

Resources

- Green net vegetable bags from market traders, greengrocers or supermarkets, or squares of old net curtain dyed green
- Coloured plastic bags
- Scraps of felt and fabric
- Wools
- Used party poppers
- Sequins
- PVA glue

Recycle Recycle Recycle

Constructing with Everyday Objects

These photographs show the fascinating *'Barking up the Right Tree'* sculpture, which is made from world-famous Sheffield cutlery. Although the artist, Johnny White (1953–present), chose to use the cutlery for a specific reason, for example, the historical background of the city, it presents everyday objects in a quite different context. Perhaps older children might enjoy hammering and flattening old cutlery into interesting shapes and making a sculpture of their own. Younger children might enjoy painting plastic cutlery and combining it with paper plates and cups to create a mobile or sculpture of 'The School Picnic'! Encourage children to look at everyday objects in a new light, assessing shape, size, colour, line and use.

© Sheffield Galleries and Museums Trust

Plastic Cutlery Wind Chime

Resources
- 13 pieces of plastic cutlery
- Acrylic paints
- Strong carton card
- Strong thread and a long, large-eyed embroidery needle
- Adhesive tape
- An oddment of narrow braid
- A compass or round object with a diameter of about 20cm
- PVA glue

Approach

1. Show the children pictures of the cutlery sculpture above and explain why the artist used that particular medium. Do they like it? Discuss the possibility of using cutlery to express other ideas. When would they use plastic cutlery? At a birthday party? A picnic? A family barbecue? Use the cutlery to express ideas or simply make interesting 3-D objects and patterns.

2. Paint white cutlery in bright colours and patterns using the acrylic paints – otherwise, use coloured plastic cutlery.

3. On the carton card, draw two circles, each with a diameter of 20cm. Cut out the circles and glue one on top of the other for strength. Paint the underside of the disc in bright acrylic paint.

4. Mark 12 points around the edge of the circle. Older children could use a protractor to make 12 lines at intervals of 30 degrees from the centre of the circle. Younger children could simply mark the points of the clock face.

5. Cut 12 lengths of thread about 30cm long. Wind one end of each thread around a piece of cutlery and tie it very tightly. Brush PVA glue over the wound thread to stop it slipping off. Leave until it is dry.

6. Pierce a hole, a little way in from the edge of the circle, at each of the 12 points with the embroidery needle. Use the needle to attach the threaded cutlery to the card disc. Knot the ends of the thread and secure them with adhesive tape.

7. Cut a slightly longer length of thread and attach this to a spoon. Make a hole in the centre of the disc and attach the threaded spoon.

8. Cut out another circle of card, sew a loop of braid through the centre and then glue this disc on top of the others, thus securing all the ends of thread attached to the cutlery. Paint the top of the chime and hang by an open window.

Recycle Recycle Recycle

What Can You Do with a Box of Coat Hangers?

Recently, a member of staff was given a box of child-sized plastic coat hangers. Not knowing what to do with them, she presented them to a group of children and asked them if they could think of a way of using them. In no time at all, the hangers were clipped together like gigantic mechano. The result was fascinating but a little boring as all the hangers were black. It was decided to unclip the hangers and paint them in bright colours before re-assembling them.

Clear Plastic Packaging

After Christmas, another member of staff found herself in possession of a number of cylindrical, clear plastic containers that had previously housed baubles and other decorations. She felt it would be a shame to waste them, so, inspired by pendant light shades, the children painted them with glass paints, stuck them together with double-sided adhesive tape and created a pendant sculpture.

Variation

Collect clear, cuboid packaging and build a painted, plastic tower; then place it in an area where the light can flood through it. If possible, to inspire the children, look at examples of stained glass in public buildings.

Plastic Milk Bottles

Such bottles are basically cuboids with bits cut away and lend themselves beautifully to construction work. They will hold together with strips of double-sided adhesive tape. Create a contemporary structure or sculpture from brightly painted bottles.

Approach

1. Paint the bottles in bright colours, either in solid colour or patterns. Alternatively, older children could choose a theme linked to environmental issues. Each class member could paint a bottle with a design based on that theme and join it to the growing structure.

2. When each bottle is dry, stick on strips of double-sided tape and press it to another bottle on the structure. Make sure that enough bottles are joined together at the base to make the structure stable. Alternatively, fill the bottom bottles with sand.

Resources

- A large number of flat-sided plastic bottles
- Wide, double-sided adhesive tape
- Acrylic paints

Cardboard Tubing 3-D structure

As well as being a very useful general construction material, cardboard tubing can be used to explore the element of 'line' in design projects.

Resources

- Cardboard tubing of all lengths and widths, from carpet roll inners to thin kitchen roll tubes
- Double-sided adhesive tape
- PVA or latex glue in a dispenser with a thin nozzle
- White matt household emulsion
- Decorating brushes
- Acrylic paints in bright colours

Approach

1. Let the children handle the different types of tubing and practise making shapes. Stress that the idea is to explore vertical or horizontal lines and that they are making a purely abstract form. This in itself is a hard concept for children who will always want to construct something concrete that they have seen. Perhaps it is best explained as a 3-D pattern.

2. Produce drawings of possible designs. Remember that contrast in a work of art makes it more interesting, so suggest turning some of the tubes the opposite way or positioning them so that they are seen 'end on'.

3. Start the construction by using several lengths of carpet tube. Join these initially with strips of double-sided tape along their lengths. This will hold the tubes together while you squirt PVA or latex glue along the joins. Latex will dry more quickly than PVA but the latter is effective given time. Do not attempt to move the structure until the seams are dry.

4. Using double-sided tape, start to add the lighter tubes to the construction. Turn some pieces around at right angles to the main construction in order to provide contrast. Cut the tubes to create different sizes.

5. When you are satisfied with the design of the structure, paint the whole thing white using household emulsion and decorating brushes for swiftness. This will clearly show off the line and form of the piece.

6. The structure could be left as a simple white form or painted in bright colours and patterns with acrylic paints. The white emulsion provides an excellent base coat for the acrylic paint.

Recycle Recycle Recycle

Wheels within Wheels

The circle is a basic element of design. Wherever we look, at school, at home or out and about in the local environment, we can see circles. Ask the children to list as many circular or cylindrical forms and objects as they can. The photograph below was taken in the local town centre and provides an excellent starting point for design.

Resources

- Oddments of tubing of various diameters, including cardboard, and rigid and flexible plastic tubing. Card inners from rolls of tape, plastic lids or anything the children can think of that would be useful for their designs
- A large, strong, shallow, cardboard tray or cut-down box
- PVA glue
- Junior hacksaws
- A bench vice for holding the tubing
- Sandpaper
- White household emulsion and decorating brushes
- Acrylic paints

Approach

1. Paint the insides of the box or tray with white paint.
2. Cut the tubes into short lengths, while taking care to observe safety precautions. Sand any rough edges until they are smooth.
3. Arrange and re-arrange the circles in the tray until satisfied with the design. Use lengths of flexible pipe or hose to introduce an element of line into the design.
4. When satisfied with the arrangement, remove the pieces one by one and glue them into the tray using PVA glue. Leave them overnight to dry.
5. Paint the whole relief white. This will have the effect of simplifying and pulling the whole design together.
6. Study the relief and decide whether or not you need to introduce colour. Maybe only certain parts of the relief need to be painted in order to make it look complete.

Fun with Plastic Bottles

Bottle-bottom Flowers

Approach

1. Following the curves of the bottle bottom, trim it into a daisy shape.
2. Using the outliner paste, draw a circle in the centre of the flower and outline all the petals on the inside of the bottle bottom. When the outline is dry, paint the flower with the glass paints.
3. Cut a length of the garden wire and, using the long-nosed pliers, coil one end into a flat spiral the same size as the flat centre at the back of the flower.
4. Attach the coil to the back of the flower, first using double-sided tape and then the clear tape over the top of the coil.

Resources

- The bottoms cut from soft drink bottles
- Outliner paste
- Glass paints
- Green plastic-coated garden wire
- Double-sided adhesive tape and clear adhesive tape
- Round-nosed pliers

Carpet Skittles

Resources

- One-litre plastic milk bottles
- Assorted tin lids and plastic tops from other containers
- PVA glue
- Sand
- Acrylic paints
- Felt-tipped pens

Approach

1. Make sure that the bottles are well washed and dry. If you wish to weigh down the bottles, add a little dry sand now.
2. Create a hat for each bottle using a combination of lids and plastic tops. Fix these securely with PVA glue.
3. When the glue is dry and the hat is firmly attached, use a felt-tipped pen to draw the character on the bottle.
4. Paint the bottle with acrylic paints.

Variations

- Create bottle 'families' by using two-litre, one-litre and half-litre bottles for the characters.
- Simply paint the bottles in colourful patterns instead of creating people.
- Organise class skittle teams and let each team design their own set of personalised skittles.

Recycle Recycle Recycle

Dancing Clowns Mobile

Resources
- Soft plastic bottles
- Felt-tipped pen
- A craft knife
- Scissors
- Acrylic paints
- Brushes
- Nylon thread
- Garden wire

Approach

1. Thoroughly wash and dry the plastic bottles.
2. Using the craft knife, make an incision below the neck of the bottle and then use the scissors to cut two-thirds of the way around the bottle. Pull the top of the bottle up and back a little to form the 'head' of the clown.
3. Bearing in mind that most of the bottle is going to be cut away and discarded, draw the arms of the clown on the bottle using a felt-tipped pen. Make use of the contours of the bottle. Draw the body, legs and feet of the clown.
4. Use the scissors to cut out the clown and then paint it with acrylic paints.
5. Tie lengths of nylon thread to the tops of the bottles and use the garden wire to make the mobile supports.

Underwater World

In the following theme, a school's arts week was devoted to turning a glass link corridor between the junior and infant buildings into an underwater kingdom. Planning was started well in advance; specialist materials were ordered from school suppliers and letters were sent out to parents requesting a wide range of recyclable materials such as the resources listed here.

Resources

- Clear soft drink bottles with fluted bottoms
- Fabric conditioner and detergent bottles
- Plastic bags and bin liners in blues and greens
- Buttons, beads and broken necklaces
- Wools in coral and seaweed colours
- Newspapers
- Net vegetable bags
- Oddments of plastic hose, flexible piping or electrical conduit
- Strawberry or fruit cage netting (the string variety for draping)
- Plastic-coated garden wire
- Grocery cartons
- Shells, gravel and small pebbles
- Coloured tissue in sea and coral colours
- Acrylic paints
- 'Peel off' window paints and outliner
- Glass paints and outliner paste
- Chicken wire
- Rolls of flexible plastic netting with holes one and a half centimetres square
- Double-sided adhesive tape, PVA glue and cellulose paste
- Rolls of clear plastic used by decorators
- Peg looms and French knitting bobbins
- Blue, green and rust-coloured, rope-like clothes line
- Toy filler
- Felt-tipped pens

Approach

A list of activities appropriate for all age groups was drawn up and staff chose which activities they thought would be most suitable for their children. Some activities were carried out by more than one age group.

Tissue Watery Panels

1. Use PVA to glue torn strips of tissue to lengths of clear decorator's plastic, sheets of clear polythene or plastic bags. Cover the plastic completely and use plenty of glue.

2. Cut fish shapes from tissue or coloured paper and add these, along with a few sequins and some glitter.

3. When completely dry, the tissue panels can be peeled off the plastic and attached to the windows using double-sided adhesive tape. Alternatively, for added strength, they can be left on the plastic sheeting. In the example shown, they were left on the sheeting because there were small gaps between the glass panels where rain could damage the tissue.

Recycle Recycle Recycle

Seaweed Panels

1. Cut blue and green plastic bags and bin liners into strips about 40cm long.

2. Cut a length of plastic garden netting and thread the strips through the holes so that both ends of each strip hang down on the same side of the netting. Continue until you cannot see the netting through the strips.

3. In this example the netting panels were threaded onto a clothes line and tied to the top of the exceedingly high glass walls. All the upper area of the atrium was covered. The strips sway and rustle in the draughts from the open doorways and are very effective.

Rock Column

1. Open out grocery cartons. Glue scraps of carton card across folds and gaps to reinforce them. Trim the sheets of cardboard into irregular shapes.

2. Scrunch up sheets of newspaper and glue them onto the shape to create bumps and hollows.

3. Cover the shape with several layers of pasted newspaper and leave it to dry. Paint in rock-like colours.

4. Glue on gravel, shells, small pebbles or even interestingly textured fabric to create further texture.

Variations

- Create the basic shape as described above but cover with snipped-up bits of carton instead of newspaper. This is a good way to use up the waste scraps and gives a good texture. The children enjoy stacking up the pieces to make outcrops. It is also less time-consuming than using papier mâché. Paint it when dry.

- Another alternative is to simply paint the flat card shape in rock-like colours and glue on shells, pebbles and so on. The columns were wired to the supports along the length of the corridor.

47

French-knitting Coral

1. Knit long lengths of French knitting using novelty yarns.
2. Thread the tubes of knitting onto thick garden wire and twist them into strange freestanding shapes or around banisters or rails.

Freestanding Underwater Plants

1. Show the children a selection of packaging and craft materials and ask them to design a freestanding plant. Ask them to consider ways of joining the various materials and then to draw annotated diagrams.
2. Place the completed plants along the corridor and at the bases of the rock columns.

Bottle-bottom Coral

1. Cut the fluted bottoms off the clear soft drink bottles.
2. The bottle bottom can be left with a straight edge or it could be trimmed into a curved or wavy edge. Use a hole punch to make holes around the rim.
3. Paint the bottle bottoms in coral colours, leave them to dry and then tie them together in bunches.
4. Suspend the bunches of coral from the ceiling.

Fan Corals

1. Pleat the chicken wire into a fan shape. Curl the sharp ends under so that no spikes protrude.
2. Use PVA glue to cover both sides of the shape with scraps of torn tissue paper, completely covering the chicken wire.

Boulders

1. For large boulders, scrunch up large pieces of chicken wire into irregular boulder-like shapes, making sure that all the sharp ends are turned inwards.
2. To make small boulders, scrunch up sheets of newspaper and tape them together with masking tape until they are the desired size.
3. Paste sheets of newspaper with cellulose paste and wrap up the boulder. Add several layers and leave it to dry.
4. Mix sand and fine gravel with ready-mixed paint and PVA glue and then paint the boulder. Another way to texture the boulder is to paint it using paint and PVA mixed together and then to roll the wet boulder in a sandpit. Glue on a few shells for added interest.

Neptune's Throne

1. Slice lengths of carpet tube to fit around chair supports. This is best done by an adult.
2. Paste the tubes with strips of brown tissue and glue on some shells.
3. Attach carton card to the sides of the chair and cover with tissue paper.
4. Drape a net seaweed panel across the top of the chair (see page 47).
5. Make tridents from papier mâché and attach them to the rear carpet tubes.
6. Drape the inside of the throne with shiny fabric.

The Shipwreck

1. Paint lengths of carpet tubing and glue on some shells.
2. Make planks from lengths of carton card and paint.
3. Arrange the above, in a corner, with a haphazard attitude to suggest a wreck.

Recycle Recycle Recycle

Octopus

1. For each octopus, cut eight strips of fabric 135cm × 15cm and sew them up into long tubes. Turn each tube the right way out and then stuff it with toy filler.
2. Cut a circle of fabric 75cm in diameter and with strong thread, sew all the way around the circle with a running stitch. Pull the thread to gather up the circle and stuff it as firmly as you can with toy filler. Sew up the remaining gap.
3. Sew the eight tentacles to the underside of the body.

The Mermaid

1. The mermaid is cut out in eight pieces: back and front tail, back and front body, and back and front arm pieces.
2. Assemble a complete front and a complete back, and then sew them together, leaving a gap for stuffing. Stuff the mermaid firmly with toy filler.
3. Six-ply rug wool was used for the hair but any chunky knitting wool could be used. Cut lengths of wool and machine sew them at the mid-point onto a strip of body fabric. Sew plenty of wool onto the strip to create a thick 'wig'. Sew the strip of fabric to the head and either glue or sew the hair into the desired style.
4. Cut the facial features from felt and glue them into position.

3-D Painted-glass Fish

1. When working with younger children, the cutting of the fish shape is best carried out by adults.
2. Remove the labels and wash and dry the bottles.
3. Carefully cut away the bottom part of the bottle and keep it for making plastic flowers.
4. Flatten the bottle at the cut-away end, creasing the sides as far as possible towards the neck. Hold the flattened end firmly and cut a V-shape out of the end of the bottle to create the tail fins.
5. Tape the edges firmly together with clear adhesive tape.
6. Now make narrow V-shaped cuts in the top and bottom edges of the fish for the other fins. Tape these securely with clear tape, paying particular attention to the points, which can be quite sharp.
7. Use the relief outliner paste to draw patterns and detail on the bottle fish. When the lines are dry, paint the fish with the glass paints.
8. Tape a length of nylon thread to the top of the fish at the point of balance and suspend it in front of a window, where the light can pass through the bottle.

Recycle Recycle Recycle

Fantastic Fish

Fabric conditioner and washing detergents often come in very interestingly shaped bottles and with a little imagination these bottles can be turned into quite fantastic fish.

1. Let the shape of the bottle dictate the patterns for the fish. Draw the patterns using a felt-tipped pen and then paint them with the acrylic paints.
2. When the paint is dry, add fins using a variety of collage material.
3. Tie nylon thread to the handles of the bottles, find the point of balance and then suspend them from the ceiling.

Peel-off Window Paint Fish

1. Draw a fish or sea creature on A4 or A3 white paper.
2. Place a piece of clear polythene over the drawing (polythene pockets are very good for this), use the outliner to trace the design onto the polythene and then leave it to dry.
3. Fill in the design with the paints. When completely dry, peel off the fish and press it onto the window above the tissue panels.

In addition to all the ideas shown in this theme, an enormous amount of black electrical conduit was brought into school (as well as a vacuum cleaner hose) and this was threaded along the corridor to enhance the feel of the shipwreck! One parent donated some very large, stuffed, fabric fish. These we hung high up in the atrium to give a feeling of deep water. The whole atmosphere was summed up as 'awesome' by one of the children!

Painting on Packaging Plastic

So many items these days are packaged in clear plastic containers; it seems a shame to waste the opportunity of either decorating the containers themselves and putting them to another use or cutting them up to make something different. Below are a few ideas for re-using the flexible type of packaging plastic.

Sun Catchers

Approach

1. Design the sun catcher on A4 paper. The sun catcher might be circular, oval, triangular or even made up of several pieces of plastic linked together.

2. Place the piece of packaging plastic over the design and trace the outline with the outliner paste. When the paste is dry, paint in the design with the glass paints. At this point, sequins and small beads such as seed beads may be dropped onto the paint for added effect. The paint acts as glue when it dries.

3. When the sun catcher is dry, trim off any excess plastic. Punch a hole at the top for the hanging thread and several holes along the bottom edge for the strings of beads.

4. Thread up the beads and tie them to the sun catcher. Hang the sun catcher in the window to catch the light.

Resources

- Pieces of clear packaging plastic
- Tubes of glass outliner paste (available in various colours)
- Water-based glass paints
- Shiny beads, sequins and seed beads
- Nylon thread
- A hole punch
- White A4 paper

Painted Flowers

Resources

- Pieces of clear packaging plastic
- Tubes of glass outliner paste (available in various colours)
- Water-based glass paints
- Shiny beads, sequins, seed beads and craft pompoms
- Nylon thread
- A hole punch
- White A4 paper
- Stem wire, sticky fixes and long-nosed pliers

Approach

1. Design the flower shapes on A4 paper. The flowers are more interesting if they are layered, so remember to graduate the sizes.

2. Place the packaging plastic over the designs and trace these with the outliner paste. When dry, paint the designs and if desired, add sequins and beads. While the designs are drying, cut a length of stem wire and, using the pliers, curl one end of the wire into a flat spiral. Bend this at right angles to the stem.

3. Cut out the flower shapes and make a small hole in the centre of each. Starting with the smallest, thread the flower shapes onto the wire. The spiral will stop them from falling off. To separate the layers slightly, place small sticky fixes behind each layer of the flower, before pushing the next one up to it.

4. To finish the flower, thread a large bead onto the wire behind the flower and bend the wire at right angles to the bead. If desired, glue a sequin or craft pompom to the spiral at the centre of the flower.

Recycle Recycle Recycle

Paint and Foil Pictures

Approach

1. Cut the carton card to the same size as the piece of packaging plastic.
2. On the A4 paper, design a motif that will fit the rectangle of plastic, yet not touch the sides.
3. Trace the motif onto the plastic with the outliner paste. Now paint all the space outside the motif with black acrylic paint.
4. Paint the motif with the glass paints.
5. Check that the first coat of black acrylic paint on the background is dry and then paint over it again. Hold the plastic up to the light to check whether you can see specks of light through the black. Touch up the paint if necessary.
6. While the picture is drying, cut a piece of kitchen foil slightly smaller than the carton card. Crumple this up slightly and then flatten it out again. Use double-sided tape to attach the foil to the carton card ensuring that the shiny side faces upwards.
7. Make sure that the picture is dry and then attach small pieces of double-sided tape to the painted side of the picture on the four sides. The tape will be hidden by the black paint. Be careful not to scratch off the paint as you are handling the tape. Turn the picture over so that the non-painted side of the plastic faces you and push the picture firmly down onto the foil. Tape all around the edges with black adhesive tape.

Resources

- A rectangle of packaging plastic
- Strong carton card
- Black adhesive tape
- Kitchen foil
- Double-sided adhesive tape
- Black acrylic paint
- Water-based glass paints
- Black outliner paste
- Brushes
- White A4 paper

Painted Fish Mobile

Resources

- Clear packaging plastic
- Outliner paste
- Water-based glass paints
- Sequins
- Nylon thread
- Lengths of garden or craft wire
- White A4 paper
- A hole punch
- A pair of pliers

Approach

1. Design fish of various sizes and patterns but do not make the patterns too complicated. Trace the fish onto the packaging plastic with the outliner paste and paint it with the glass paints, adding sequins (if desired) to represent scales.
2. Make a support for the mobile from lengths of garden or craft wire. Punch a hole at the top of each fish, thread them with nylon thread and then suspend them from the wires, balancing shoals of smaller fish with larger ones.

53

Beads and Buttons

I still find that, even in this hi-tech age, children are delighted with a tin full of buttons or beads. Tins of buttons are perhaps not as easy to acquire now as they used to be but if the children ask older members of the family to turn out their cupboards they may be rewarded. Failing this, charity shops and car boot sales are a good place to go hunting. If unwanted clothing is going to the recycling box rather than the charity shop, make sure that all the buttons are removed and saved for future use.

Resources

- A selection of small and large beads, these could be wooden, glass or plastic, or a mixture of all three
- Stiff garden or craft wire
- Fine flexible wire
- Long-nosed pliers suitable for jewellery making
- Wire cutters

Beaded Collar

Approach

1. Cut a length of the thicker wire, no shorter than 116cm. Bend this in half and twist the looped end to create a fastening loop.
2. Thread a small bead onto one of the ends of wire and push it up towards the loop. Twist the two wires to secure the bead. Repeat this several times using small beads.
3. Start to add on larger beads in the same way. The largest beads need to be halfway along the length of wire. Complete the other half of the collar to balance the first half. It doesn't have to be exactly the same.
4. Twist one of the remaining ends of wire back along the beaded length of wire, securing it so that the sharp end does not protrude.
5. Using the long-nosed pliers, curl the remaining end into a flat spiral, which will fit into the loop on the other end of the collar, thus creating a fastening.
6. Cut a length of fine wire and secure this to the collar a little way down from the fastening. Start to thread on small beads and then twist this fine wire around the collar at intervals, continuing to add on more beads as you go.
7. Fasten the end of the wire securely to the collar at the other side.

Recycle Recycle Recycle

Variations

- Start by cutting a longer length of fine wire. Fold in half (as above) and create the loop. Use very small beads at the back of the neck, then thread both strands of wire with slightly larger beads, occasionally twisting the strands together. Add a larger bead after each twist before continuing to thread the two strands with beads. Complete the necklace by wiring on a fastener to hook into the loop.
- Using the techniques described above, add buttons to the beads to create original jewellery or simply use three or four special buttons together to create an original centre piece.
- Create bracelets by twisting several beaded wires together and interspersing with very large beads.

Button-covered Trinket Box

Resources

- A strong cardboard carton (such as a washing tablet box with a hinged lid)
- Scraps of fabric
- PVA glue
- A hot gun
- Carton card
- Buttons of all sizes and colours
- Scraps of ribbon

Approach

1. Measure the dimensions of the box and then cut pieces of carton card half the depth of the box to fit all the way around the interior. Glue these to the lower half of the interior sides. These extra pieces of card will support the lift-out tray.

2. Cut pieces of fabric to fit the insides of the box (not the lid) and glue them into position, taking particular care to glue the fabric to the ridge caused by the extra card lining.

3. Close the box and draw a pencil line around it to mark the lower edge of the lid. **Below** this line, cover the box with fabric. **Above** the line, paint the sides of the box with acrylic paint in order to cover the box markings. If the box is completely covered with fabric, there is a danger that the lid will not fit.

4. To make the tray, cut a piece of sturdy carton card to fit snugly inside the box so that it rests on the card supports. If desired, glue narrow strips of card around the edges of this to create sides to the tray – otherwise, simply cover the piece of card with fabric. Glue loops of ribbon to two opposite sides of the tray so that it is easy to lift out. When all the glue is dry, position the tray in the box.

5. Cover the top and sides of the lid with fabric and then glue brightly coloured buttons all over it. The sides of the box could also be covered or simply trimmed with braid.

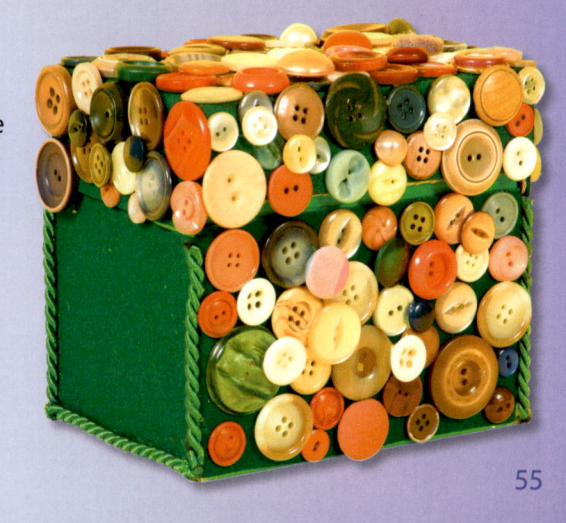

Tree Decorations

Approach

1. To make a tassel, first cut a piece of card the required length. Wind enough glittery thread around the card to ensure a thick tassel.

2. Cut a length of wire or nylon thread and slip one end under the wound threads where they pass over the card. Twist the wire to secure the threads. Then cut the threads off the card along the other fold and tie a little thread around the top of the tassel.

3. Thread a selection of beads onto the wire.

4. Twist the end of the wire over and secure it to make a hanging loop.

Variations

- Wind the tassel and then slip a longer length of wire through the threads, pulling it through to create two lengths of wire for beading. Twist the two lengths together just above the tassel to secure it.

- Add a further length of wire through the tassel to create four strands for beading. When beaded, twist the four strands together and bend the wire over to create a hanging loop.

- Instead of making a tassel, use a decorative button for the base of the decoration. Thread the wires through the buttonholes.

- Add a bow ribbon to the top of the decoration.

- Gather up some ribbon into a frill and add that to the top of the decoration.

Resources

- Fine wire or nylon thread
- Assorted beads and buttons of various sizes
- Glittery threads or knitting yarns
- Oddments of card
- Short lengths of ribbon

Button and Bead Cards

Approach

1. Fold the piece of A5 card in two, either vertically or horizontally.
2. Choose buttons and beads that complement the colour of the card.
3. Thread each button onto a length of thin wire, passing the wire through two holes of the button. Use the round-nosed pliers to safely curl up the protruding end of wire.
4. Attach sticky fixes to the back of the buttons and position them on the card.
5. Make a small bow from silk or parcel ribbon and attach a sticky fix behind the knot. Then, pull the button wires together and stick them in place with the bow.
6. Glue a few sequins onto the card between the buttons.

Variations

- Wire the button and then thread seed beads, sequins or other small beads onto the wire. Curl the wire ends to stop the beads from slipping off.
- Glue a small piece of wrapping paper, wallpaper or handmade paper to the card before attaching the buttons.

Resources

- Brightly coloured buttons, seed beads or other small beads, and sequins
- Thin craft or garden wire
- Scraps of handmade paper
- Scraps of decorated papers such as wrapping or wallpaper
- Oddments of silk, parcel ribbon or florist's ribbon
- A5 coloured card
- Glue sticks
- Foam adhesive pads (sticky fixes)
- Round-nosed jewellery pliers
- Wire cutters

Make It with Magazines

How much junk mail falls through your door in a week? How many magazines does the average family buy in a week? These are ready-made resources of colour and construction material. Some weekend supplements contain whole pages of glorious colour just waiting to be cut up. Here are a few ideas for doing just that.

Magazine Flowers

Approach

1. Cut out several circles in each of the three sizes. Experiment with different numbers of circles but obviously the greater the number of circles, the fuller the flower. Snip around the edges of the circles to create a fringed effect.
2. Cut a length of stem wire and use the pliers to curl one end of the wire into a flat spiral. Bend this at right angles to the wire.
3. Starting with the smaller circles, poke a hole in the centre of each and thread them onto the wire. The circles will rest against the spiral. When all the circles have been threaded onto the wire, slip a large bead onto the wire and glue it to the last large circle. Bend the wire down at right angles to the bead.
4. Complete the centre of the flower by gluing a craft pompom or a large sequin to the wire spiral.
5. Bend and curl the fringing to give a fuller effect.

Resources

- Coloured pages from glossy magazines
- Compasses or small, medium and large circle templates around which to draw
- Stem wire
- Large wooden beads, craft pompoms or large sequins
- Long-nosed pliers
- Wire cutters

Flower Baskets

These simple baskets make attractive gifts when planted up with winter pansies, spring bulbs or summer bedding plants.

Approach

1. Cut a handle for the basket from card and tape it to the deep plastic container. It might be necessary to trim away a little of the container edge to allow the handle to fit snugly.
2. Tear the scrap paper into strips and paste these all around the outside of the container. Push the strips under the container rim. Do not paste them over the rim and into the basket. Do not paste under the container either. Paste longer strips around the handle to strengthen it. Add two more layers of papier mâché. Allow them to dry.
3. Cut out pictures of flowers and greenery from the magazines and paste them around the basket but not on the handle. Also leave these to dry.
4. Paint the rim of the basket and also a little way down into the basket, with acrylic paint. Then paint the handle with acrylic paint.
5. When everything is dry, paint with varnish to make it waterproof.
6. If a container with holes has been used, it will be necessary to paint a tray in which to stand the basket. Do not paint the base of the food tray.

Resources

- Deep plastic food containers, preferably with holes in the bottom (for drainage)
- Shallow plastic food trays
- Card from cereal boxes or something similar
- Scrap paper
- Cellulose paste
- Gardening magazines and catalogues
- Masking tape
- Acrylic paints and varnish

Recycle Recycle Recycle

Collages after Rousseau

Approach

1. Look carefully at the paintings of Henry Rousseau (see page 37 for an example). Note the variety of leaf shapes, flowers and animals he includes in his pictures. Encourage the children to hunt through gardening magazines looking for bold images of plants and flowers. Search other magazines for animals and insects. Build up a selection of smaller green imagery for the background of the picture.

2. Cut a background board from stiff carton card. Collage this with a background of greenery cut from magazines.

3. Cut pictures of larger plants and exotic flowers from magazines and then cut leaf shapes from scraps of coloured paper. Glue these onto the background.

4. Add cut-outs of insects, birds and animals, partially hiding them amongst the greenery. Try to create a pictorial adventure. The finished boards could be used as the stimulus for written work.

5. Spray the finished picture with varnish or clear acrylic for a glossy appearance.

Resources

- Scraps of green and brown paper and card (any shades)
- Magazines and garden catalogues
- Glue sticks or cellulose paste
- Stiff paper or card for backing
- Examples of the work of Henri Rousseau and pictures of exotic landscapes
- Varnish or acrylic spray

Cut It from Card

Why spend money on construction card when we have resources such as cereal packets and supermarket cardboard cartons to hand? These materials can be used to create a whole array of interesting and decorative objects. Here are just a few ideas.

A Fruit Bowl

Resources

- Strong carton card
- A compass or large lid or plate
- Scrap paper or newspaper
- Cellulose paste or dilute PVA
- Gardening magazines and catalogues
- Masking tape
- A ruler
- Varnish

Approach

1. Cut a large circle from strong carton card. Draw in the vertical and horizontal diameters.
2. From the point where the lines cross, measure outwards to the same number of centimetres on each line and draw a dot. Then join these dots to form a square.
3. From the edge of the circle, cut along each line to the corner of the square. Score along the sides of the square to make it easy to bend the cardboard. Cut a wedge of card from each corner of the circle to allow the sides to fold up neatly. Tape the corners, pulling the flat circle into a bowl shape.
4. Cover the bowl in several layers of papier mâché, finishing with a layer of paper cut-outs of flowers or fruit.
5. When completely dry, apply several coats of varnish.

Card and Fabric Flowers

The flowers can be made in various sizes and used as fridge magnets, brooches, pendants, embellishments for cards, hair ornaments or simply as household decorations.

Resources

- Thin card from cereal boxes or something similar
- Scraps of plain and patterned fabric
- Glue sticks and PVA
- Buttons, beads and sequins
- Strong thread
- Fridge magnets
- Small safety pins
- Adhesive tape
- Small hair combs

Approach

1. Practise drawing simple flower petals of different sizes and shapes on scrap paper. When satisfied with the design, cut several petals from some card, in the same shape but different sizes.
2. Using glue sticks, glue the petals, one at a time, to the scraps of fabric. Trim around the petals, leaving enough fabric to fold over to the back of each one.
3. Snip the fabric around each petal to allow it to fold neatly around the curve. Glue this to the back of the petal with a little PVA glue.
4. Cut a circle of card for the centre of the flower and glue the largest petals onto this. Glue on the next layer of petals and so on.
5. Thread beads, sequins and small buttons to create an interesting centre and sew or glue this into position.
6. When the flower is completely dry, fix a magnet, safety pin or comb to the back of it.

Recycle Recycle Recycle

Create an 'Old Master'

Approach

1. Look at pictures of old flower paintings or, if possible, visit a local museum or art gallery. Focus on the heavy gilded frames.

2. Cut a large rectangle from some carton card. Cut narrow strips of card to fit around this and glue them into position to create a frame. Several layers will be needed to build a deep frame. Decorate the frame by gluing on string and other collage materials. Then paint the frame gold.

3. Paint the background in a dark colour and when dry use the flower cut-outs to create an arrangement in the style of the old paintings. 'Age' the picture with a thin wash of brown paint and when completely dry, spray with clear acrylic to give it a shiny surface.

Resources

- Strong carton card
- Thick string
- PVA glue
- Pictures of flowers cut from magazines
- Paints
- Collage materials such as pasta, artificial flower heads and braid
- Gold acrylic paint or spray paint
- Clear acrylic spray or varnish

Festive Decorations

Whatever the celebration, card shapes can be cut from strong carton card and decorated in various ways, be it with papier mâché, collage materials (such as pasta, rice, screwed up tissue paper or wool) or they can simply be painted in vibrant colours.

Approach

1. Draw the shapes on carton card and then cut them out. Younger children will need templates to draw around and will also need help with the cutting out. The very young can use pre-cut shapes.

2. Decide how the shape is going to be decorated and paint around its edge with an appropriately coloured paint in order to disguise the cardboard.

3. Spread PVA glue over the shape and glue on the collage material. A moistened toothpick is useful here for holding down bits and pieces without getting in too much of a mess!

4. Paint pasta and rice-covered shapes in metallic paints.

5. If you are covering a shape with beads, paint the background first and let it dry before gluing on the beads.

Resources

- Strong carton card
- Acrylic paints
- PVA glue
- A range of collage materials including pasta and rice
- Oddments of wool and braid
- Beads from broken jewellery
- A toothpick

61

Art in a Public Place

Inspired by Holiday Photos

'CowParade', by Jurrian van Hall, 'THE GALLERY' Donkersloot

The photograph above, was taken by a teacher on a weekend break to Amsterdam. The very colourful cow was standing in a doorway of an art gallery. It was originally part of the world's largest public art event, 'CowParade', which started in Chicago in 1999, moved on to New York in 2000, to Kansas City and Houston in 2001 and on to London in 2002. It has shown in Edinburgh and arrived on the streets of Paris in spring 2006. There are now plans for the show to appear in Russia and China. 'Why cows?' you might ask. The model cows are merely fun 3-D canvases on which the artists can explore the unique culture and history of their city. The shape and surface area of the models make them an ideal canvas.

Model cows are not the only large animals that have been chosen as vehicles of artistic expression in public places. In 2006, the cities of Turin (whose emblem is a bull) and Lyon (whose emblem is a lion) joined together to present the first 'Lyon Biennial Festival', an urban open-air exhibition which showed in both cities. 69 artists from all over the world were each given a model bull or a lion on which to express their ideas, in their own particular art form.

Look at your locality. Is there an animal particularly associated with your own town? Look carefully at the facades of old public buildings. Images are often carved above windows and doorways. Some animals appear in quite unexpected places, such as the pig shown here on the pillars at the entrance to the market area in Doncaster. The sculptures remind the public of the importance of the livestock market to the town. Choose an animal related to your town and create an art event similar to the 'CowParade'.

Art in a Public Place

Pig Parade

Approach

1. Show pictures of the various 'CowParade' exhibitions around the world. Identify the venues on a globe or world map in order to establish the scale of the exhibition. Discuss the aim of the exhibitions: to make art accessible to everyone, to break down barriers and pre-conceived ideas, to make people think, to have fun, to act as a vehicle for the artists' own expressive ideas and to express something of the venues' characters and history.
2. Discuss an animal that is significant to your local area – in this example it was the pig. After an initial brainstorming, use templates or pre-printed sheets (the artists start with a blank model cow) to let children explore their ideas. These can be developed into finished pieces of work and then displayed.
3. Wearing protective gloves, roll up the chicken wire and squeeze it into a basic animal shape. Add more chicken wire to shape the head.
4. Cover this armature with layers of pasted sheets of newspaper. Time permitting, allow these to dry between adding each layer. Make necessary adjustments to the shape as the work progresses. Add sufficient layers to make a strong structure.
5. For the legs, tape on lengths of cardboard tubing and cover them with pasted paper, building up the shape.
6. Finish the model with a layer of white paper or two coats of white emulsion.
7. When it is dry, customise the model to suit your area – paint with the local coat of arms or images of a local industry. A smaller-scale exhibition could be mounted in the classroom using balloons as a base for the papier maché work. This would allow for individual expression of ideas.

Resources
- Chicken wire
- Newspapers
- Strong cardboard tubes
- Cellulose paste
- Thin white paper or white household emulsion
- Acrylic paints
- Varnish
- Decorators' brushes

Relief Pictures

Approach

1. Cut the required base shape from wood or use several layers of carton card glued together for strength.
2. Tightly scrunch up sheets of newspaper and glue them to the baseboard with PVA glue. Cover the whole surface. Build up the shape by adding extra layers of scrunched-up paper where necessary.
3. Now cover the whole shape with layers of pasted newspaper.
4. Finish as you did for the 3-D model above.

Resources
- Strong cardboard or plywood
- Newspapers
- Cellulose paste and PVA glue
- Paints
- Off-cuts of timber
- Hinges and screws

Variation

Create ceramic pigs by joining two thumb pots and adapting the shape. It would be fun to turn the pigs into decorated money boxes, which could later be given as gifts.

63

Antonio Gaudi (1852–1926)

The organic forms and colourful mosaics of Antonio Gaudi could be the starting point for many exciting art projects. The photograph below shows *'Gaudi's Lizard'* in the Parc Guell, Barcelona, which is a wonderful source of interesting shapes and starting points for art projects. The ceiling roses of the colonnade in the park are fascinating, not only for their design and colour, but because it is possible to clearly see how Gaudi has used discarded objects such as wine bottles, saucers and other old crockery in his mosaics.

Mosaic Lizards

Gaudi's Lizard, by Antonio Gaudi (1852–1926), Parc Guell
© iStockphoto/Carri Keill

Approach

1. Show the children pictures of the mosaic lizard in the Parc Guell and pictures of different types of lizards from around the world. Let them draw pictures of lizards.

2. Start modelling the lizard by rolling a fat sausage shape from the clay. Shape the nose and cut a slit for the mouth. Pinch along the top of the sausage shape to modify the top of the lizard. Try to shape the legs by gently drawing clay from the sides of the sausage. If this is too difficult, add extra clay at this point but blend the legs well into the body. Shape the tail and then leave the model to dry and harden.

3. Paint a mosaic pattern on the dried model using acrylic paints.

4. Alternatively, paint the model with PVA glue a little at a time and cover it in lines of square sequins. Paint any areas that are too difficult to cover, such as the claws.

Resources

- Self-hardening clay
- Acrylic paints
- PVA glue
- Square sequins

64

Art in a Public Place

Crockery Mosaics

This project is more suitable for older children and every care must be taken to ensure their safety whilst working with broken ceramics. Protective goggles and gloves must be worn.

Approach

1. Obtain a collection of broken or chipped cups, beakers, saucers, dishes and plates.
2. Place the items, a few at a time, in a strong polythene bag. Ensure that the bag is securely tied and tap the crockery sharply with a hammer. Do not break the crockery into very small pieces.
3. If possible, show the children photographs of the mosaic ceiling roses and let them discuss how they think Gaudi constructed them. Decide upon the pattern and colours of the mosaic and if necessary, draw the design first.
4. Spread a layer of PVA glue or plaster of Paris in the tin lid (or tray) and arrange the pieces of crockery to suit. Work quickly if using plaster of Paris before it begins to set. PVA glue on the other hand, will take several days to dry out and harden.

Resources

- Broken crockery
- Biscuit-tin lids or old trays
- A strong polythene bag
- A hammer
- PVA glue or plaster of Paris
- Protective gloves and goggles

Paper Mosaics

Younger children could use paper plates, cups and dishes to make Gaudi-style mosaics.

Resources

- Strong carton card
- Coloured/patterned paper plates
- Cups and dishes
- PVA glue
- White acrylic paint

Approach

1. Cut a circle from some carton card and paint it white.
2. Show the children pictures of Gaudi's mosaic works.
3. Cut up the paper plates and so on, into pieces.
4. Spread the card with PVA glue and arrange the pieces appropriately.

Josep Guinovart (1927–present)

This photograph was taken in Barcelona a few years ago. It shows part of an installation called *'Entorn-Contorn'* by Josep Guinovart, which is situated in the exhibition hall at the Poble Espagnol. The installation is a fascinating mixture of the natural and surreal. Brightly painted metal and plastic shapes are juxtaposed with logs and natural carved wooden forms. The whole installation fills a glass atrium spanning the space between two floors. It is an unlikely mix of the natural and the unnatural and yet brought to my mind the fungal forms and seedling growths that can be seen on the woodland floor, captured in the speeded up film of time-lapse photography.

Entorn-Contorn, by Josep Guinovart (1927–2007), Poble Espanyol

The artwork for this theme, inspired by Guinovart's work, was designed for a woodland setting but could be sited in any grassy area at school. It would also be fun to share it, however briefly, with the general public. Contact the local council's parks department or Neighbourhood Services to see if it is possible to site the work in a public space. In this instance, the work was sited at the 'Visitor Centre' in a local wood, where there were plenty of opportunities to gather natural materials to supplement the work carried out in school.

Woodland Installation

Start collecting well in advance so that there is a wide selection of materials available for the children to choose from.

Approach

1. Copy and enlarge the photograph above. Show it to the children along with photographs of fungi, seedling growth and various plant forms found in woods, forests and jungles – the more exotic the better.

2. Let the children examine the collection of materials so that they can start to formulate ideas based on the shapes and forms available. Ask each child to design one part of the installation, explaining what he or she will use and how it will be constructed. Show all the designs to the group and encourage them to make constructive comments regarding necessary modifications.

Resources

- Strong carton card
- Yogurt pots and plastic packaging of all shapes
- Paper plates
- Acrylic paints
- Outdoor varnish
- Strong garden wire
- Masking tape
- Long cardboard tubes such as those from rolls of fabric
- Flexible hose or conduit
- Garden stakes and canes
- Ornamental seed heads and fir cones
- Any oddments of shaped wood such as stair spindles, door knobs, the tops of newel posts – in fact, any recyclable object that is available and fits the theme

Art in a Public Place

The individual elements of the installation will depend very much upon the resources gathered but here are a few ideas to consider.

- Cut large bean-like shapes from strong carton card and paint both sides with acrylic paint. Pierce a hole in the centre of each shape and slot it onto a long cane or garden support.

- Cut small (about 10cm in diameter), circular or oval shapes from card. Paint both sides with acrylic paint, then pierce a hole in the centre of each shape and slot them onto lengths of strong garden wire. Support the wires by pushing them into a length of metal tubing that has been pushed into the ground.

- Pierce holes in the bottom of plastic bottles and thread them onto garden canes. Tape the bottles together with masking tape and paint the whole thing with acrylic paint. Maybe glue a paper plate or card shape to the topmost bottle.

- Use coloured water or soft drink bottles as the centre of flowers. Paint both sides of a fluted paper plate. Glue the bottle to the front of the plate. Glue a yogurt or similar-shaped pot to the back of the plate. Then tape a garden cane to the back of the pot. Paint the pot and tape green. Alternatively, pierce a hole in the bottom of the pot before gluing it to the plate and then thread it onto a short length of strong garden wire. Curl one end of the wire into a spiral and tape it inside the pot. Bend the wire at 90 degrees to the pot. Glue the pot to the plate and then tape the wire to the garden cane.

- Pierce holes in the centre of plastic lids and the bottom of variously-shaped plastic pots. Glue the pots together in twos, open end to open end. Thread the glued pots onto garden canes, alternating them with the lids. Paint them with acrylic paint.

- Paint fluted paper plates with acrylic paint on both sides and slot them onto green garden supports. Cut double-leaf shapes from card, then paint and slot them onto the support below the plates.

- Cut large, irregular leaf or flower shapes from strong carton card. Measure the diameter of a long cardboard tube and cut holes of this diameter in the centre of each shape. Paint the tube and the shapes. Slot the shapes onto the tube.

- Pierce holes in the bottom of attractively shaped yogurt drink bottles and slot these onto canes interspersed with plastic lids. Paint with acrylic paints.

- Trim the top off a plastic bottle so that it fits snugly over the end of a length of cardboard tubing. Tape it in place. Then spread PVA glue around the join and a little way along the tube. Wind thick string, rope or washing line around the join and along the tube. Hold the ends in place with masking tape until the glue has dried and the rope is secure.

- Wire fir cones and ornamental seed heads onto garden canes. Tape over the wire with masking tape and then paint it.

- If the installation is to be outside for any length of time, spray all the pieces with several coats of varnish. Assemble all the different elements of the installation and push the canes firmly into the ground. Add any pieces of natural wood that you may have gathered.

Your Town in Bloom

This particular community project was initiated by Doncaster council, in an attempt to raise awareness of and stimulate interest in, the local environment and issues affecting the community. However, there is no reason why the initiative should not come directly from the school. Try contacting the local Neighbourhood and Community Services department of the local council to see if there are any projects in which the school could become involved. Suggest projects of your own. You will probably find that the area team is delighted to help in setting up local projects that the community wish to be involved in. After all, they are there to listen to the community, forge links and get people involved.

The community boards featured here were part of the 'Doncaster in Bloom' project. Doncaster council wished to involve the schools and community groups in the central urban area and about 80 boards in all were completed and sited around the town. The size of each board was determined by the height of the safety railings on which it was to be attached. All groups were invited to choose an environmental theme that had relevance to the local community. Subjects chosen ranged from litter and recycling, to advertising features of the town, to issues relating to climate change. The project was run in tandem with the 'Doncaster in Bloom' competition that invites groups and individuals in the community to enter various categories such as 'best front garden', 'best back garden', 'best hanging basket' and so on. Schools and youth groups became involved with their environmental gardens, wildlife areas and school allotments.

68

Art in a Public Place

Your School in Bloom

Resources
- **Outside boards:** Rectangles of marine ply with holes drilled for hanging, acrylic paints or household emulsion, yacht varnish
- **Inside boards and posters:** Strong carton card and stiff white card, good quality paper for posters, school paints

Approach

1. Discuss with the children any issues that they feel are relevant to the school and the wider community. This might include local litter problems, unsightly areas nearby, bullying, drug abuse, lack of local amenities or issues relating to local plant, bird and wildlife.
2. Decide where the boards are going to be sited and check with the authorities that there is no problem with hanging boards on school railings and so on.
3. Let all children draft out ideas for the boards and vote for the final choices or amalgamate various ideas into individual boards.
4. Paint outside boards with acrylic paint and/or household emulsion and apply several coats of yacht varnish.

Gardening Suggestions

Even with little or no outside space, much can be done to encourage the growing of flowers and vegetables.

Some ideas for doing this are listed below:

Resources
- Grow bags
- Jars
- Willow or cane
- Various seeds

- Start a gardening club to work on a regular basis in the school grounds.
- Create a wildlife or environmental garden. This does not have to be large.
- Stage a 'Grow the tallest sunflower' competition.
- Grow beans in jars.
- Have a window box/planter competition within year groups.
- In large pots, grow beans up cane or willow wigwams. The flowers are attractive and the children can cook and eat the beans. Grow sweet peas in a similar way.
- Plant tomato plants in 'grow bags'.
- Stage a miniature garden competition. This could be with real seeds and plants in a seed tray or it could be a craft project.
- Paint flowers on classroom windows that look out onto the street for passers by to admire. Let the school burst into bloom!

The Dream Tree

Ask the children what they think of their local environment. Is there anything that they would like to change about it? Can they think of ways to improve it? Draw up a wish list for the local area. Does the school have links with the local community groups? Design a questionnaire and carry out a survey to find out what people think about the local area.

The project shown in this theme started in school and was then taken out into the community to the local youth club, a church drop-in centre, a home for the elderly, a centre for adults with learning difficulties and a multicultural centre. At each venue, the people were asked to think about the local environment and to consider ways in which it could be improved and what they could do to help.

At the planning stage, many ideas were discussed but it was finally decided to create a tree that would carry all the dreams of the community and hopefully bear fruit! The tree had to be bright and eye-catching and as it was a 'dream tree' it could look quite unnatural. We opted for a shocking pink tree trunk and bright red, yellow and orange leaves. It was important that all the techniques involved were very simple and that the project itself was extremely portable and environmentally friendly. On the underside of each leaf, a wish for the community was written.

Wall Hanging

Approach

The Trunk

1. Make as many lengths of French knitting and stick weaving as possible (see pages 28 and 29).
2. Twist up these lengths and glue them to the background fabric with latex glue.

The Grass and Lettering

1. Using a felt-tipped pen, draw the letters to spell 'DREAMTREE', in reverse, onto rectangles of Hessian.
2. Using the peg rugging technique, work the letters in red and the surrounding areas in shades of green.
3. Glue these rectangles across the bottom of the background fabric.

The Leaves

1. Iron the interfacing onto the back of the red, yellow and orange fabrics.
2. Draw and cut out many leaves. Write each dream or wish on the white side of a leaf using marker pen. Glue sequins to the coloured side of the leaf.
3. Glue the finished leaves, only at the stalk end, to the background fabric. By doing this you will be able to turn the leaves to read the messages.

The Slogan

1. Choose a slogan appropriate to your location, using alliteration if possible, for example 'Wishes of Wheatley', 'Dreams of Doncaster', or as here, 'Rooted in Rotherham'.
2. Cut the letters out of bright fabric and glue them to the wall hanging.
3. Work out a programme for displaying the finished work at venues in the local area.

Art in a Public Place

Resources

- A large piece of donated black fabric – perhaps an old blackout curtain
- Unwanted clothing, curtains and sheets in all shades of green, red, yellow and orange
- Bright pink wools in all shades and weights – all donated
- Hessian – old sacking would do
- Sequins
- Latex glue
- Rug prodders, if you have them, otherwise half a dolly peg sharpened to a point or even a pencil would suffice
- Weaving sticks – available from school suppliers
- French knitting bobbins
- White iron-on interfacing
- Fine permanent markers or fabric pens

'Collages after Rousseau' (page 59)

Essential SCIENCE STAGE 8
FOR CAMBRIDGE SECONDARY 1

Darren Forbes | Ann Fullick | Lawrie Ryan
Richard Fosbery | Viv Newman | Roger Norris | Editor: Lawrie Ryan

Oxford excellence for Cambridge Secondary 1

OXFORD

OXFORD
UNIVERSITY PRESS

Great Clarendon Street, Oxford, OX2 6DP, United Kingdom

Oxford University Press is a department of the University of Oxford.
It furthers the University's objective of excellence in research, scholarship,
and education by publishing worldwide. Oxford is a registered trade mark of
Oxford University Press in the UK and in certain other countries

Text © Darren Forbes, Richard Fosbery, Ann Fullick, Viv Newman, Roger Norris
and Lawrie Ryan 2013
Original illustrations © Oxford University Press 2015

The moral rights of the authors have been asserted

First published by Nelson Thornes Ltd in 2013
This edition published by Oxford University Press in 2015

All rights reserved. No part of this publication may be reproduced,
stored in a retrieval system, or transmitted, in any form or by any
means, without the prior permission in writing of Oxford University
Press, or as expressly permitted by law, by licence or under terms
agreed with the appropriate reprographics rights organization.
Enquiries concerning reproduction outside the scope of the above
should be sent to the Rights Department, Oxford University Press, at
the address above.

You must not circulate this work in any other form and you must
impose this same condition on any acquirer

British Library Cataloguing in Publication Data
Data available

9780198399834

10 9 8

Printed in Great Britain by CPI Group (UK) Ltd., Croydon CR0 4YY

Acknowledgements

Cover photograph: © Getty Images/Jose Elias/Lusoimages
Illustrations: Edward Fullick and Tech-Set Ltd
Page make-up: Tech-Set Ltd, Gateshead

Although we have made every effort to trace and contact all
copyright holders before publication this has not been possible in all
cases. If notified, the publisher will rectify any errors or omissions at
the earliest opportunity.

Links to third party websites are provided by Oxford in good faith
and for information only. Oxford disclaims any responsibility for
the materials contained in any third party website referenced in
this work.

Contents

Introduction ... 1

Unit 1 Biology

Chapter 1 Obtaining food ... 2

Science *in context!* Healthy diets for healthy people ... 2
1.1 A balanced diet ... 4
1.2 Carbohydrates ... 6
1.3 Proteins and fats ... 8
1.4 Vitamins, minerals and fibre ... 10
1.5 Plants make food ... 12
1.6 Finding out about photosynthesis ... 14
1.7 Factors affecting photosynthesis ... 16
1.8 The digestive system ... 18
1.9 Digestive enzymes ... 20
1.10 More about digestion ... 22
End of chapter questions ... 24

Chapter 2 Circulation and respiration ... 26

Science *in context!* The history of the heart ... 26
2.1 Absorption of water and minerals in plants ... 28
2.2 Transport systems in plants ... 30
2.3 Transport in humans ... 32
2.4 The heart ... 34
2.5 The blood ... 36
2.6 Problems of the circulatory system ... 38
2.7 The respiratory system ... 40
2.8 Breathing in and out ... 42
2.9 Respiration in cells ... 44
2.10 Smoking and health ... 46
End of chapter questions ... 48

Chapter 3 Reproduction and growth ... 50

Science *in context!* Finding the causes and cures of disease ... 50
3.1 The female reproductive system ... 52
3.2 The menstrual cycle and fertility ... 54
3.3 The male reproductive system ... 56
3.4 Fertilisation and development of the early embryo ... 58
3.5 Pregnancy and birth ... 60
3.6 Growth and the factors that affect growth ... 62
3.7 The changes during adolescence ... 64
3.8 Drugs affecting reproduction and growth ... 66
3.9 Drugs affecting behaviour ... 68
3.10 The impact of disease ... 70
End of chapter questions ... 72

Unit 2 Chemistry

Chapter 4 Elements, mixtures and compounds ... 74

Science *in context!* Chemical giants ... 74
4.1 Revisiting the particle model ... 76
4.2 Gas pressure ... 78
4.3 Diffusion ... 80
4.4 Atoms, molecules and elements ... 82
4.5 Chemical symbols and formulae ... 84
4.6 Introducing the Periodic Table ... 86
4.7 Elements and compounds ... 88
4.8 Forming compounds from elements ... 90
4.9 Investigating elements, mixtures and compounds ... 92
End of chapter questions ... 94

Chapter 5 Metals, non-metals and corrosion ... 96

Science *in context!* Interesting elements ... 96
5.1 Metals, non-metals and the Periodic Table ... 98
5.2 Properties of metals and non-metals ... 100
5.3 Exceptional elements ... 102
5.4 Elements from compounds ... 104
5.5 Making and testing hydrogen ... 106
5.6 Rusting ... 108
5.7 Investigating rusting ... 110
5.8 Preventing rust ... 112
5.9 Corrosion of other metals ... 114
End of chapter questions ... 116

Chapter 6 Chemical reactions ... 118

Science *in context!* Chemistry in the kitchen ... 118
6.1 Preparing a chloride ... 120
6.2 Preparing a sulfate ... 122
6.3 Preparing oxides ... 124
6.4 Preparing metal hydroxides ... 126
6.5 Carbonates plus acid ... 128
6.6 Flame tests ... 130
6.7 Reactions with water ... 132
End of chapter questions ... 134

iii

Contents

Unit 3 Physics

Chapter 7 Light — 136

- Science *in context!* An illuminating story — 136
- 7.1 Rays of light — 138
- 7.2 Transmitting, absorbing and reflecting — 140
- 7.3 Reflection of light — 142
- 7.4 Refraction — 144
- 7.5 Dispersion and the spectrum — 146
- 7.6 Investigating colour — 148
- 7.7 Coloured light and filters — 150
- 7.8 Sight — 152
- 7.9 Lenses and cameras — 154
- 7.10 Using lenses to magnify — 156
- End of chapter questions — 158

Chapter 8 Sound — 160

- Science *in context!* Beautiful sounds — 160
- 8.1 Making sounds — 162
- 8.2 Describing sound waves — 164
- 8.3 Analysing sound waves — 166
- 8.4 The speed of sound — 168
- 8.5 Sound in solids and liquids — 170
- 8.6 Hearing sounds — 172
- 8.7 The dangers of sounds — 174
- 8.8 Beyond our range of hearing — 176
- End of chapter questions — 178

Chapter 9 Forces and magnets — 180

- Science *in context!* From super fast to super small — 180
- 9.1 Speed — 182
- 9.2 More about the speed equation — 184
- 9.3 Measuring speed electronically — 186
- 9.4 Showing movement with graphs — 188
- 9.5 Forces and movement — 190
- 9.6 Magnets — 192
- 9.7 Making and testing magnets — 194
- 9.8 Magnetic fields — 196
- 9.9 Electromagnets — 198
- 9.10 Electromagnetic devices — 200
- End of chapter questions — 202

Glossary — 204

Index — 208

Photo acknowledgements — 211

Access your support website:
www.oxfordsecondary.com/9780198399834

Introduction

Welcome to *Science for Cambridge Secondary 1!*
This Student book covers Stage 8 of the curriculum and will help you to prepare for your Progression test and for studying Stage 9, and later, your Cambridge IGCSE® Sciences (Biology/Chemistry/Physics).

Using this book

This book is divided into the three main disciplines of science, **Biology**, **Chemistry** and **Physics**, though you will find overlap between the subject areas. Each chapter starts with Science *in context!* pages. These pages put the chapter into a real-world or historical context, and provide a thought-provoking introduction to the topics. You do not need to learn or memorise the information and facts on these pages; they are given for your interest only. Key points summarise the main content of the chapter.

The chapters are divided into topics, each one on a double-page spread. Each topic starts with a list of learning outcomes. These tell you what you should be able to do by the end of that topic.

Learning outcomes

Key terms are highlighted in **bold type** within the text and definitions are given in the glossary at the end of the book. Each topic has a list of the key terms you should understand and remember.

Key terms

Summary questions at the end of each topic allow you to assess your comprehension before you move on to the next topic.

Summary questions

Expert tips are used throughout the book to help you avoid any common errors and misconceptions.

Expert tips

Practical activities are suggested throughout the book, and will help you to plan investigations, record your results, draw conclusions, use secondary sources and evaluate the data collected.

Practical activity

At the end of each chapter there is a double page of examination-style questions for you to practise your examination technique and evaluate your learning so far.

Answers to Summary questions and End of chapter questions are supplied on a separate Teacher's CD.

Student's website

The website included with this book gives you additional learning and revision resources in the form of interactive exercises, to support you through Stage 8.
www.oxfordsecondary.com/9780198399834

IGCSE® is the registered trademark of Cambridge International Examinations.

1 Obtaining food

Science *in context!*

Healthy diets for healthy people

Fatou is a dietician in the Gambia. She works to help people keep healthy by making sure they eat a balanced diet. Here are two of her case studies that show how important it is to eat the right food.

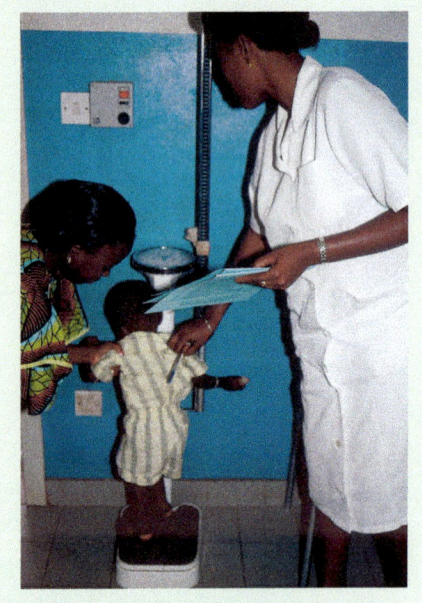

Fatou is well known by the people she works with

Modou needs protein

Without the advice of Fatou, Modou could easily have died from lack of protein

Modou is only two years old and it is not long since he started eating solid foods instead of having his mother's milk. He was a healthy baby but now he is thin and weak and his belly is swollen. Fatou sees that he has kwashiorkor. He needs more protein in his diet very quickly. Fatou talks to Modou's mother. She gives her some extra protein to add to Modou's food, and explains that he needs more meat or fish or pulses in his diet. Next time she visits, Modou runs up to see her. He is recovering fast. Fatou helped him in time.

Malik needs iodine

When Fatou visits the village where Malik is headman, she sees that he has a swelling in his neck called a goitre. Many of the villagers also have this condition. Malik tells her that many villagers feel tired and the work in the fields is not going well. Fatou knows that the problem is the lack of the mineral iodine in their diet. She brings the village salt with added iodine, and asks Malik to make sure everyone buys this in future. Several months later, Malik is full of energy again and his village is working well.

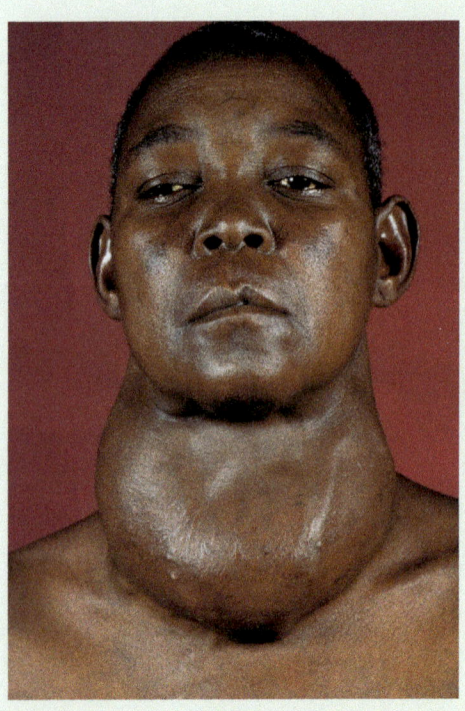

Goitres can easily be cured using iodised salt

1 Obtaining food

Many diseases which affect people all over the world are caused by a poor diet. It may be too little food or too much food, or just one single part of the diet that is missing. In each case a change in the diet can make people much healthier. Fatou wants people everywhere to learn about how the food they eat affects their health. It would make a big difference and there would be many healthier people!

In this chapter you will find out about the process of photosynthesis, what makes a balanced diet, the functions of various nutrients and what happens in the body if some of them are missing. You will also learn about the relationship between diet and fitness, the organs of the digestive system and how they work, and about enzymes.

Key points

- All organisms need food to give them energy and the raw materials for growth, repair and reproduction.
- A balanced diet is important for good health. A balanced diet contains carbohydrates, proteins, fats, vitamins, minerals and fibre.
- Carbohydrates are food molecules made up of simple sugars which the body can use very easily. They contain a lot of energy. Foods containing carbohydrates include bread, rice and potatoes.
- Proteins are food molecules made up of amino acids. They are used for growth and repair. Foods containing proteins include meat, fish, milk and pulses.
- Fats (lipids) are very high energy foods. They are made up of fatty acids and glycerol. It is easy to gain weight by eating too much fat.
- Food tests – iodine test, Benedict's test, biuret test, filter paper test – allow you to identify experimentally the different food types in your diet.
- Vitamins and minerals are needed in very small amounts but if they are lacking we suffer from deficiency diseases, e.g. vitamin C – scurvy, iron – anaemia.
- Fibre cannot be digested but it is needed to keep the digestive system working healthily.
- The energy in the food we eat is very important. Too little and we will lack the energy we need to work and live, too much and we could become obese and at risk of diseases such as heart disease and diabetes.
- Plants make their own food in a process called photosynthesis. They use carbon dioxide from the air, water from the soil and light energy from the Sun to make simple sugars, plus oxygen as a waste product. The light energy is captured by the green chemical chlorophyll found in the chloroplasts.
- There are a number of different experiments which can be used to demonstrate that plants need different substances or produce substances such as starch and oxygen during photosynthesis.
- Humans have to break down or digest their food in their alimentary canal (digestive system). This consists of the mouth, oesophagus, stomach, liver, pancreas, small intestine, large intestine and anus.
- The mechanical breakdown of the food is the physical chopping up of the material done by the teeth and by peristalsis, which also moves the food through the gut.
- The chemical breakdown of the food is carried out by enzymes, which are biological catalysts that speed up the breakdown of food.
- The small, soluble molecules produced by digestion are absorbed into the blood in the small intestine by villi.
- The undigested material along with dead cells and micro-organisms is passed out of the body as faeces.

1.1 A balanced diet

Learning outcomes

After this topic you should be able to:
- identify the constituents of a balanced diet
- explain the link between diet and fitness.

A balanced diet is important for health

Expert tips

The photo above shows a food pyramid. You should eat more foods that are shown at the base of the pyramid and much fewer of the foods shown at the top.

People need food! To get the energy and the raw materials we need to live and grow, we can eat plants and other animals. The food we eat is broken down into small particles (called molecules – see page 83) that our bodies can take in and use. This process is called **digestion**.

Eating the right things

The food we eat is an important part of staying healthy. We need a lot of different substances in our food. Here are some of the main ones:

- **Carbohydrates** are full of energy, which the body can use very easily.
- The body uses **protein** to grow and repair itself.
- **Lipids (fats)** have much more energy than carbohydrate. We need some fat to give us energy but too much can cause health problems.
- We only need tiny amounts of substances called **vitamins** and **minerals** but they are vital in keeping us healthy.
- We can't digest (break down) **fibre** but we need it to keep our digestive systems healthy.

Eating the right amount

It isn't just what we eat that is important to keep us healthy. We need to eat the right amount of food as well. The food we eat contains energy which is measured in **kilojoules**. Your body needs energy for keeping warm, moving about, growing, repairing any damaged body tissues and growing new babies. People need different amounts of energy from their food at different stages of their lives.

Person	Daily energy needs / kJ
13-year-old girl	8900
13-year-old boy	9500
female office worker	9500
male office worker	11 500
male farm worker	15 000
pregnant office worker	10 000

If we eat too much, we store the extra energy as a layer of fat. This acts as an energy store, but too much fat is very unhealthy. It is linked to many health problems including heart disease and diabetes. However, if people don't get enough to eat they will become very thin. They will catch diseases easily because their immune systems cannot work properly. If someone has little or no food for a long period of time they will die.

1 Obtaining food

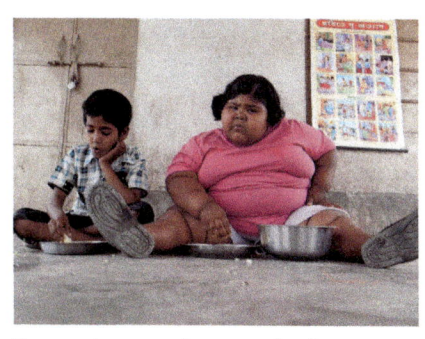

Too much energy from your food over a long time leads to obesity

Too little energy from your food over a long time leads to starvation

Looking at labels

Processed food is sold with labels which tell you exactly what is in the food. You can see the balance of the different types of food and the energy it contains has also been worked out for you.

Food is the energy source for your body – it is your fuel. Like any other fuel, it will burn. To work out how much energy is in a food, scientists burn a sample of the food in a **calorimeter** and measure how much heat is released.

Foods are labelled to show the types of food they contain and their energy content in kilojoules

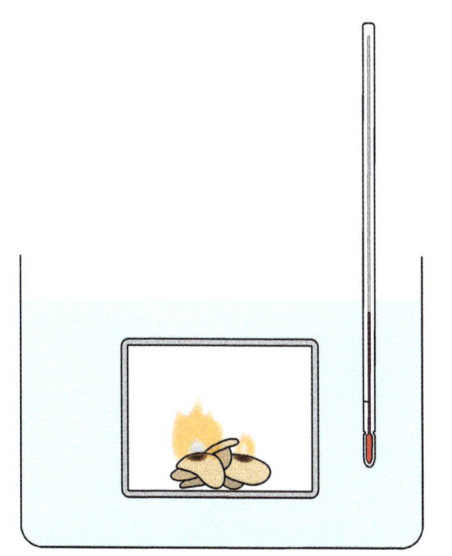

A sample of food is burned inside a closed container; the surrounding water gets hot. The bigger the temperature rise is, the more energy the food has released

Key terms

- **calorimeter**
- **carbohydrate**
- **digestion**
- **fat**
- **fibre**
- **kilojoule**
- **lipids**
- **mineral**
- **protein**
- **vitamin**

Summary questions

1. Using three different examples each time, name:
   a) three foods that contain lots of carbohydrates
   b) three foods that are rich in protein
   c) three foods that contain lots of fats.
2. Look at the table opposite. Suggest why:
   a) a 15-year-old boy needs more energy than a 15-year-old girl
   b) a pregnant office worker needs more energy than a female office worker who is not pregnant
   c) a male farm worker needs more energy than a male office worker.

5

1.2 Carbohydrates

Learning outcomes

After this topic you should be able to:
- describe the importance of carbohydrates in a balanced diet
- describe how to test for carbohydrates, using the equipment correctly and discussing any risks involved
- take accurate measurements when burning carbohydrates.

Carbohydrates are a very important food group. For much of the population of the world, carbohydrates make up most of their everyday diet.

What are carbohydrates?

There are two main types of carbohydrates: sugars and starches. Sugars are small energy-rich molecules. Starches are long chains of sugar molecules joined together. Bread, potatoes, rice, pasta and cereals are all good sources of starches. Biscuits, cakes, fizzy drinks and sweets are often high in sugars.

Carbohydrates are used in the body to provide energy from respiration. This energy is then used for movement, growth, reproduction, keeping warm and all our body processes. If you eat more carbohydrate than you need, your body stores the extra energy in the form of fat.

Foods rich in carbohydrates

Testing for carbohydrates

We can use simple chemical tests to discover if a particular food contains carbohydrates. There are two different tests, one for starches and one for sugars.

Practical activity — Tests for starches and sugars

The **iodine test** for starch: Add iodine solution to the food. If the yellow or orange colour of the iodine solution changes to blue-black, then the food contains starch.

The **Benedict's test** for sugars: Add blue Benedict's solution to the food and heat to above 70 °C in a water bath. If the food contains sugar, the solution will change from blue to green, then yellow, orange and red.

Test a variety of foods for starch and sugars. Present your results in a table.

⚠️ Wear chemical splash-proof eye protection. Avoid contact with iodine as it stains skin and clothing. If you have a food allergy tell your teacher before handling food samples.

Benedict's test for sugars. The more it changes colour, the more sugar the food contains. Green means there is very little, red means there is a lot

1 Obtaining food

You can also measure the energy in different types of carbohydrate foods. Later you can do the same thing for other types of food and compare your results. In this activity you will make a simple calorimeter.

> **Practical activity** — The energy in carbohydrates
>
> Measure out a small sample of a starchy carbohydrate food and a sugary food.
>
> Place a known volume of water in a boiling tube.
>
> Carefully burn one of the samples of food. Hold the sample carefully in some tongs and use it to heat the water as shown.
>
> Measure the rise in temperature of the water.
>
> Repeat the experiment with a sugary food – be very careful with this one. Your teacher may demonstrate it.
>
> Think carefully about your experiment. Does all of the energy from the burning food heat the water? Think of some ways you could improve your experiment.
>
> ⚠️ **Wear eye protection. If you have a food allergy, tell your teacher before handling food samples.**

Obesity, fitness and health

It is easy to eat too much carbohydrate because most people like sweet and starchy foods. The extra energy is stored as fat. This can result in **obesity**. An adult is obese when they weigh 20% or more above the ideal weight for their height. If people become so fat, it affects their health.

Obesity increases your risk of developing heart disease. You are also more likely to suffer from diabetes and many other diseases. It is a good idea to monitor how much food you are taking in and to keep yourself active so you do not get fat in the first place. This is much easier than dealing with the health problems later.

> **Key terms**
>
> - **Benedict's test**
> - **iodine test**
> - **obesity**

> **Summary questions**
>
> 1. Make a list of as many foods rich in carbohydrate as you can. Split them into the starchy foods, the sugary foods and those which contain both.
> 2. Look at the experiment above 'The energy in carbohydrates'. What do you think would happen if a bigger sample of food was used? Why do you have to be very careful burning sugar-rich foods?
> 3. Make a poster about carbohydrates. Find out as much as you can about them and the different types of food from around the world which contain carbohydrates.
> 4. Make a leaflet about obesity for school lessons in health awareness.

1.3 Proteins and fats

Learning outcomes

After this topic you should be able to:
- describe the importance of proteins and fats in a balanced diet
- describe how to test for proteins and fats, using the equipment correctly and discussing any risks involved
- present the results of your investigations in tables.

Proteins and fats are important food groups. They are both important for health but they are very different.

Protein in food

Protein is needed in your body for growing and building new cells. Meat, fish, cheese, beans and lentils are all foods that contain lots of protein. Protein molecules are made up of long chains of smaller molecules called **amino acids**. Different proteins are made up of different combinations of these amino acids. We can make some amino acids in our bodies but some of them have to be taken in with our food. These are called **essential amino acids**.

All of these foods are rich in protein

If you are growing fast you will need plenty of protein in your diet. This is why it is very important that children have a diet containing plenty of protein. Athletes who are training hard and building lots of muscle also need plenty of protein in their diet.

Practical activity — Testing for protein

Biuret test for protein: Put your food sample in a test tube and add 1cm³ blue biuret solution. Alternatively, add 1 cm³ sodium hydroxide solution (NaOH) and then add a few drops of blue copper sulfate solution.

If a purple colour appears, the food contains protein.

Try this test on a number of different foods and record your results in a table.

⚠ **Wear chemical splash-proof eye protection. Sodium hydroxide is corrosive.**

Fats in the diet

Fats contain lots of energy. 1 g of fat contains almost twice as much energy as 1 g of carbohydrate. You need some fat in your diet for your body to make cell membranes and nerve cells. However, fats contain so much energy that if you eat more than you need it is easy to become overweight.

1 Obtaining food

The scientific name for fats is **lipids**. They are made up of chemicals called fatty acids and glycerol. Butter and cooking oil are examples of fats, and fatty foods include chips, samosas and donuts.

Only eat small amounts of fat rich foods like these

Fats and health

Too much fat in your diet can lead to obesity which increases the risk of many illnesses. Overeating fatty foods also increases the risk of problems in the circulatory system. Fat can be deposited in the walls of your arteries forming an **atheroma**. This makes the arteries narrower so it is harder for the blood to pass through. Blood clots can form and block the blood vessel.

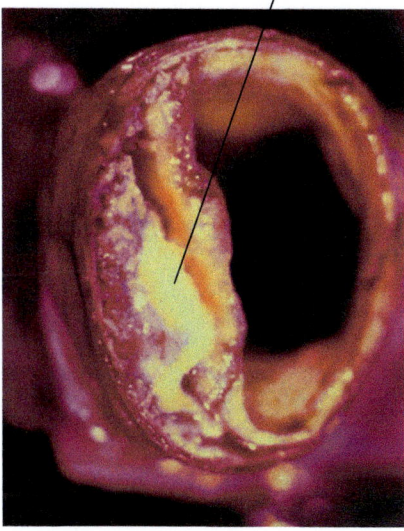

Eating a lot of fat increases your risk of developing an atheroma like this

Practical activity — Testing for fats

Rub a piece of food on a filter paper. Leave the paper to dry for a few minutes. Hold the paper up to the light. If it becomes translucent (lets the light pass through) the food contains fat.

Try this test on a number of different foods and record your results in a table.

Key terms

- amino acid
- atheroma
- essential amino acid
- lipid

Summary questions

1. Do some research about proteins. Make a poster to explain to mothers what proteins are and why they are important in a child's diet.

2. Record all the different foods you eat for two days. Make a table with three headings: carbohydrate, protein and fat. Put the foods in the different columns. They may go in more than one, e.g. milk goes in fat, carbohydrate and protein.

3. a) Use your data from question **2**. Make a bar graph to show how many of your foods contain each of the three food groups.
   b) Which of the food groups do you eat most of? Is this what you expected?
   c) In what ways might you improve your investigation? What would you need to do to investigate how much of each food group you eat?

1.4 Vitamins, minerals and fibre

Learning outcomes

After this topic you should be able to:
- describe the importance of vitamins, minerals and fibre in a balanced diet
- use secondary sources to find out about the amounts of different nutrients needed each day.

Everything that small babies need to eat and drink comes from their mothers' milk or from special milk in a bottle. As babies get older, milk is no longer enough. For the rest of our lives we need a range of foods to give us a balanced diet. In addition to carbohydrate, protein and fat we also need vitamins, minerals and fibre to remain healthy.

Vitamins

Vitamins are chemicals that we need in tiny amounts but without which we soon become very ill. We don't digest vitamins – they are just taken straight into our bodies from our food.

If we don't get enough vitamins in our diet, we get illnesses called **deficiency diseases**. For example, vitamin C is found in oranges, lemons and limes and lots of green vegetables. We need it for healthy gums and skin. Centuries ago, sailors on long sea voyages didn't get fresh fruit and many of them died of scurvy, the disease caused by lack of vitamin C. Once citrus fruits were taken on voyages, deaths from scurvy stopped.

Citrus fruits are rich in vitamin C

Expert tips

Carbohydrates, proteins and fats are the food substances that we need in large quantities. They make up most of the food we eat every day. Vitamins and minerals are very important food substances but the body only needs tiny quantities each day.

Vitamin	How it is used by the body	Deficiency disease	Good sources
A	For healthy skin and good night vision	Night blindness	Oily fish, green vegetables, dairy products, carrots
B1	Healthy nerves and the release of energy from food	Beriberi – exhaustion and loss of weight	Wholegrains, eggs, nuts, yeast, liver, pulses
C	Protection of the cells and absorption of iron	Scurvy	Citrus fruits, blackcurrants, tomatoes
D	For absorbing calcium	Rickets	Dairy produce, oily fish, eggs and it is made in the skin in the sunshine

Minerals

You also need tiny amounts of minerals in your diet to keep healthy. As you grow, your bones get bigger. The mineral calcium makes bones hard and strong. You get lots of calcium when you drink milk or eat dairy products.

You can run fast because your blood carries lots of oxygen to your muscle cells. You need the mineral iron for your blood to carry oxygen properly. Without it you feel tired and weak. You get iron by eating foods, such as red meat and apricots.

Regular habits

The food we can't use is usually pushed out of our bodies as faeces within about 24 hours. If our food doesn't move through the body

1 Obtaining food

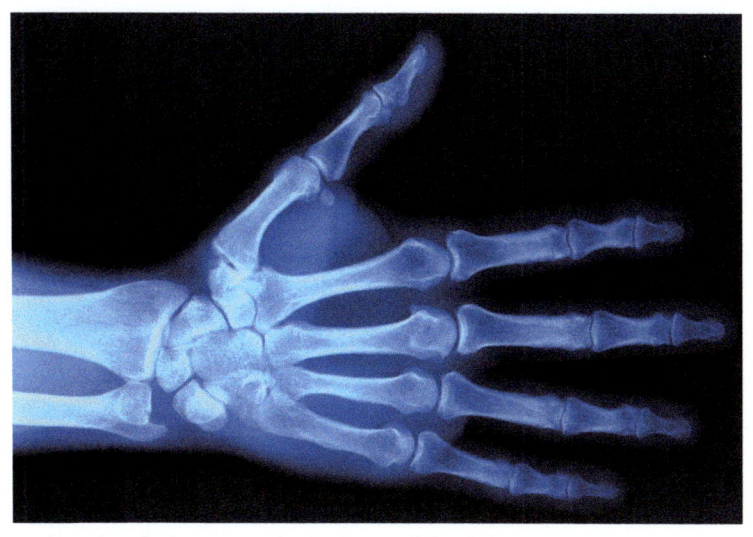

It takes a lot of calcium to make the bones of the skeleton strong

quickly, the result is constipation. Some people take medicines, called laxatives, to make themselves go to the toilet regularly.

However, there is a much healthier way of keeping things moving in your gut. We don't use all the food we eat, for example we cannot digest the cellulose from plant cells. We call this material **fibre**, and it helps to keep the food moving through the digestive system. Fruit, wholemeal bread, bran, beans and sweetcorn have a lot of fibre.

Practical activity   Daily doses

It is important to get just the right amount of all the different nutrients. Guideline daily allowances (GDA) are published. Your teacher will give you some tables showing the GDAs for different parts of the diet.

- Look up the food types you have met so far and make a list of the amounts of each you should eat every day to remain healthy.

Key terms

- deficiency diseases
- fibre

Summary questions

1. Make a table to show three different minerals, their importance in the diet and some good sources. Make your table like the one for vitamins in this topic.
2. Lack of vitamin D and lack of calcium both cause rickets. Explain why deficiencies of vitamin D and calcium cause rickets.
3. Make a poster explaining why fibre is an important part of a healthy diet.

11

1.5 Plants make food

Learning outcomes

After this topic you should be able to:
- describe how plants carry out photosynthesis.

You have looked at the balanced diet that people need to keep them well. Now think about the plants you see at home or at school. What do they need to keep them healthy and make them grow?

Photosynthesis

All living things need food for energy, but plants don't eat food! Plants need three main things – water, light and air – and they use them to make their own food.

To make their food, plants need water and carbon dioxide from the air. Carbon dioxide is only a small part of the air, but it is very important to a plant.

Light provides the energy to turn water and carbon dioxide into food, a bit like the heat energy in an oven turns flour and water into bread. The plant uses the carbon dioxide and water to make carbohydrates.

When carbohydrates are formed, another gas called oxygen is produced. This is the waste product of the process.

Making food by using energy from the Sun is called **photosynthesis**.

The leaf factory

Photosynthesis happens in the leaves of plants. Water enters the plant through its roots and travels up the stem to the leaves. Carbon dioxide from the air enters through **stomata** (tiny holes) in the leaf.

Light energy, usually from the Sun, hits the leaf. The **chloroplasts** (packets containing a special green substance) trap it to use in making food. Carbohydrates are made in the leaf and transported all over the plant to use for growth. Oxygen escapes through the stomata in the leaf's surface.

This orchid plant needs energy to produce these beautiful flowers

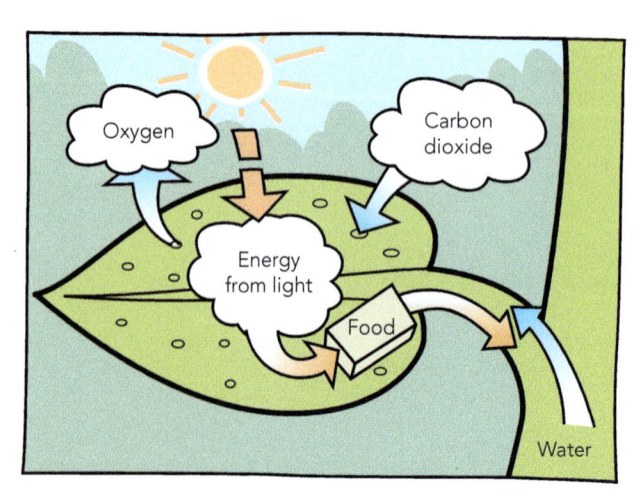

The photosynthesis production line

1 Obtaining food

Water vapour also escapes from the stomata. The plant can open and close these tiny holes so it can control:

- the amount of carbon dioxide which moves into the leaf from the outside air, and
- the amount of oxygen and water vapour which is lost from the leaf.

The structure of the leaf

Leaves are adapted so they can photosynthesise and make food as efficiently as possible.

- They are broad and flat to absorb as much energy from the Sun as possible.
- They are thin so carbon dioxide can get to the cells easily and oxygen can move out of the cells easily.
- They have veins which carry water to the cells.
- They have lots of chloroplasts in the cells to carry out photosynthesis.
- They have stomata which allow gases to move into and out of the leaf.

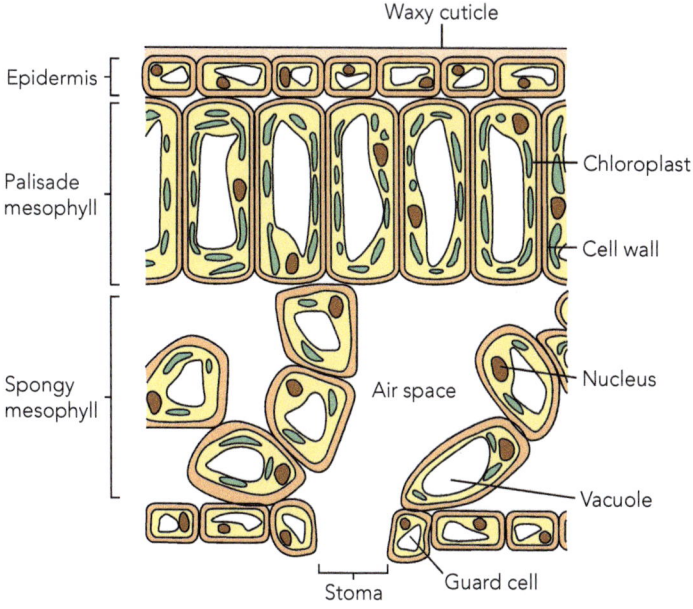

The internal structure of a leaf

Key terms

- **chloroplasts**
- **photosynthesis**
- **stomata**

Summary questions

1 What is photosynthesis and why is it so important for plants?

2 A scientist called Jean-Baptiste van Helmont (1577–1644) carried out a famous experiment in plant growth. He planted a tree weighing 5 lb (about 2 kg) in a pot and watered it regularly for 5 years. After 5 years it weighed 169 lb (about 76 kg). (lb represents the imperial unit pounds.) He thought the tree had grown from the water. Explain why he was right and also why he was wrong.

1.6 Finding out about photosynthesis

Learning outcomes

After this topic you should be able to:
- describe how you can test a leaf for the presence of starch
- explain how you can show experimentally that plants need light for photosynthesis
- describe an experiment to show that plants need chlorophyll to make food.

Testing a leaf for starch

To investigate how plants make food by photosynthesis, you need a way of showing that photosynthesis has taken place. Some of the sugar the plants make is turned into starch and stored in their leaves. You can use iodine solution to test for the presence of starch (see page 6) but you need to prepare the leaf first.

The leaves of a tree are arranged to capture as much light as possible

Practical activity — Using iodine solution to test a leaf for starch

1. Take a leaf from a plant which has been kept in a sunny place for several days.
2. Put the leaf in a beaker of boiling water from a kettle and leave it in the hot water for about 2 minutes. This will break down the cell membranes so the iodine solution can reach any starch in the cells.
3. Put the leaf in a test tube of ethanol and then stand the tube in the beaker of hot water. The ethanol will boil. The green colour comes out of the leaf which makes it much easier to see the colour of the iodine solution.
4. Take the pale leaf and run it under the cold tap to remove the ethanol and soften it.
5. Spread the leaf out on a white tile and cover it with iodine solution.
6. A dark blue-black colour shows that the leaf contains starch.

⚠ **Wear eye protection. Avoid contact with iodine as it stains skin and clothing. Don't use naked flames – ethanol is very flammable.**

Light and photosynthesis

Practical activity — Is light needed for photosynthesis?

For this investigation use a plant that has been kept in the dark for about a week, so it will have used up all the starch in its leaves.

1. Cover part of the leaf with a piece of aluminium foil or black card – you can cut a shape out of the card if you like.
2. Leave the plant in a sunny place for at least 24 hours.
3. Remove the covered leaf and draw it with the cover still on it. Make sure you draw the outline of the leaf even if it is obscured by the cover.

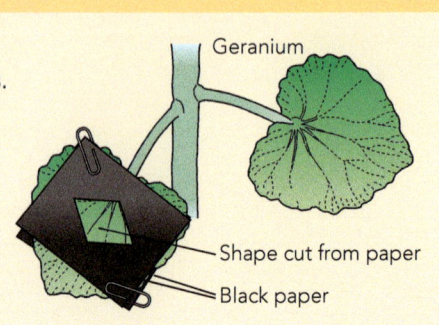

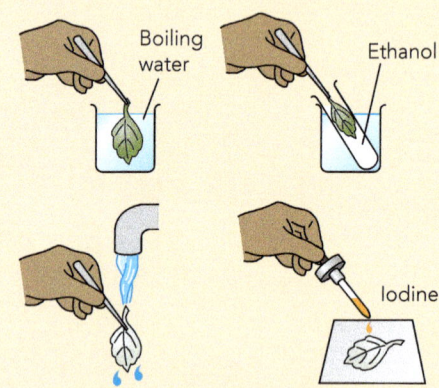

1 Obtaining food

4 Remove the foil or card and test the leaf for starch using iodine solution, as in the previous experiment.

Make a drawing of the leaf after you have added iodine solution and compare it to the drawing showing the covered leaf.

What does this investigation tell you?

⚠️ **Wear eye protection. Avoid contact with iodine as it stains skin and clothing. Don't use naked flames – ethanol is very flammable.**

Why are leaves green?

The green colour in plants comes from a special green chemical called **chlorophyll** found in the chloroplasts. Not all plants are completely green – some have leaves which are partly white or yellow. This can cause problems if the plant does not get plenty of light. In poor light the leaves may turn completely green again or the plant may die. The following investigation shows you why.

Variegated leaves

Practical activity — Do plants need chlorophyll for photosynthesis?

Take a variegated plant that has been kept in the dark for a week and put it in a sunny place for several hours.

Take a leaf from the plant and draw it carefully to show the pattern of green and white areas.

Test the leaf for starch using iodine solution, as in the previous experiments.

Draw a diagram of the leaf after you have added the iodine solution and compare it with the diagram you drew earlier.

What does this tell you about the importance of chlorophyll in photosynthesis?

⚠️ **Wear eye protection. Avoid contact with iodine as it stains skin and clothing. Don't use naked flames – ethanol is very flammable.**

Key terms
- **chlorophyll**

Summary questions

1. When you test a leaf for starch using iodine, explain why it is important to:
   a) put it in hot water for 2 minutes
   b) put it in ethanol in a water bath to boil for several minutes.
2. Why is it important to keep a plant in the dark for about a week before you use it for experiments on photosynthesis?
3. Plan a different investigation to show that plants need light for photosynthesis.

1.7 Factors affecting photosynthesis

Learning outcomes

After this topic you should be able to:

- describe an investigation to show that oxygen is produced in photosynthesis
- identify variables in your investigation and choose variables to change, control and measure.

Photosynthesis is very important because plants make food from carbon dioxide, water and energy from the Sun. All animals depend on the food made by plants. Plants are not just important because they make food – they also make oxygen.

Photosynthesis

Almost all living organisms need oxygen to get the energy from their food in the process of respiration. So plants not only make the food, they also make the oxygen needed to break the food down in living cells. Plants are very important!

We can summarise what happens in photosynthesis in a simple word equation:

$$\text{carbon dioxide} + \text{water} \xrightarrow[\text{chlorophyll}]{\text{light energy}} \text{glucose (sugar)} + \text{oxygen}$$

Making oxygen

Oxygen is a very useful waste product of photosynthesis. We can easily test and show that starch is made in the leaves of land plants. It is much more difficult to show that those same leaves produce oxygen. The air already contains lots of the gas oxygen. So we would need very sensitive instruments to measure the **change** in concentration of oxygen near leaves. However, if we use water plants such as *Cabomba* or *Elodea*, the oxygen given off in photosynthesis can be seen. It appears as little bubbles coming off the cut stems or the leaves.

Practical activity — Oxygen production in photosynthesis

1. Put some *Cabomba* or *Elodea* in a large beaker of water.
2. Cover the plant with a glass funnel.
3. Put a test tube full of water over the funnel and put the beaker in a bright light.
4. After a few minutes in the bright light you will see bubbles of gas coming off from the water plant. In a few hours you should have collected enough gas to test.
5. If the gas is oxygen (or rich in oxygen), it will relight a glowing splint.

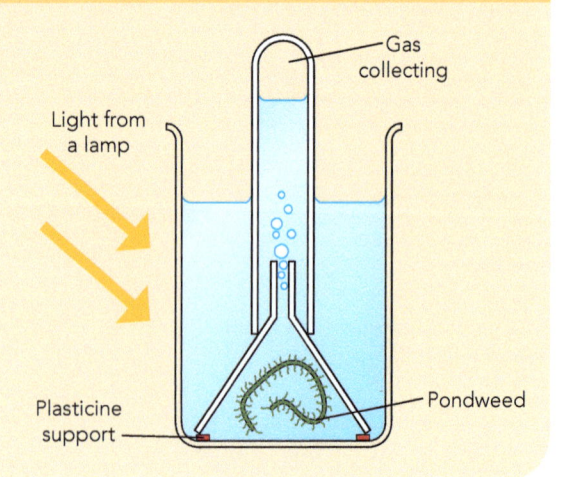

1 Obtaining food

Variables

Many different factors will affect the rate at which a plant carries out photosynthesis. You can investigate this using the experiment above. If you move the lamp closer to the plant in the beaker, what do you think will happen to the rate of photosynthesis? You can measure the rate of photosynthesis by counting how many bubbles are given off in a minute. As you move the lamp closer or further away, does the stream of bubbles get faster or slower?

Other factors affect how quickly photosynthesis takes place as well. The lamp used to produce the light for this experiment may also make the water in the beaker warmer. Does a change in temperature affect the rate of photosynthesis? What would you need to do to control the temperature of the water in the beaker? What do you think would happen if the amount of carbon dioxide in the water was made higher or lower?

Practical activity — Investigating variables that affect photosynthesis

Choose a factor that affects photosynthesis.

Produce a plan showing how you would investigate the effect this factor has on photosynthesis.

Expert tips

Too much light can damage plants so they do not photosynthesise well. Growers in the tropics often cover the plants with netting to provide shade. Greenhouses are ventilated when they get too hot to make sure the plants do not die.

Many different factors will affect how quickly these rice plants photosynthesise. That in turn will affect how fast they grow

Summary questions

1. Plant growers in some Northern countries use natural gas or oil heaters to keep commercial greenhouses warm during the colder days of winter. When natural gas or oil burns in the air it produces carbon dioxide and water. In what ways are the workers helping the plants to grow?
2. Plants need water to make food. Explain why we do not carry out experiments to show that without water plants cannot photosynthesise.
3. Make a big poster to summarise all the experiments you have done to investigate photosynthesis.

1.8 The digestive system

Learning outcomes

After this topic you should be able to:
- explain the need to digest food
- recognise the main organs of the digestive system.

The wood we get from a tree is useful to us in many ways. But before we can use the tree, we have to cut the wood into smaller pieces. Think of five different uses of wood – how many of them need the wood to be cut up first?

In the same way, we need food to provide our body cells with energy and with materials for growth and repair. But a mango, a bowl of rice, or a biscuit can't travel round your body in the blood. Even if they could, a single cell couldn't use them!

To be able to use the carbohydrates, proteins and lipids (fats) from our food, they must be broken down in the **alimentary canal**, also known as the digestive system. Small useful molecules are sent to the cells of the body, and any food that is undigested is passed out of the body.

The digestive system

Food comes into your digestive system through your mouth. Your digestive system (gut) is a tube 8–9 m long which runs from your mouth to your anus, so food doesn't really get into your body until it passes through the intestine walls into the blood.

In your mouth, your teeth start to break up the food into smaller pieces. Your mouth also produces **saliva**, a liquid which makes your food easier to swallow. It also starts the chemical breakdown of some of your food.

Into the gut

Once you have swallowed your food, it is moved steadily through your gut. Muscles squeeze to keep the food moving and to mix it to a paste. The muscles contract and relax in waves and this is called **peristalsis**.

The job of the gut is to break down your food into small, soluble molecules. These can be taken into your blood and carried to the cells of your body. The digestive system has different parts which each do a different job. The whole gut is coiled into your abdomen, the part of your body below your ribs.

The teeth are important for chopping the food into small pieces

The effect of peristalsis is rather like squeezing a tube of toothpaste

The parts of the digestive system

The chewed food is swallowed and goes into the oesophagus. This is a muscular tube that can squeeze food down to the stomach in about seven seconds.

1 Obtaining food

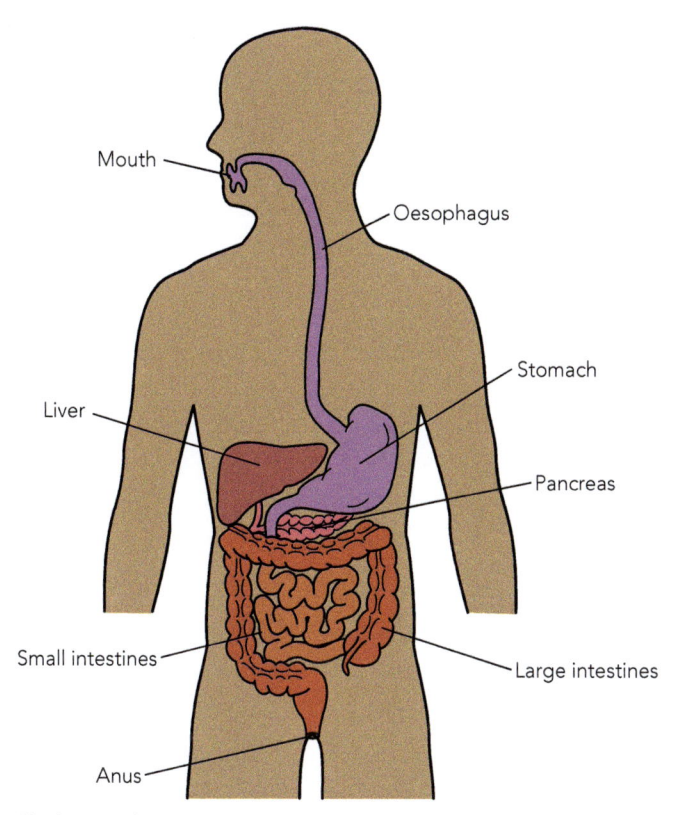

The human digestive system

Labels: Mouth, Oesophagus, Liver, Stomach, Pancreas, Small intestines, Large intestines, Anus

> **Expert tips**
>
> To help you learn about the digestive system, make a very large copy of this diagram, add the labels and then write about each organ underneath your labels. You could put together answers to question **3** from the members of the class into a big poster.

Your stomach is a muscular bag containing acidic juices. It stores food for about three to four hours, mixing up the food with the digestive juice made by the stomach wall and breaking down the protein. Small useful molecules are sent to the cells of the body, and any food that is undigested is passed on.

From the stomach, the partly digested paste moves into the small intestine. The liver and pancreas make juices which are squirted onto the food in the small intestine. They help to break it down. It takes food about six hours to travel along the 6 m length of your small intestine.

In the small intestine the final breakdown of your food takes place. The small food molecules made are absorbed, which means they are taken into your blood through your gut wall.

All of the undigested food such as fibre collects in your large intestine. Some of the water is removed back into your body to leave a thick, semi-solid waste. This is passed out through the anus as faeces.

> **Key terms**
>
> - **alimentary canal**
> - **peristalsis**
> - **saliva**

Summary questions

1. What is digestion and why is it important?
2. Draw a table to summarise the main parts of the digestive system and what they do.
3. Find out more about one area of the digestive system and make a poster or a presentation to explain it to the rest of the class. Different groups could find out different parts of the digestive system.

1.9 Digestive enzymes

Learning outcomes

After this topic you should be able to:
- explain how enzymes act as biological catalysts
- describe an experiment to demonstrate enzyme activity.

Expert tips

This photo shows that a piece of meat is digested far quicker if put into pepsin and hydrochloric acid, which are both produced by the stomach. The photo was taken about an hour after adding the piece of meat.

The food you put in your mouth is cut up into smaller pieces by your teeth. They increase the surface area of your food greatly before you swallow it, which makes it easier to break down. The teeth, along with the action of peristalsis, make up the mechanical or physical breakdown of your food. But most digestion of food takes place further down your digestive system and it involves chemical breakdown.

Enzymes

If you put a piece of meat in a beaker of acid like this and leave it for several days it will disappear! The large protein molecules of the meat are broken down by the acid into much smaller molecules called amino acids. These then dissolve. But this would take several days.

Different parts of the gut make different chemicals that speed up the breakdown of carbohydrates, proteins and fats. These chemicals are called **enzymes**. An enzyme is a biological **catalyst**. A catalyst speeds up a chemical reaction by making it easier for it to happen. Food molecules break up slowly in acids and other substances, so it would take far too long to be of any use to your body. Enzymes make things happen much faster.

The enzymes in your gut make it possible for you to break down food in a few hours rather than several days

1 Obtaining food

Enzymes at work

Your pancreas makes lots of enzymes and so does the small intestine. These enzymes speed up the breakdown of proteins, carbohydrates and fats into smaller, simpler molecules which pass into the blood.

The physical breakdown of your food – the chewing of your teeth and the squeezing by the gut muscles – gives your food a very big surface for the enzymes to work on. This in turn means they can do their job of chemical breakdown much faster.

The enzymes that break down carbohydrates into simple sugars are called **carbohydrases**. The enzyme amylase which is found in your saliva is an example of a carbohydrase.

The enzymes that break down proteins to amino acids are called **proteases**.

The enzymes that break down the lipids you eat into fatty acids and glycerol are called **lipases**.

Practical activity   Digesting starch

1. Put 10 cm^3 of starch solution in a test tube labelled A and put it in a beaker of water kept at 37 °C.
2. Put another test tube with 10 cm^3 starch solution labelled B into the warm water.
3. Add 2 cm^3 of water to test tube A and mix well.
4. Add 2 cm^3 of amylase solution to test tube B and mix well. Every two minutes remove some of the mixture from tube A and test it for starch using iodine solution.
5. Do the same thing for the contents of test tube B.
6. Continue until there is no longer any starch in one of the test tubes.

⚠ **Iodine solution stains skin and clothing – avoid contact and wear eye protection.**

Not everything you eat is affected by enzymes. Some things simply can't be digested – you don't have the enzymes to do it. Others just don't need any digestion.

Minerals and vitamins are not broken down because they can be taken directly into the blood stream and sent to the cells where they are needed.

Fibre cannot be digested but it gives the muscles of the gut something to work on.

Key terms

- carbohydrase
- catalyst
- enzyme
- lipase
- protease

Summary questions

1. Explain the difference between physical digestion and chemical digestion.
2. When you eat a piece of bread it contains carbohydrates, proteins and some vitamins and minerals. Your body treats the carbohydrates and proteins very differently to the minerals and vitamins. Why?
3. Make a table to summarise digestion in the alimentary canal. The headings for the table should be: type of food molecule, type of enzyme, products of digestion.

1.10 More about digestion

Learning outcomes

After this topic you should be able to:
- summarise the working of the alimentary canal.

As the food you have eaten is squeezed through your gut, it is mixed with several litres of digestive juices. These juices contain enzymes to break down the food. This is a rather noisy process and the rumbles and gurgles made by your gut are sometimes very easy to hear! As your meal moves along your small intestine, all that is left is a chemical soup. You need a lot of the soup, but some of it is rubbish. Your body needs to sort out which is which.

Keeping the food

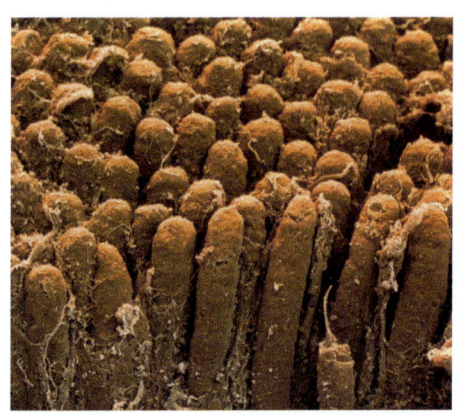

This is a highly magnified piece of the lining of your small intestine. The strange finger-like **villi** play an important part in making sure that all the digested food molecules make it into your blood, to be carried to your cells.

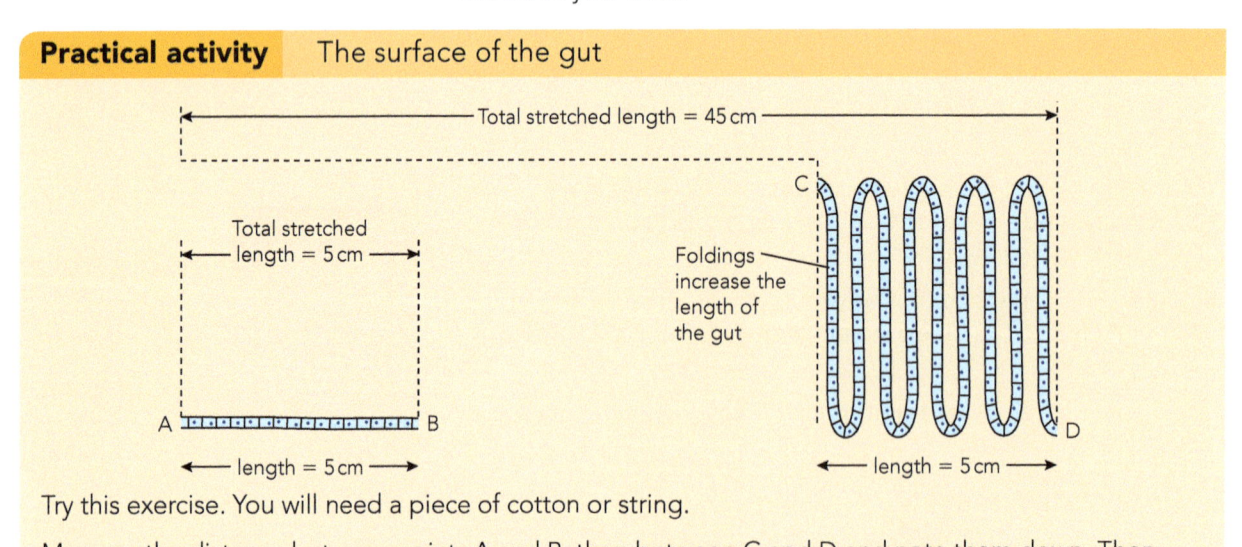

Practical activity — The surface of the gut

Total stretched length = 45 cm

Total stretched length = 5 cm

Foldings increase the length of the gut

length = 5 cm

length = 5 cm

Try this exercise. You will need a piece of cotton or string.

Measure the distance between points A and B, then between C and D and note them down. Then measure the length of the line joining A and B, then the length of the line joining C and D.

What is the effect of the 'villi'?

The villi of the small intestine give it a much bigger surface than if it was a smooth tube. Villi have a good blood supply and thin walls. This ensures that the products of digestion – glucose, amino acids,

1 Obtaining food

fatty acids and glycerol – can be absorbed easily. Once these small, useful molecules get into the blood they are carried away to the liver and then off round the body.

Big molecules, bits of undigested food and micro-organisms which live in the gut can't be absorbed by the villi. They are left in the small intestine.

Getting rid of the waste

All of the useful digested food and most of the water is absorbed into the body in the small intestine. The thin, watery liquid left is squeezed along to the large intestine. This acts as the waste disposal unit of the body. No digestion takes place in the large intestine, but the rest of the water is absorbed back into the body. Where do you think all the water has come from?

What is left is semi-solid waste called **faeces**. It is made up of food that can't be digested (such as fibre, lots of dead gut cells and micro-organisms). When your large intestine gets full, messages go to your brain and you pass the faeces out of your body through a ring of muscle called your anus. This is called **egestion**. The waste from a meal should leave your body within about 24 hours if your gut is working well.

If you are constipated, waste stays in the large intestine far too long and almost all the water is removed. This makes the faeces dry and hard. People spend a lot of money trying to relieve constipation but more fibre in the diet is the best solution.

If you have diarrhoea, your large intestine is irritated and waste is not held long enough for the water to be reabsorbed.

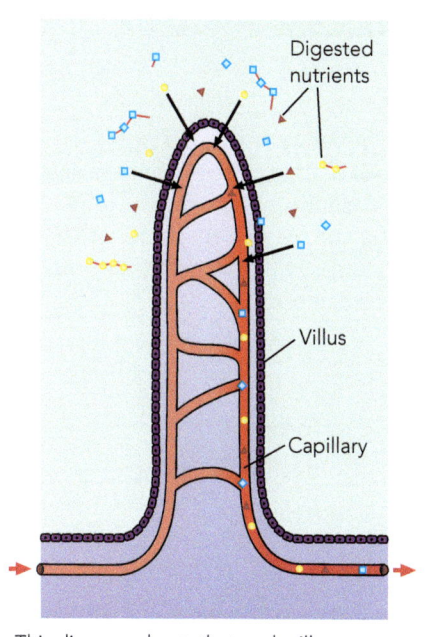

This diagram shows that each villus has many capillaries so all the digested nutrients are absorbed into the blood

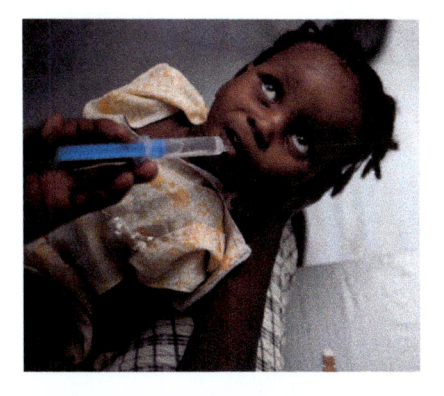

More children in the world die of diarrhoea than any other disease, because water is lost so fast. The water, and the minerals it carries with it, cannot always be replaced quickly enough without special solutions like these.

Key terms

- egestion
- faeces
- villi

Summary questions

1. Here are two sayings about digestion. Can you give a scientific explanation for them?
   a) Chew every mouthful of food 30 times before swallowing.
   b) A noisy gut is a healthy gut.
2. Make a large flow chart to show the process of digestion of the food from beginning to end.
3. Work in a group to make a large model of the digestive system with labels on each region explaining what it does in the process of digestion.

Chapter 1 — End of chapter questions

1 Seven terms to do with the nutrition of animals and plants are listed below. Definitions of these seven terms are also given. Match the letters that represent the terms with the numbers that represent the descriptions.

   A calorimeter
   B kilojoule
   C chlorophyll
   D digestion
   E enzyme
   F fibre
   G amino acid

   1 biological catalyst
   2 part of the human diet that helps to prevent constipation
   3 used to make proteins
   4 the unit of energy in foods
   5 green pigment in plants that absorbs light
   6 apparatus for measuring energy content of foods
   7 the breakdown of foods in the alimentary canal [7]

2 An unbalanced diet can have effects on the body. The table below shows some of the conditions associated with unbalanced diets. Copy and complete the table with the likely causes. You should choose your answers from the list below the table.

Effect of an unbalanced diet	A likely cause
obesity	
anaemia	
rickets	
tooth decay	
scurvy	

lack of vitamin C, too much sugar, not enough iron, too much fatty foods, not enough vitamin D [5]

3 The diagram below shows the human digestive system.

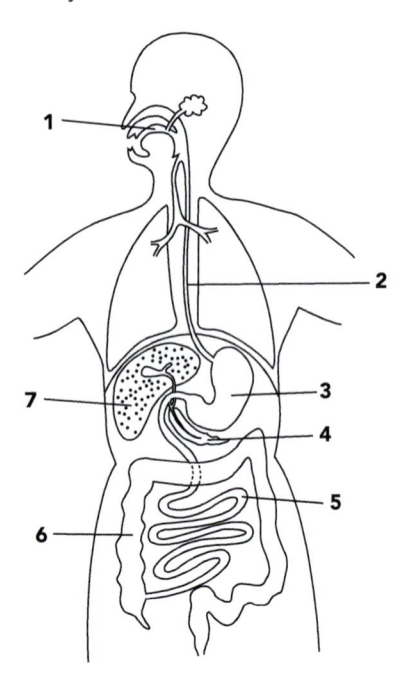

Copy and complete the table.

Structure labelled on the diagram	Name of the part of the digestive system	Function
	mouth	
2		moves food by peristalsis
3		
	pancreas	makes enzymes that work in the small intestine
	liver	makes alkaline fluid that neutralises acid from the stomach
5		absorbs soluble food into the blood
	large intestine	

[10]

4 An oxygen sensor detects changes in the oxygen concentration in water. Prem and Ayesha used an oxygen sensor to measure

1 Obtaining food

the changes in oxygen concentration in a beaker of water that contained some pond weed, as shown below. A data logger made a continuous record of the readings.

a Name the process that occurs in the pond weed to produce oxygen. *[1]*

Prem and Ayesha arranged the lamp so that it shone directly at the pond weed. After a while, they placed a piece of black paper in front of the lamp. After 10 minutes, they removed the black paper so that the bright light shone on the pond weed again. The figure below shows the print-out from the data logger.

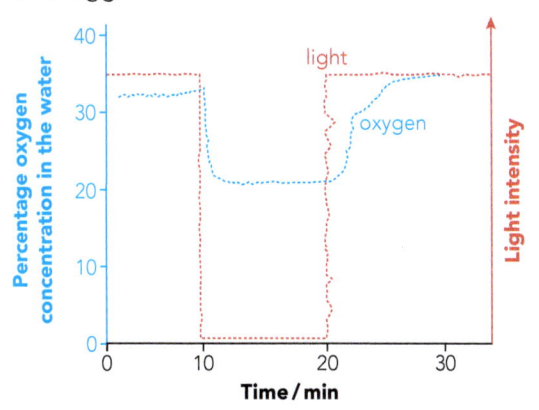

b Prem and Ayesha investigated the effect of changing a factor on the pond weed.
  i State the factor that Prem and Ayesha changed during their investigation. *[1]*
  ii State the variable that they measured. *[1]*

c Look carefully at the print-out.
  i How long after the start of their experiment, did the students cover the lamp with black paper? *[1]*
  ii Describe the effect on the pond weed of covering the lamp. *[5]*

5 In an investigation of amylase, Sam and Hilary placed starch solution, water and amylase solution into separate flasks and put them in a water bath at 40 °C for 10 minutes.

Visking tubing is a material that is similar to the lining of the alimentary canal. Sam put 15 cm³ of starch solution into each of two bags made of Visking tubing. Hilary added 1 cm³ amylase solution to bag **A** and 1 cm³ water to bag **B**. They sealed the bags at the top with paper clips and put them inside test tubes as shown in the diagram.

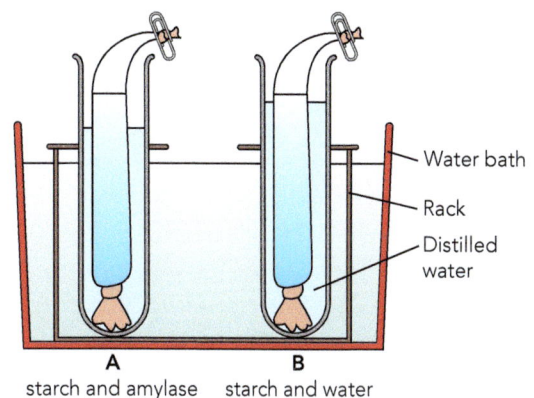

a Explain why:
  i Hilary put 1 cm³ water in bag **B** *[1]*
  ii they put the test tubes into a water bath at 40 °C. *[1]*

After 30 minutes, Sam and Hilary took samples of the contents of each Visking tubing bag and the water around each bag. They tested these samples for starch and for sugar. The results are in the table below.

Sample	Final colour with	
	Starch test	Sugar test
inside bag **A**	yellow	orange
water around bag **A**	yellow	orange
inside bag **B**	blue-black	blue
water around bag **B**	yellow	blue

b Explain the way in which the two students would test for **i** starch, and **ii** sugar. *[4]*

c Explain what has happened inside bag **A** to give the results shown in the table. *[2]*

d Explain why Sam and Hilary set up bag **B** as part of their investigation. *[2]*

25

2 Circulation and respiration

Science *in context!* The history of the heart

We know a lot about the circulation and the heart today. But it has taken scientists hundreds of years to work out how it all works. Here are just some of the discoveries.

Ancient China: People in China understood how the blood flows round the body about 2000 years before anyone else. They made a model with bamboo and bellows.

Galen c.130 – c. 200 ACE: Galen was a Greek doctor who taught his students there were two types of blood and that blood passed from one side of the heart to the other through invisible holes. He did lots of dissections of animals but none of people so he got lots of things wrong.

Ibn-El-Nafis 1208–88 ACE: This brilliant Arab doctor worked out the correct anatomy of the heart and the lungs and how the blood flowed between them. He was the first person to work out the blood flow to the heart itself. Once his work was translated into Latin, hundreds of years after his death, people in Europe began to have the same ideas!

William Harvey 1578–1657 ACE: This British doctor treated the Kings of England and also carried out a lot of research into the flow of blood. He decided Galen was wrong and carried out many experiments on animals and people to show that his ideas were right. Harvey spent many years getting data to back up his ideas before he wrote a book which clearly described the circulation of the blood. He explained how the heart, the arteries and the veins worked. People did not accept his ideas at first because he disagreed with Galen, but in time other doctors realised how important Harvey's ideas were for treating their patients.

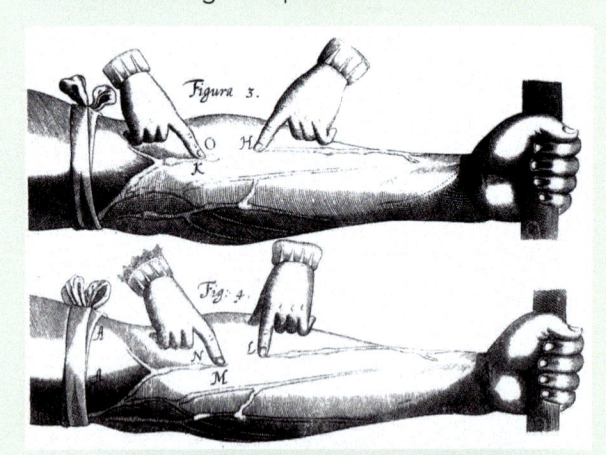

Ala'El-Deen Ibn-El-Nafis was the first person to work out and record the circulation of the blood in detail

William Harvey and one of his diagrams explaining how the valves in the veins stop blood flowing backwards

2 Circulation and respiration

In this chapter you will find out about transport systems in both plants and animals. You will discover how flowering plants take in water and mineral salts and then transport them up to the leaves and flowers. You will also look at the transport system which moves the sugars made in the leaves of a plant to all the other parts. You will look at the heart and the circulation of the blood in humans, and the way the blood transports chemicals to and from the cells of the body. You will also explore the respiratory system, how gases are exchanged and the process of respiration which provides energy for every living cell.

Key points

- Large multicellular organisms need a transport system to bring the cells what they need and to take away the waste products made by the cells.
- Plant roots are covered in tiny root hairs which increase the surface area for the absorption of water and mineral ions.
- Plants often actively move mineral ions from the soil into the root cells.
- The xylem and phloem are the transport tissues in plants.
- Xylem vessels are dead cells. The xylem transports water and mineral ions from the roots around the plant.
- The phloem is living tissue and transports food (sugars) from the leaves around the plant.
- The heart, the blood and the blood vessels make up the transport system of the human body.
- The main blood vessels are the arteries, the veins and the capillaries.
- The heart is a four-chambered pump which beats about 70 times a minute forcing blood around the body.
- The right-hand side of the heart pumps blood to and from the lungs, the left-hand side pumps blood to and from the body. This is a double circulation because blood flows through the heart twice during one complete circulation of the body.
- The heart sounds are made by the heart valves closing.
- The main components of the blood are red blood cells, white blood cells, platelets and plasma.
- Exercise helps to maintain a healthy heart.
- The coronary arteries may become narrowed so the blood does not flow to the heart, causing a heart attack.
- The respiratory system consists of the nose, mouth, trachea, bronchi, bronchioles, alveoli and lungs.
- Exercise increases the heart rate and the breathing rate so more oxygen can be supplied to the tissues of the body and more carbon dioxide can be removed.
- Inhaling: the ribs are moved up and out and the diaphragm flattens. The chest volume increases so air is forced in.
- Exhaling: the ribs fall and the diaphragm flexes upwards so the chest volume gets smaller and air is forced out.
- Aerobic respiration in all cells can be summarised as:

  glucose + oxygen $\longrightarrow$ carbon dioxide + water (+ energy)
- If the airways become narrowed in asthma or infections, less air reaches the lungs and so less oxygen gets into the blood, which can cause problems.
- Cigarette smoke contains the addictive drug nicotine and the cancer-causing chemicals in tar.
- Smoking is linked to an increased risk of lung, throat and mouth cancer, shortness of breath, heart attacks and of having premature, small or even dead babies.
- Smoking paralyses the cilia in the airways so they cannot move mucus full of dirt and bacteria away from the lungs.

2.1 Absorption of water and minerals in plants

Learning outcomes

After this topic you should be able to:
- describe the absorption of water and mineral ions by the roots of flowering plants
- explain how root hair cells are suited to their function.

The leaves of plants make food by photosynthesis and so are very important. Most plants also have parts which are not green and are hardly ever seen, but are just as important as the leaves. These are the roots. Without their roots plants cannot survive. Look at the picture of the tree after a storm and make a list of the jobs you think plant roots might do.

This tree was uprooted during a tropical storm

Holding on

Plants need to be held firmly in one place. Then they can spread their stems and leaves to trap as much sunlight as possible and the wind does not blow them over. The roots spread underground and act as an anchor both for the plant and for the soil. Without plant roots the soil is blown away and only bare rock is left.

Water is important

Plants need water for photosynthesis to make their food and to move soluble substances all around the plant. How do plants get the water they need? The answer is in the roots.

As roots grow they are covered in tiny **root hairs**. This is where water enters the plant. Water moves from the soil into the **root hair cells**. The water moves through the root and into the plant itself.

The transport system of the plant carries the water all around the plant to where it is needed (see page 30). The 'hair' of the root hair cell reaches out into the soil. It gives the cell a much bigger surface area so there is a lot of surface exposed. This means a single root hair cell can absorb a lot of water for the plant – and there are lots of root hair cells.

The root hairs can be seen clearly on these newly germinated clover seeds

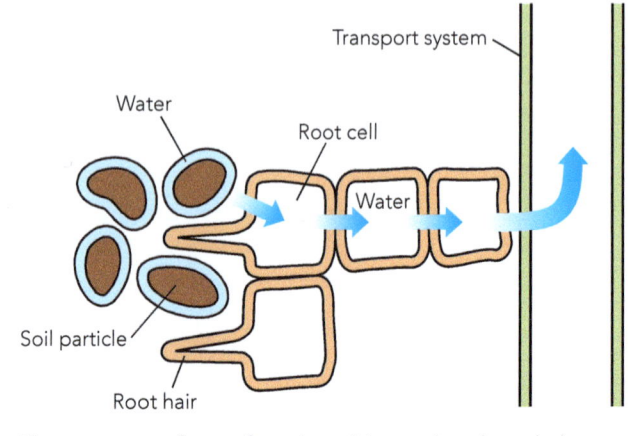

The movement of water from the soil into a plant through the root hair cells

2 Circulation and respiration

Mineral ions from the soil

When plants photosynthesise, they make carbohydrates. However, to be healthy and make new plant growth, they need other things too, particularly nitrogen, phosphorus and potassium. These **mineral ions** all come from well-fertilised soil. Plants take up the mineral ions from the soil through their roots. The roots sometimes absorb the mineral ions along with the water, but sometimes they actively move them into the root cells.

This is why farmers regularly put **fertiliser** on their fields. The fertiliser may be manure from animals or special chemicals which the farmer can buy. Gardeners fertilise their soil to keep their vegetables growing large and their flowers blooming. People even give house plants special solutions of fertilisers often called 'plant food'. All of the fertilisers provide the following elements needed by the plants which are absorbed as mineral ions.

- Nitrogen – needed to give strong stems and big leaves.
- Phosphorus – needed for the roots to grow so the plants are not stunted. Without phosphorus, the roots don't grow and the leaves are yellow and can't make food properly.
- Potassium – needed to help plants use water, grow well and flower.

Potassium deficiency in a potato plant

Practical activity — Looking at roots

There are a number of ways in which you can look at the roots of plants and see how well suited they are to the uptake of water and mineral ions from the soil.

Set up some pea or bean seeds and let them germinate in a jar. Observe the growth of the root hairs. You could look at them with a magnifying lens or a microscope and measure them to see how far they go. Draw your observations.

Grow an onion suspended over water in a transparent jar and watch the development of the roots. Draw your observations.

Look at a prepared slide of a root hair cell under the microscope. Draw your observations.

Key terms
- fertiliser
- mineral ions
- root hair
- root hair cell

Summary questions

1 The roots of a plant have three main jobs. What are they?
2 Work in a group. Make a model of a root hair cell with labels explaining the different things that it does.
3 Make a poster to explain to people why it is so important to make sure that both gardens and farmers' fields are both well watered and well fertilised if possible.

2.2 Transport systems in plants

Learning outcomes

After this topic you should be able to:
- describe the role of the xylem in moving water and minerals up a plant
- describe the role of the phloem in moving food around a plant.

Plants make food in their leaves by photosynthesis. However, the sugars they make are needed all over the plant. The root hair cells take in water and mineral ions, but they are not just needed in the roots. Every cell in the plant depends on water to survive. So the transport systems of a plant are very important in moving substances all around the plant. There are two main transport systems, the **xylem** and the **phloem**.

The xylem

Most of the wood of a tree is made up of xylem vessels. The xylem carries water and mineral ions from the soil all around the plant. Xylem vessels are dead, but the water and minerals still move up them. Xylem cells have very thick walls so xylem is very important in supporting the stems of plants.

Practical activity — Investigating water transport

Take a celery stalk or the transparent stem of a plant such as *Impatiens*.

Add enough food colouring to water in a jar to give the water a strong colour, e.g. red or blue.

Place the base of the celery stalk in the coloured water and leave it for several hours or overnight.

Make observations of the external appearance of the celery. Then cut across the stalk in a number of places to see where the food colouring has stained. These are the xylem vessels.

The xylem vessels carry the water coloured by the dye up the stalks

The phloem

The phloem carries the sugars made by photosynthesis from the leaves to the rest of the plant, including the growing areas of the roots and shoots. This is where the sugars are needed to make new plant cells. The food is also transported to the plant's storage organs. It is needed to make an energy store to help the plant survive the winter. The phloem is a living tissue and it uses energy to move the food around.

2 Circulation and respiration

Expert tips

Plants have two transport systems – the xylem and phloem. Mammals, like us, only have one. An important role of our transport system is the transfer of oxygen and carbon dioxide. In plants these gases diffuse through the air spaces inside the plant; they are not transported in the xylem or phloem.

Aphids are plant pests. They stick their sharp mouthparts into the living phloem of plants and feed on the sugary liquid inside

Vascular bundles

The xylem and phloem in plant stems, roots and leaves are often arranged together in **vascular bundles**. When you look at a **section** of a plant stem under a microscope, it very easy to see the xylem and the phloem.

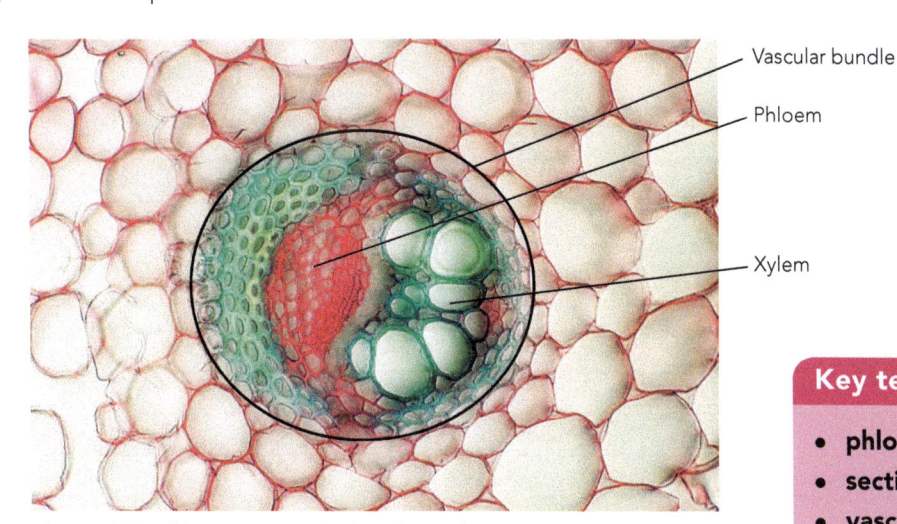

The xylem and the phloem in a vascular bundle in a buttercup stem

Key terms

- **phloem**
- **section**
- **vascular bundle**
- **xylem**

Summary questions

1 Make a table to show the similarities and differences between xylem and phloem.
2 If you repeated the celery experiment but placed the stem of a white flower, e.g. a gerbera, in the coloured water, what result would you expect and why?
3 Animals such as antelopes and deer can kill young trees by eating the bark all around the base of the tree. Using your knowledge and the figure above, explain why this happens and suggest ways in which it might be prevented.

2.3 Transport in humans

Learning outcomes

After this topic you should be able to:
- name the main parts of the circulatory system
- describe the main functions of the circulatory system.

Expert tips

A good way to learn the circulatory system is to make a very large diagram on the floor of your classroom, a playground or on a field. Show the heart and all the other large organs and the large blood vessels. Walk around the diagram deciding what happens to blood as it goes through each organ.

Think about all the things that go on in the village, town or city where you live. A whole complicated transport system makes sure that all the needs of the people are met. Make a list of as many of these needs as you can.

Just like your community, your body has many needs. The cells of your body must have food and oxygen. Carbon dioxide and other wastes need removing. Repairs must be made, diseases need fighting, and messages need carrying. Amazingly your body has one big system to carry out all of these functions and to move materials to and from the cells.

The transport system of the body

The heart, the blood and the blood vessels make up the transport system of your body. This table shows you some of the things carried around the body in the blood.

What is transported	Where it is transported
oxygen	from lungs to all the cells for respiration
carbon dioxide	from all the cells to the lungs in order to be removed
food	from the gut to all the cells for respiration
waste products like urea	from all the cells to the kidneys in order to be removed
chemical messages	from the places where they are made to the whole body
repair system of the body	to wherever damage takes place
defence system of the body	to wherever disease causing organisms have entered the body

The blood vessels

The heart pumps your blood around a system of tubes called blood vessels. Some blood vessels carry blood away from your heart around your body. These are called **arteries**. The blood they carry is usually rich in oxygen and bright red. They have a pulse from the force of the heart beat.

Other blood vessels bring blood back to the heart. These are called **veins**. The blood they carry is usually loaded with carbon dioxide so it is a dull red, and they do not have a pulse.

Connecting the arteries to the veins is a network of very tiny blood vessels called **capillaries**. The capillaries run through the tissues

2 Circulation and respiration

Practical activity — Discovering blood vessels

Arteries

There is an artery that runs down your wrist. You cannot see the artery but you can feel the pulse and use it to work out how many times your heart beats in a minute.

Use the diagram to help you find your pulse.

Once you can easily find your pulse, sit quietly for a few minutes and then take your pulse. Count the beats of your pulse for 15 seconds and then multiply your result by 4 to find your heart rate per minute.

Veins

Open and close your fist a few times. Now look on the inside of your wrist or in the crook of your elbow. You should be able to see some veins close to the surface.

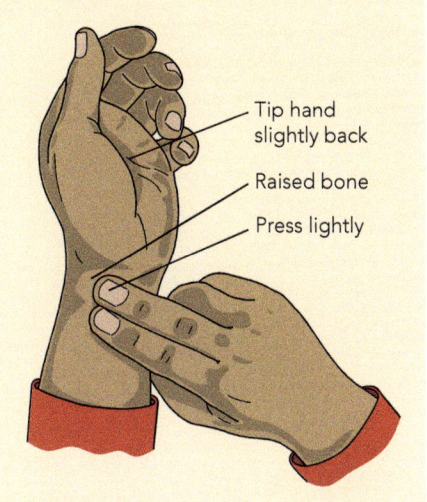

- Tip hand slightly back
- Raised bone
- Press lightly

Your pulse is found where an artery passes close to your skin

of your body, carrying substances to and from the cells. Capillaries have very thin walls so that substances can be exchanged between the blood and the tissues very easily.

Blood moves quite slowly in the capillaries. Food and oxygen dissolved in the blood move out into the cells that need them. At the same time, substances that are not needed in the cells move out into the blood. Substances often move from places where they are plentiful to places where they are in short supply. You will see this clearly when you look at what happens in the lungs (see page 42).

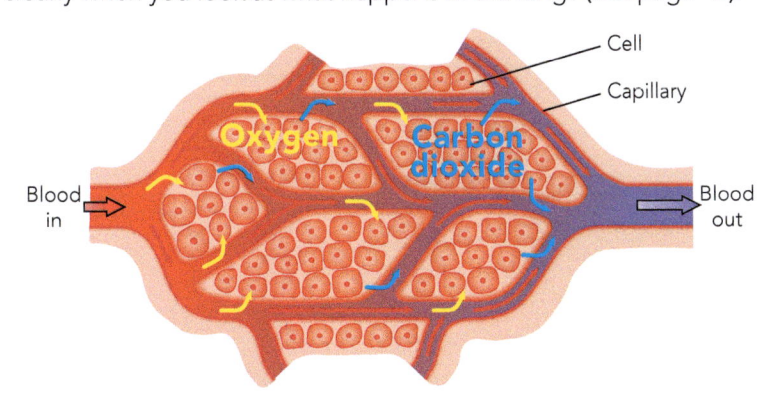

All cells have capillaries close by so substances can move in and out

Key terms

- arteries
- capillaries
- veins

Summary questions

1. a) Describe the functions of arteries, veins and capillaries.
   b) Name two substances that pass from the blood to the cells and one substance that passes from the cells to the blood.
2. Work in a group. Do some research into the structure of arteries, veins and capillaries. Make a model or a poster about these important blood vessels.

2.4 The heart

Learning outcomes

After this topic you should be able to:
- describe the structure of the human heart
- explain how the heart beats
- describe how to investigate the heart rate.

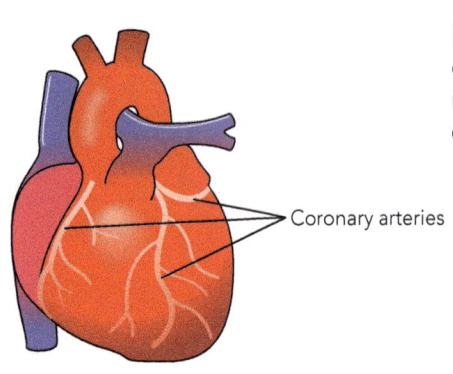

Your heart is a bag of muscle which contracts, forcing the blood around your body about 70 times each minute. The heart has its own blood supply. The **coronary arteries** bring food and oxygen to the muscles of the heart itself.

The structure of the heart

Your heart is made up of two pumps that pump together. The right-hand side of your heart collects blood from around the body and pumps it to your lungs. This blood is low in oxygen and contains lots of carbon dioxide and other waste products. It is called **deoxygenated blood**.

In the lungs carbon dioxide passes from the blood to the air and oxygen passes from the air into the blood. This **oxygenated blood** returns to the left side of the heart which fills and then pumps the oxygen-rich blood around your body.

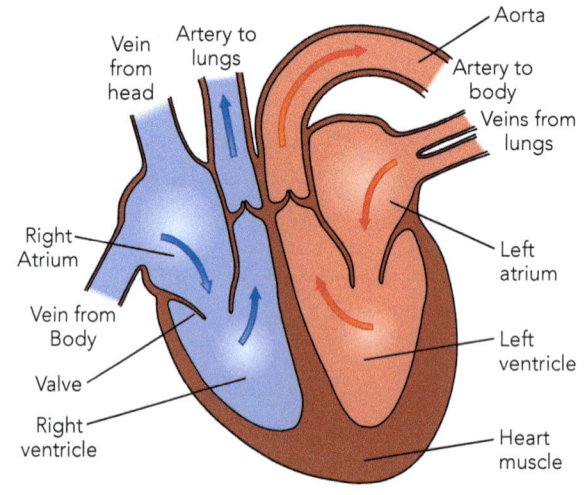

The coronary arteries

The structure of the heart

Practical activity   Amazing heart muscle

Use the class clock or a stopwatch. Clench and unclench your fist once every second for five minutes.

What does your hand feel like?

Your heart beats about once a second throughout your life. Fortunately it is made of special muscle that does not get tired like the muscles which move your hand!

The heart valves act as one-way gates to make sure the blood always flows the right way around the heart. If you listen to the heart through a stethoscope, the sounds of the heartbeat you hear are made by the valves closing.

2 Circulation and respiration

> **Practical activity**   Listening to the heart
>
> You can listen to the sound of a heart beating using an instrument called a stethoscope. You can make a simple stethoscope using a filter funnel and a cardboard tube or roll of paper.
>
> Place the filter funnel on the chest of a classmate. Put one end of the cardboard tube over the end of the funnel and put your ear at the other end. You should be able to hear the 'lub-dub' sound of the heart beat.
>
> Count how many times the heart beats in a minute.

Circulation and blood pressure

The human circulation is known as a double circulation because the heart pumps the blood twice in one complete circulation – once to the lungs and once to the body. A double circulation makes sure that the cells of the body get blood which is really rich in oxygen. Trace the pathway of the blood around the circulation shown in the diagram.

A double circulation like this is very important in warm-blooded, active animals like human beings because it is very efficient. It lets our blood get fully oxygenated in the lungs before it is sent off to the different parts of the body. In animals such as fish that have a single circulation, very few parts of the body receive fully oxygenated blood.

Every time your heart beats, it pumps blood into your arteries and around your body. The pressure of blood in your arteries is quite high. You can feel this when you take your pulse. After the beat, your heart must fill up with blood before it can pump again, and so the pressure in your arteries is lower. When a doctor measures your blood pressure, they measure the pressure both when the heart is emptying and when it is filling.

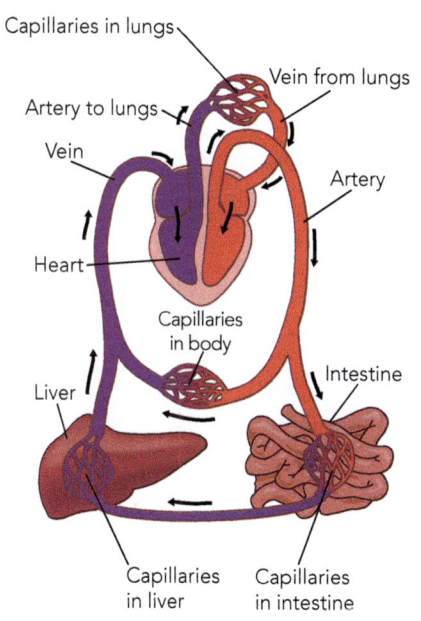

The double circulation to the lungs and to the body

> **Key terms**
>
> - **coronary arteries**
> - **deoxygenated blood**
> - **oxygenated blood**

> **Summary questions**
>
> 1 Your heart beats about 70 times a minute. How many heartbeats will you have had by the time you are 15 years old? (Don't forget the leap years!)
> 2 Make a flow diagram to show the flow of blood through the heart, starting with the blood entering the heart in the vein from the body.
> 3 Most arteries carry oxygenated blood and most veins carry deoxygenated blood. Which are the exceptions to this rule and explain why?

2.5 The blood

Learning outcomes

After this topic you should be able to:
- explain the functions of the blood
- recognise red blood cells and white blood cells
- explain how the structure of the blood cells is related to their function.

Expert tips

'Blood is the most important tissue in the body.' Do you agree with this statement? Discussing this with your teacher and your friends may help you to remember all the jobs that blood does for us.

If you cut yourself, you bleed. A red liquid called blood comes out of the wound. Blood is an amazing substance that carries out many different jobs in your body.

The functions of the blood

Blood is part of the transport system of the body. It carries oxygen and dissolved food to the cells where they are needed. It carries carbon dioxide and other waste products away from the cells so they do not build up and cause problems. The blood also carries chemical messages which control growth, reproduction and the day-to-day balance of your body.

Blood forms clots which dry into scabs after you have cut yourself. This stops you from bleeding to death and also stops disease-causing micro-organisms from getting into your body. The blood contains cells which can destroy many disease-causing micro-organisms and protect us from illness. If you lose some blood, your body can make some more.

What is blood made of?

A single drop of blood contains millions of tiny blood cells in a pale yellow liquid called plasma. Different types of blood cells do different jobs. The yellow liquid has its own jobs to do as well. Together they all make up the mixture we call blood.

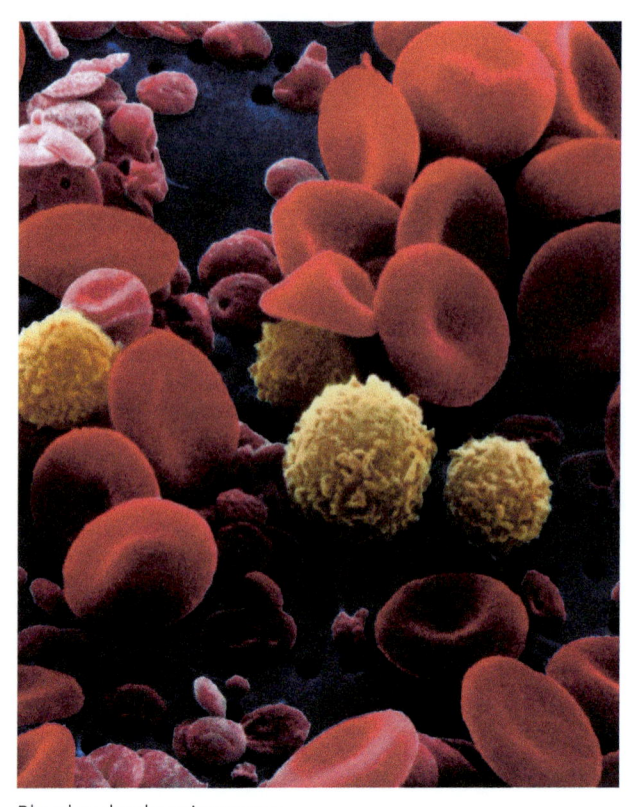

Blood under the microscope

2 Circulation and respiration

- There are more **red blood cells** than any other cells in the blood. They carry oxygen around your body. It is the red blood cells that give the blood its red colour.
- **White blood cells** are bigger than red blood cells. They come in different shapes and sizes. Their main job is to defend your body against disease. They look white when there are lots of them in one place.
- **Platelets** are tiny bits of cells. They help make clots and scabs over cuts, and repair your body.
- **Plasma** is the pale yellow liquid that makes up most of the blood. It is mainly water. The blood cells are suspended in the plasma. It also carries dissolved food, chemical messages and waste products such as carbon dioxide. The plasma also helps to make clots and scabs.

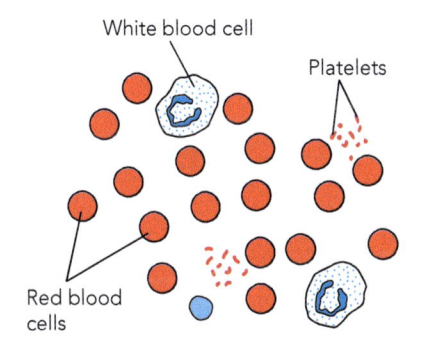

These are the cells that are found in the blood

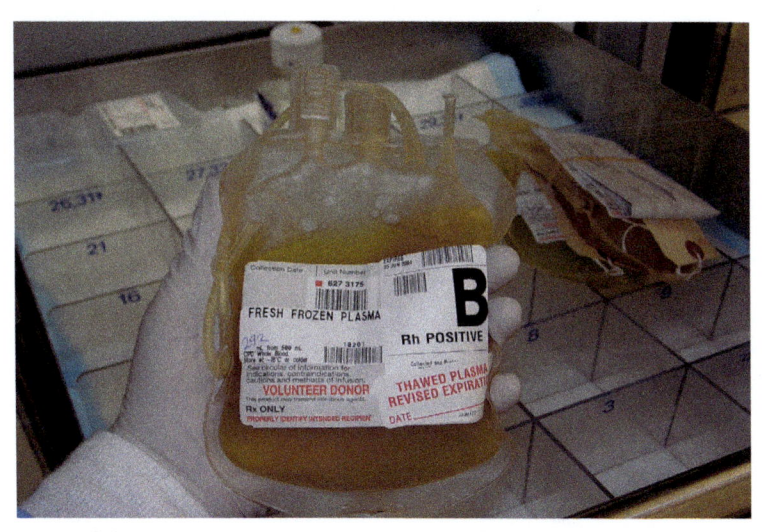

A bag of plasma, the yellow liquid that carries all of the blood cells and more around the body

Key terms

- plasma
- platelet
- red blood cell
- white blood cell

Summary questions

1. Make a table to show the main components of blood and their functions in the body.
2. Read this paragraph and answer the questions that follow:
   When people are hurt in accidents or have big operations they may be given blood. This blood has been given (donated) by other people. Great care is taken to make sure that the blood doesn't clot.
   a) Why do you think people might need to be given blood?
   b) Why is it so important that the blood doesn't clot?
3. Working in a group, make a collage of red blood cells, white blood cells, platelets and plasma.

2.6 Problems of the circulatory system

Learning outcomes

After this topic you should be able to:
- explain ways of keeping your heart healthy
- interpret data from an investigation about heart rate
- describe how heart problems can develop through fat being deposited in the coronary arteries
- research heart problems using secondary sources.

A fit heart can keep going for many years and lets you do everything you want to. However, if you have problems with your heart it can be very serious and even lead to death. In this topic you are going to look at what helps to make a fit, healthy heart, and what happens when things go wrong.

A healthy heart

When you first start exercising, your heart beats hard with the effort. But your heart is made of muscle. When it has to work hard regularly, it gets bigger and stronger. It beats more strongly and efficiently as you get fit. It can supply all the food and oxygen you need without beating too hard or too fast. Fitness affects your whole body. If you are fit it is easier to cope with the demands of being alive.

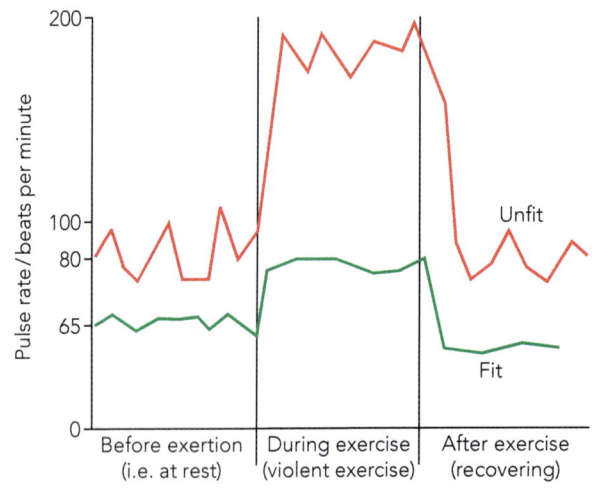

How exercise affects the heart rate

Practical activity — How exercise affects your heart rate

Remember how to take your pulse? Look back to page 33 and remind yourself. Now you are going to investigate what happens to your heart when you exercise.

Sit quietly for a couple of minutes and then take your resting pulse. Collect data from everyone in your class and display it in a suitable graph or chart.

If it is safe, exercise on the spot for 1 minute, e.g. run on the spot. Retake your pulse as soon as you stop exercising.

- Describe the change in your pulse. Collect the data from the whole class again and display it on a suitable graph or chart.
- What can you say about the effect of exercise on the heart rate, and about the differences between people in your class?
- Explain your conclusions using your scientific knowledge and understanding.

2 Circulation and respiration

Heart problems

Many people do not have a very healthy lifestyle. Many things can affect the health of your heart. One of these is exercise. If you exercise regularly, your heart will be strong and muscular and is more likely to be healthy. Also you are less likely to develop an atheroma (see topic 1.3, page 9) if you take regular exercise.

As you get older your coronary arteries may get narrower. They can also get narrower because of atheromas – fatty material building up on the walls of the blood vessels. The risk of the blood vessels getting blocked in this way goes up when people eat a lot of fat in their diet or become obese. When the coronary arteries get narrower, not so much blood can flow through them. This means that not enough food and oxygen reaches the muscle of the heart. This can cause pain, a heart attack or even death. A heart attack is when part of the heart muscle dies because it does not get enough oxygen.

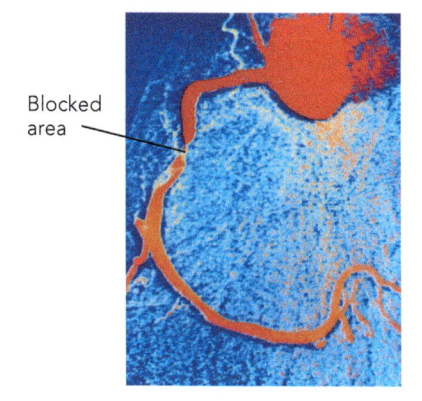

Stent and balloon in place

Fatty deposits narrow artery

Balloon inflated to open stent and artery

Stent holds artery open

You can see the difference made by the blocked area of the coronary artery

The problem of diseased coronary arteries can be solved using a **stent**. A stent is a metal mesh which is put into an artery to hold it open and let the blood flow normally (shown on the right). Doctors can also do bypass surgery. They carry out an operation to replace the 'furred up' artery with a piece of a healthy blood vessel taken from somewhere else in the body.

The best idea is to keep your risk of having these problems as low as possible. You can do this by not smoking, eating a healthy, low fat diet and taking plenty of exercise.

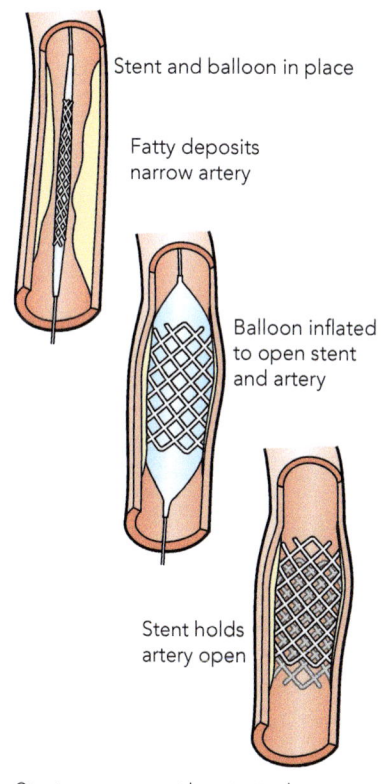

Stents can prevent heart attacks

Key terms

- **stent**

Summary questions

1 Why are the coronary arteries so important for the health of your heart?
2 Make a poster or a presentation to tell people in your community how to take care of their hearts and avoid furring up of the arteries and increasing the risk of heart attacks.
3 Work in a group of three, each finding out about one of the following:
   Leaky heart valves and how they can be treated; heart pacemakers; heart transplants.
   Make a short presentation to the rest of the group about it.

2.7 The respiratory system

Learning outcomes

After this topic you should be able to:
- describe the human respiratory (gas exchange) system
- explain the structure of the lungs
- plan an investigation to test ideas about the effect of exercise on your breathing rate.

People need to breathe to stay alive. When you **inhale** you breathe air into your lungs, taking in oxygen. When you **exhale** (breathe out) you are getting rid of carbon dioxide waste as you do so.

Practical activity — Counting your breaths

Use the classroom clock or a stopwatch. Count how many breaths you take in a minute. Breathing in and out again counts as one breath.

Record your breathing rate three times and work out the mean number of breaths you take each minute.

Plan and carry out an investigation into the effect of exercise on your breathing rate. Make and test a prediction, collecting data which is as reliable as possible.

The respiratory system

Your lungs are protected inside your rib cage. The lungs and the tubes which join them to your nose and mouth are known as the **respiratory system**.

You can't see the air you breathe out normally, but when it is very cold, the moisture in your breath condenses to form a 'cloud'

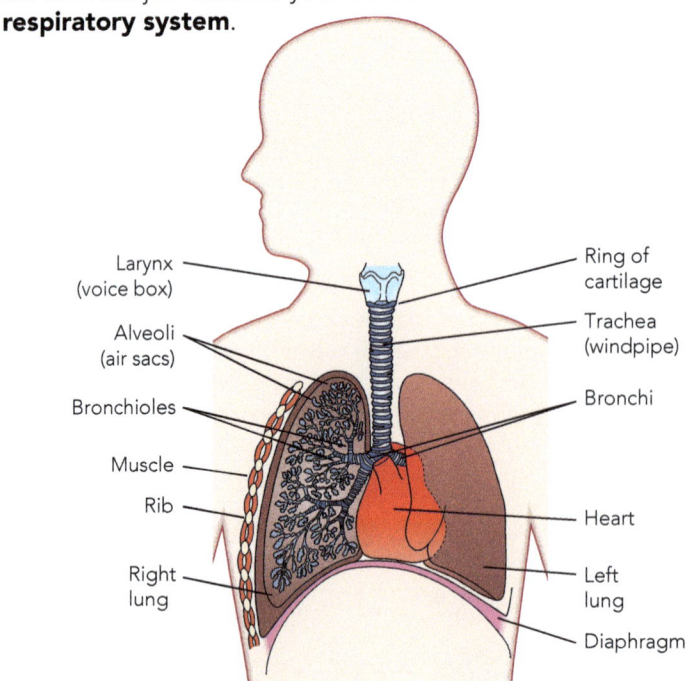

The human respiratory system

Usually, when you breathe in, air enters through your nose. The inside of your nose is warm, wet and hairy. So the air coming into the nose gets warmed and moistened, and is cleaned as dust gets trapped in the hairs.

The air goes down the windpipe which is lined with **cilia** (tiny hairs) to move dust, dirt and bacteria away from the lungs. In the chest, the windpipe divides into two bronchi which then split into smaller and smaller tubes called bronchioles. The air travels along these tubes into the lungs.

2 Circulation and respiration

The lungs are made of tiny air sacs called alveoli. This is where oxygen comes into your body and you get rid of waste carbon dioxide from the blood.

When you breathe out, the air travels back the way it came. However, it may leave your body through your mouth when you talk / or through your nose.

Breathing and exercise

How many times do you breathe in one minute? Predict what would happen to the number of breaths you take in a minute if you walked around the classroom for two minutes first. What do you think would happen if you jogged hard on the spot for a minute?

The volume of oxygen we need varies with what we do. Normally our body copes by breathing more deeply so a bigger volume of air goes into the lungs. We also breathe more quickly so the lungs fill and empty more often.

If you exercise hard and regularly, your lungs get bigger – they grow more alveoli – to supply the oxygen needed by your muscles.

Key terms
• cilia
• exhale
• inhale
• respiratory system

Practical activity — Measuring the volume of your lungs

You will need a large measuring cylinder full of water and a water bowl. You will need a piece of rubber tubing passing through the water in the trough into the full measuring cylinder.

Breathe in normally and then breathe out normally into the rubber tube.

Measure the volume of your normal breath in the measuring cylinder and record it.

Breathe in as deeply as you can. Then breathe out as hard as you can through the rubber tube to measure the maximum volume of air you can breathe out of your lungs. Record your result.

Share your results with the rest of the class and display your data on a chart or graph.

Measuring the volume of air you can exhale

Summary questions

1. If your nose is blocked, you may breathe in through your mouth. This is not as good for you as breathing in through your nose. Discuss the problems for:
   a) the lungs
   b) the whole body.

2. a) Why do people who live at altitude have bigger lungs than people who live at sea level?
   b) Pearl divers in Japan can stay below water for several minutes at a time searching for oysters on the sea bed. They manage without air tanks. Give a scientific explanation for this.

3. If you suffer from asthma, the tube leading into your lungs gets narrower. If you have bronchitis, the bronchi and bronchioles produce lots of thick, sticky mucus. Both of these illnesses make you feel short of breath because you can't get enough oxygen. Explain why each illness makes it hard to get the oxygen you need.

41

2.8 Breathing in and out

Learning outcomes

After this topic you should be able to:
- describe the movement of the ribs and diaphragm when you breathe in and out
- explain how gas exchange takes place in the alveoli of the lungs
- explain why it is important to keep the airways clear.

People often imagine their lungs like two pink balloons filling with air and then emptying as they breathe. But in fact your lungs are much more like a pair of pink sponges. You need to get as much oxygen out of the air as possible. Why do you think sponges might be better for this than balloons?

Alveoli – the air sacs of the lungs

Each of your lungs is made up of millions of tiny air sacs called alveoli that make it look like a sponge. The alveoli have very thin walls so that the air and the blood are as close to each other as possible. Oxygen goes from the air into the blood and carbon dioxide goes from the blood into the air to be breathed out. This **gas exchange** occurs all the time, not just when you breathe in.

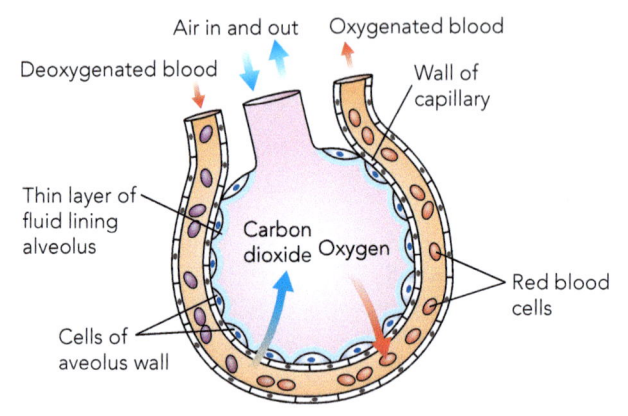

Gas exchange in a single alveolus

We need lots of oxygen for respiration to supply all the energy we need. We also have to get rid of the carbon dioxide produced so that we don't poison ourselves. The alveoli give our lungs an enormous surface area to exchange the gases we need. In each lung we have about 300 million alveoli. If all the alveoli in both the lungs could be spread out flat, they would cover a tennis court!

Breathing in and out

Put your hands on your ribs. Breathe in deeply, then breathe out hard. What happens to your ribs?

Breathing uses special muscles between your ribs, and your diaphragm. The diaphragm is a domed sheet of muscle across the bottom of your ribcage. It separates the organs of your chest from your digestive system. When you inhale, the muscles lift your ribs upwards and outwards. The diaphragm muscle contracts and flattens. This means the space inside your chest gets bigger and so air moves into your lungs. You breathe in.

When you exhale, the muscles between the ribs and the diaphragm muscle all relax. The ribs move down and the diaphragm flexes upwards again. This makes the space in the chest smaller again and squeezes the air out of the lungs. You breathe out.

2 Circulation and respiration

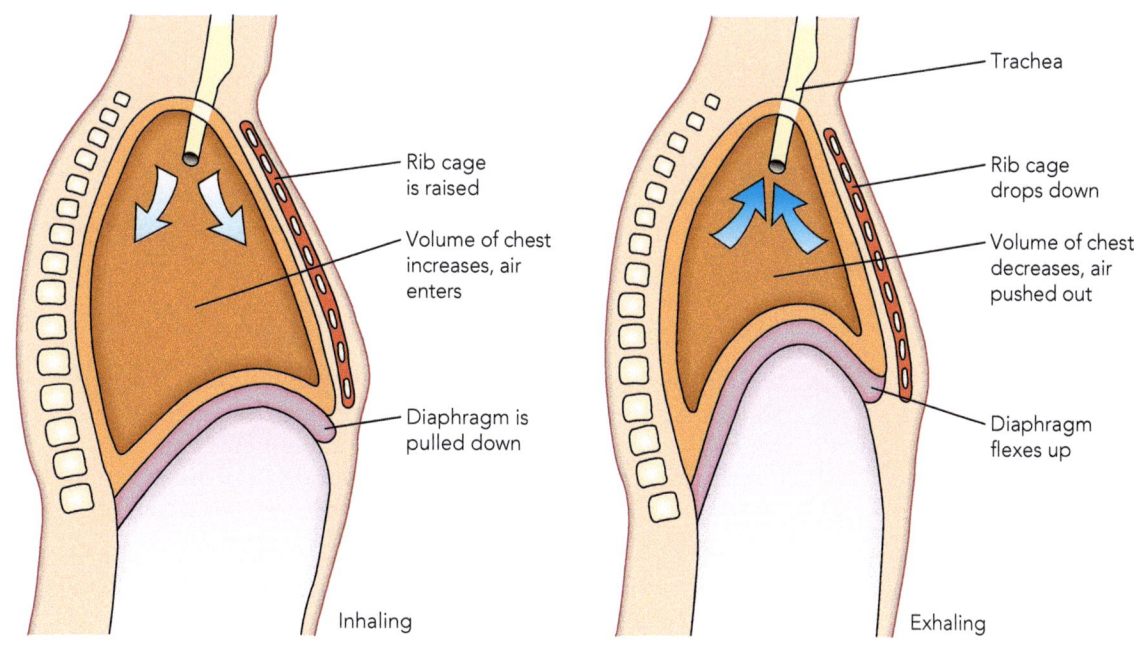

Inhaling — Rib cage is raised; Volume of chest increases, air enters; Diaphragm is pulled down

Exhaling — Trachea; Rib cage drops down; Volume of chest decreases, air pushed out; Diaphragm flexes up

The way you move air in and out of your lungs

Practical activity — A model of breathing

Your lungs are not balloons. However, you can use a model chest made with balloons to demonstrate how the movements of the diaphragm move air in and out of the lungs.

You may have the chance to examine a set of animal lungs. Try to see and draw the main parts of the respiratory system. Your teacher may blow air into a section of the lungs.

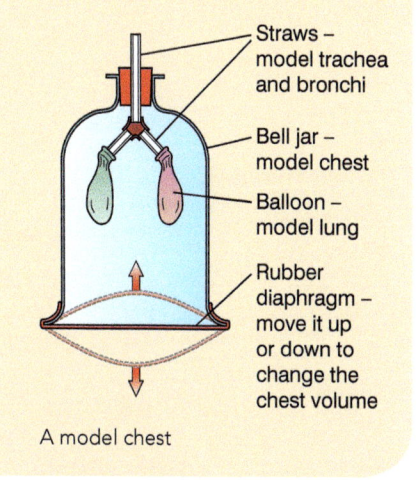

Straws – model trachea and bronchi
Bell jar – model chest
Balloon – model lung
Rubber diaphragm – move it up or down to change the chest volume

A model chest

Key terms
- **gas exchange**

Summary questions

1. An exchange of gases takes place in the alveoli. Which gases are exchanged?
2. Make a flow diagram to show the way in which air is moved into and out of the lungs.
3. Look at the model chest shown in the figure above. Explain carefully the ways in which it is a good model of breathing and the ways in which it is a very poor model.

2.9 Respiration in cells

Learning outcomes

After this topic you should be able to:
- explain the difference between respiration and breathing
- explain that aerobic respiration needs oxygen
- describe how glucose and oxygen reach every cell in the body and how waste products leave.

You will remember that respiration is one of the characteristics of all living things. Respiration is the way cells get energy from their food, and this often uses oxygen. In this chapter you have looked at breathing and the exchange of gases in the respiratory system. There is a link between breathing and respiration – try and work out what it is.

Aerobic respiration in cells

Respiration takes place in every cell of your body. Your cells use glucose as their energy source. They use oxygen to break down glucose and release the energy you need for everything you do. Carbon dioxide and water are produced as waste products. Respiration using oxygen is called **aerobic respiration**. The reaction can be summarised as a word equation:

glucose + oxygen $\longrightarrow$ carbon dioxide + water (+ **ENERGY**)

For aerobic respiration to take place, glucose and oxygen have to reach every cell in your body.
- The oxygen comes into the blood from the air breathed into the lungs through gas exchange in the alveoli. It moves into the cells from the blood in the capillaries.
- The glucose comes into the blood from the small intestine. It moves into the cells from the blood in the capillaries.
- Glucose and oxygen move from the blood in the capillaries into the cells of the body.

The reactions of respiration take place in the **mitochondria** in the cells of the body. The energy released in aerobic respiration is used in many different ways. The carbon dioxide produced as a waste product is poisonous and must be removed.
- The carbon dioxide leaves the cells and goes into the blood in the capillaries. It is carried to the lungs and moves out into the air in the alveoli to be breathed out and removed from the body.
- The water remains in the cells as it is useful.

Expert tips

Make sure that you do not confuse respiration and breathing. You are fully aware that you are breathing air in and out of your lungs. Respiration goes on inside all the cells of your body and is not something you are aware is happening.

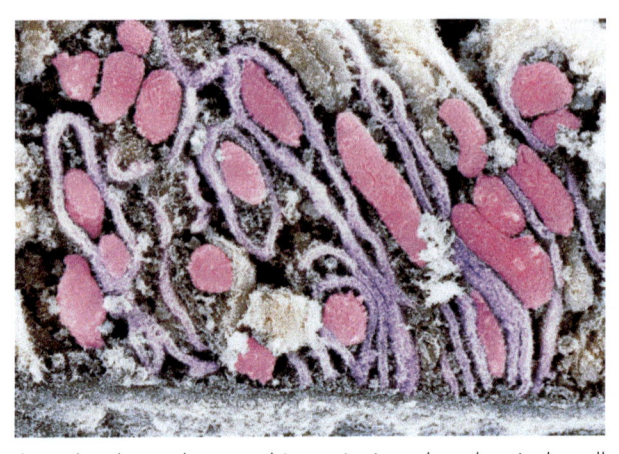

Mitochondria – the places where aerobic respiration takes place in the cells. The mitochondria in this scanning electron micrograph are coloured pink

2 Circulation and respiration

Use	How the energy is used
Growth	Making new cells, making new biomass (e.g. proteins, enzymes), growing babies
Energy stores	Animals make fat stores, plants store oils and starch
Movement	Energy is used to make our muscles contract. These are the muscles that we use to move about and the muscles that work all the time in the heart and the gut
Keeping the body temperature the same	Mammals and birds use energy to keep their bodies the same temperature whatever the outside temperature might be
Transport	Cells need energy to move some chemicals into the cell or out of it, and it takes energy to move substances around the body of a plant or an animal
Reproduction	All organisms use energy when they reproduce to form gametes. Some also provide food for the developing offspring.

The use of energy in the body

Airway problems

As you can see, a good supply of oxygen to the cells of your body is vital for aerobic respiration to take place. You also need to get rid of the poisonous carbon dioxide. To do this it is very important to be able to move air in and out of your lungs. Sometimes the airways become narrow or blocked and this makes it very difficult for you to get air in and out. You are short of oxygen and cannot get rid of carbon dioxide.

- In asthma the lining of the breathing tubes swells up so the tubes become narrow. It is often caused by an allergy. Drugs inhaled into the lungs are used to treat asthma. Left untreated it can be fatal.
- In chest infections, such as bronchitis and pneumonia, the lining of the breathing tubes produce thick, sticky mucus that fills and blocks the tubes. This makes it very difficult to get air in and out of the lungs and can cause breathlessness and even death.
- If a piece of food is inhaled and gets stuck in the airway, it can cause choking and death unless it is forced out of the body by coughing or by a sharp blow or squeeze.

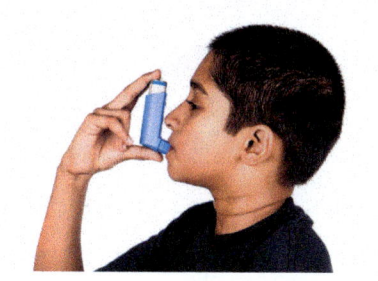

This boy is taking a drug using an inhaler. The drug makes the breathing tubes widen and so allows him to breathe more easily

Key terms

- **aerobic respiration**
- **mitochondria**

Summary questions

1. **a)** List two substances that are used up in respiration and two substances that are produced.
   b) Write out the word equation for respiration.
2. Some poisons work by stopping the mitochondria from working. People first become paralysed and then die. Suggest why these poisons kill people so quickly and why they become paralysed before they die.
3. Make a big poster to show exactly what happens to oxygen and carbon dioxide during breathing and aerobic respiration. Include a table on your poster to show the differences between inhaled and exhaled air (you will need to use secondary sources to find this).

45

2.10 Smoking and health

Learning outcomes

After this topic you should be able to:
- describe some of the problems that can arise from smoking
- explain the effect of paralysed cilia on the air reaching the lungs.

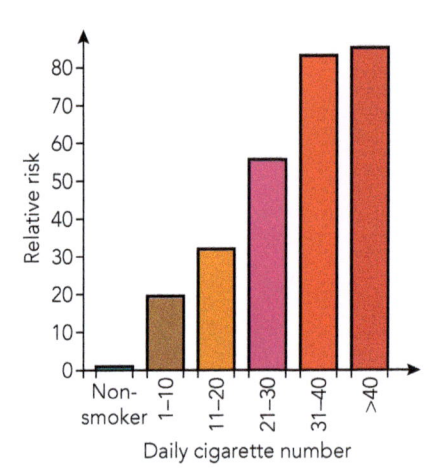

Many millions of people around the world smoke. Cigarette smoke contains the drug **nicotine** which is addictive, so once you start smoking it is difficult to stop. Smoking is expensive and has many negative effects on the human body, but people still keep smoking.

The lungs of a newborn baby are pink and clean. So are the lungs of many adults. But the lungs of smokers are grey. With each cigarette they are taking tar-laden smoke down into their lungs. This smoke also stops the normal air-cleaning system from working.

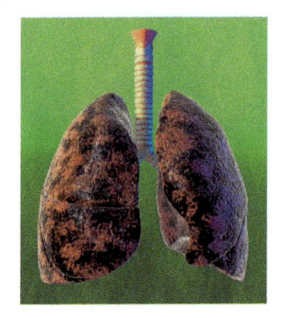

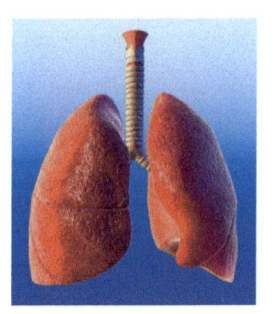

The effect of smoking on the lungs is very clear to see

This bar chart shows the effect of smoking different numbers of cigarettes each day on the risk of developing lung cancer

Tar and lung cancer

Tar is a thick, sticky black substance. It is made up of many different chemicals which get right into the delicate alveoli of the lungs. As tar builds up, the alveoli are damaged. The damaged tissue thickens until it is too thick for gas exchange to take place properly.

Some of the chemicals in tar can cause cancer. Lung cancer can grow 'silently' in the lung without causing problems until it is too late for doctors to help. Look at the bar chart – what is the effect of smoking on your chances of getting lung cancer?

Practical activity   Using a 'smoking machine'

You may get the chance to see a 'smoking machine' in your lessons.

This apparatus allows you to collect the tar from a cigarette and see how acidic the smoke is. There are lots of different versions of this apparatus.

More smoking related problems

Cancer of the mouth and throat are more common in smokers, but cancer isn't the only health risk from smoking. The lungs become thinner and weaker so that the alveoli break down to form larger sacs which fill up with fluid. Gas exchange cannot take place. This is emphysema. Coughs, shortness of breath and lots of phlegm are also more common in smokers. Smoking also has a very damaging effect on your heart. Smokers are much more likely to have a heart attack than non-smokers.

2 Circulation and respiration

Paralysed cilia

The lungs of many adults remain healthily pink. Cilia line the respiratory system moving dirt and mucus out of the tubes, keeping the lungs clean (see page 40). Tobacco smoke paralyses the cilia. Without the cilia working, tar as well as other dirt, bacteria and mucus get down into the lungs. Smokers cough to try and clear their lungs.

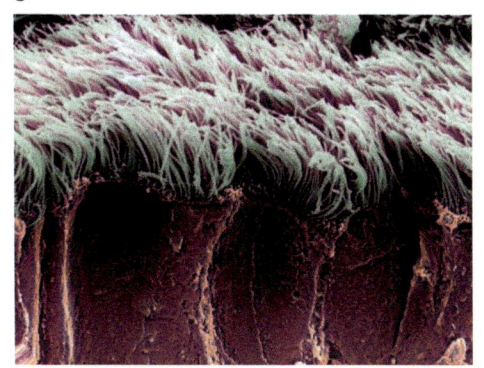

These are healthy cilia. In a smoker they would be paralysed and unable to keep the lungs clean

Who is affected?

Every cigarette has an effect. Your alveoli can't exchange gases easily with the air if they are covered with tar. You will smell of stale smoke and you won't be as good at physical activities as you would be if you didn't smoke.

The blood of smokers carries less oxygen than the blood of non-smokers. So if a pregnant woman smokes it means her growing baby is short of oxygen all the time. This affects the growth and development of the baby. Pregnant women who smoke are more likely to have a very small baby or a baby that dies before or soon after it is born.

Even if you don't smoke you can still be damaged by breathing in smoke from other people's cigarettes. But as soon as you stop smoking, or keep away from smoky places, the damage stops. Your lungs will gradually repair themselves until the damaging effects of smoking are gone for good.

Key terms

- **nicotine**
- **tar**

Summary questions

1. Name three diseases that can be caused by smoking.
2. Make a big poster to explain to other students in your school why smoking is bad for your health.
3. Work in a group. Make two lists. Collect all the reasons you can think of why people smoke. Then list all the reasons why smoking is not a good idea. Write an article for your school magazine explaining as much as you can about the dangers of smoking.

Chapter 2 — End of chapter questions

1 Seven structures involved with transport in animals and plants are listed below. The functions of each are also given. Match the letters that represent the structures with the numbers that represent the functions.

   A artery
   B phloem
   C plasma
   D platelets
   E root hair cell
   F vein
   G xylem

   1 absorbs water and minerals from the soil
   2 transports water and minerals in plants
   3 carries blood away from the heart
   4 stimulates blood to clot when exposed to the air
   5 transports sugars in plants
   6 carries blood towards the heart
   7 contains dissolved nutrients in the blood
   [7]

2 The diagram is a section through the human heart. It also shows the body's main blood vessels.

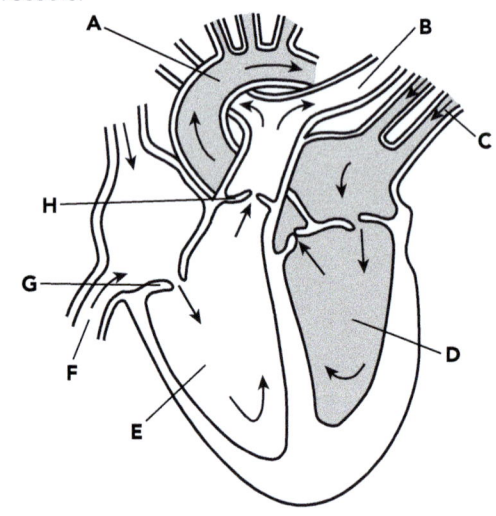

   a Copy and complete the table below.

Blood vessel	Type of blood	Where the blood travels	Blood pressure
A	oxygenated	brain, liver, kidneys, stomach	
B			low
C		heart	
F	deoxygenated		low

   [6]

   The structures labelled G and H are valves.

   b Explain why there are valves in the heart. [2]

   c Explain why the two chambers of the heart labelled D and E have thick walls. [2]

   d Explain why the circulation system is described as a *double circulatory system*. [2]

3 The diagram shows the respiratory system.

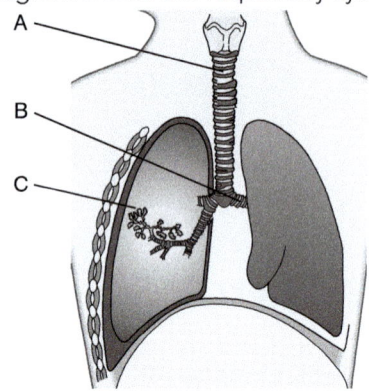

   a Name the structures labelled A, B and C. [3]

   b Movement of the diaphragm and the ribs causes air to flow in and out of the respiratory system.

   Copy and complete the table to show how the diaphragm and the ribs move when you breathe in and out.

	Breathing in	Breathing out
Diaphragm		
Ribs		

   Jaime and Carla looked at a model of the respiratory system and decided to make their own. They used a syringe and a balloon. They sawed off the nozzle of the syringe barrel and inserted a bung with a piece of plastic tubing through it. Their model is shown below.

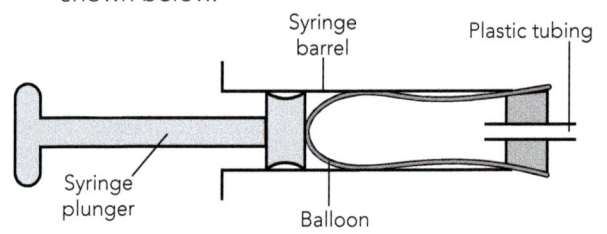

2 Circulation and respiration

c i What do the following parts of the model represent?
syringe barrel
syringe plunger
balloon
plastic tubing [4]

ii Describe what would happen to the model if the syringe plunger is pulled to the left and then pushed in to the right. [2]

iii Explain the way in which the model shows what happens during breathing. [3]

iv Other students in the class said that Jaime and Carla had not made a very good model to show breathing. Give two reasons why you think this is not a good model. [2]

4 At the beginning of a physical education lesson, a class of students was told to sit down for five minutes and then to take their pulse. Each student counted the number of heart beats in one minute.

a Describe the method used to take your own pulse. [2]

Here are the results that the class collected.
49, 52, 55, 57, 60, 60, 62, 63, 63, 63, 67, 67,
67, 68, 68, 69, 69, 69, 71, 71, 72, 73, 77, 78, 80

b Calculate the mean average of these results. [1]

c Make a table to show how many students had pulse rates in the 40s, 50s, 60s, 70s and 80s. Use your table to draw a histogram to show the variation in pulse rate in the class. [5]

d The students went to a physical education lesson where they did many different types of exercise. Explain what you would do to find out the way your heart rate changes when you do different types of exercise. [5]

5 Each 1 mm³ of your blood contains about five million red blood cells. The diagram shows some of these cells.

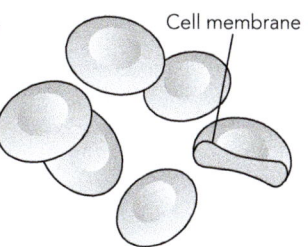

a Specialised cells such as red blood cells are adapted for the functions that they carry out.

i Describe two ways in which red blood cells are adapted for carrying oxygen. [2]

ii State what happens to red blood cells as they travel through capillaries in the lungs and in the muscles. [2]

b Some athletes go to training camps that are at high altitude, for example in the Rocky Mountains in the US and the Kenyan Highlands.

Explain why athletes train at altitude even though they may be competing in events at sea level. [3]

6 The diagram shows some cells from the lining of an airway in the lungs.

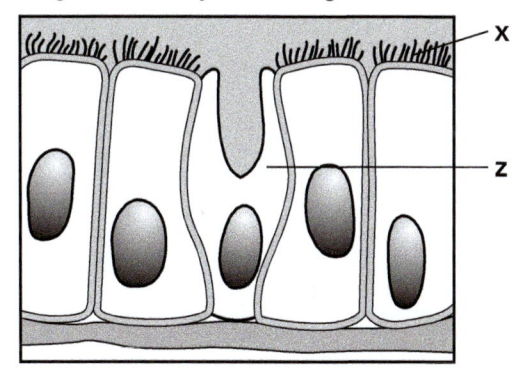

a i Name the structures labelled **X** and the substance made by cell **Z**. [2]

ii Explain the way in which these cells work together to protect the lungs. [2]

b Describe the effects of cigarette smoke on the cells that line the airways. [4]

c Many people who smoke say that they find it hard to stop. Suggest why this is so. [2]

49

3 Reproduction and growth

Science *in context!* Finding the causes and cures of disease

Sometimes the only way to discover what is causing a disease is to look at a whole population and discover who gets ill. The scientists who do this are called epidemiologists. They have to be detectives. It takes a lot of care. Just because two things happen does not mean they are linked. Global warming has increased as the numbers of pirates on the seas has fallen – but the two are not linked in any way. Finding cures isn't easy either.

Sir Richard Doll and smoking

Sir Richard Doll was a very famous epidemiologist – one of the first. In 1951, in the UK, Richard Doll noticed that many of the people he saw in hospital for cancer had lung cancer and many of them were men. Richard Doll and his colleague Austin Hill interviewed 1357 men with lung cancer – and they discovered that 99.5% of them were smokers. This suggested that smoking was linked to a very high risk of developing lung cancer. All of the research done since has shown exactly the same thing. Now people can be told clearly that if they smoke they have a much greater risk of developing lung cancer (and heart disease) so they can make a choice.

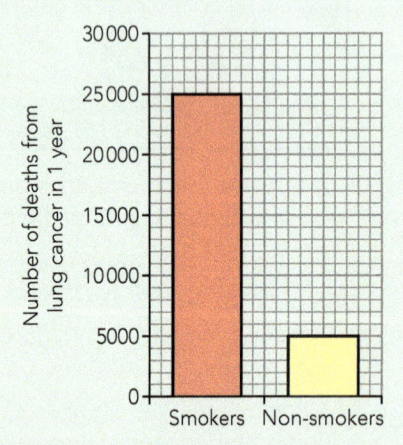

Sir Richard Doll

Number of cigarettes smoked per day	Annual death rate per 100 000 population	Relative risk
0	14	–
1–14	105	8
15–24	208	15
25+	355	25

Evidence like this helped scientists such as Sir Richard Doll find the link between cigarette smoking and lung cancer

In this chapter you will find out about the human reproductive system and adolescence. You will also see how a fetus grows in the mother and the factors that affect growth. Finally you will discover how conception, growth, development, behaviour and health can all be affected by diet, drugs and disease.

3 Reproduction and growth

Dr Aklilu Lemma and snails

In the 1960s, people knew that freshwater snails were involved in spreading the terrible disease schistosomiasis. The disease affects about 300 million people in tropical and sub-tropical parts of the world. It makes people weak and ill and stops them working. The only way to control the snails was to use expensive chemicals.

Aklilu Lemma noticed in his research in Ethiopia that when women had been washing clothes in a stream using the local soapberry called Endod, the snails in the water downstream were dead. He showed that a very dilute solution made from the crushed berries could kill the snails. He did local trials to show that the numbers of young children infected dropped from 50% to 7% where he had treated the water. It has taken many years to convince the world, but now the use of Endod to control schistosomiasis is spreading fast.

Key points

- Sexual reproduction is reproduction involving the joining of two special sex cells or gametes from two parent organisms.
- The main parts of the human female reproductive system are the ovary, uterus, oviduct, vagina and cervix.
- The menstrual cycle is the 28 day cycle in women when an egg ripens and is released from the ovary and the lining of the uterus builds up to support a pregnancy and is then shed as the monthly period.
- Female sex cells are ova or eggs. They are large, there are relatively few of them and they do not move themselves.
- The male gametes are sperm. They are very small, there are millions of them and they can swim.
- The main parts of the human male reproductive system are the penis, testes, scrotum, the glands and the sperm duct.
- In sexual intercourse the penis is placed inside the vagina and semen is ejaculated.
- Fertilisation takes place when the nucleus of the sperm and the ovum fuse.
- The cell divides and the tiny embryo moves through the oviduct and implants into the uterus.
- The fetus develops in the uterus for 40 weeks. The placenta supplies it with food and oxygen from the mother and removes carbon dioxide and other wastes.
- Growth involves the production of more cells and the permanent increase in size of the cells.
- Growth charts show the growth of an average child from babyhood to adulthood.
- Puberty is the stage in the teenage years when the body grows and becomes sexually mature.
- Drugs can be used to prevent pregnancy and to help a woman ovulate.
- Drugs can affect a developing fetus and stop it growing normally. Drugs can be used to help children grow healthily.
- Drugs can affect health, well-being and behaviour. Addiction to a drug can lead to changes in behaviour and damage.
- Disease can affect reproduction, growth, development and behaviour. It usually has a negative effect.

3.1 The female reproductive system

Learning outcomes

After this topic you should be able to:
- name the main parts of the female reproductive system
- describe the function of the female reproductive system.

All living things eventually die. So while they are fit and strong, all living organisms need to reproduce (make more of themselves). If plants and animals didn't make baby plants and animals, then soon there would be no living things at all!

Different generations of a family

Some living organisms make more of themselves simply by splitting in two. However, most living things use some form of **sexual reproduction**.

In sexual reproduction there are two parents, one female and one male. A special cell or **gamete** from the female joins with a gamete from the male to make a new and different cell. This cell will grow into a new person or plant.

In mammals, including people, the fertilised egg develops inside the mother. The **fetus** grows and develops until the baby mammal can live outside the body of the mother. Mammals look after their young once they are born. Mammals even make milk, a special food to feed their babies on.

Female reproductive organs

The female reproductive organs have two main jobs:
- they produce the female sex cells, and
- they provide a home for a growing baby when it is needed.

By the time a baby girl is born, her ovaries contain all the eggs she will ever need. After puberty, an egg matures and is released each month. Eventually, when she is 45–55 years old, she will run out of eggs and can no longer have babies.

When the egg leaves the ovary each month, it travels down the oviduct towards the uterus. This is where a baby grows and develops during pregnancy. The passageway leading from the outside of the body to the uterus is called the vagina.

3 Reproduction and growth

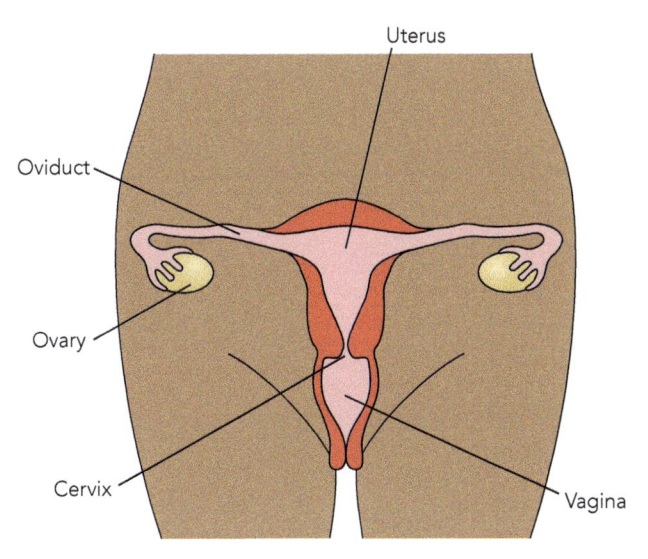

The female sex organs

The functions of the female reproductive organs

- The **ovary** contains eggs or **ova (singular ovum)** (eggs) and releases one every month. It also makes female sex **hormones**, special chemicals that affect how the body works.
- The **uterus** or womb is the organ where a baby grows during pregnancy. It has strong muscular walls.
- The **oviduct** carries the eggs from the ovary to the uterus. The male gametes called sperm meet the eggs in the oviduct. The oviducts are lined with cilia which beat and move the eggs towards the uterus.
- The **vagina** is the part of the body where the penis fits into the woman and where the sperm are left when they leave the penis.
- The **cervix** is the narrow opening of the uterus into the vagina.

An ovum in the oviduct – you can see the cilia clearly

Key terms

- **cervix**
- **fetus**
- **gamete**
- **hormones**
- **ova (singular ovum)**
- **ovary**
- **oviduct**
- **sexual reproduction**
- **uterus**
- **vagina**

Summary questions

1 What is sexual reproduction?
2 Explain the job of the ovaries in the body.
3 Make a large poster showing the female sex organs labelled with their functions.

53

3.2 The menstrual cycle and fertility

Learning outcomes

After this topic you should be able to:
- describe the menstrual cycle in women
- explain at which part of the menstrual cycle a woman is most fertile.

Expert tips

An important role of the hormones that control the menstrual cycle is to make sure that the uterus is ready to receive an embryo if fertilisation should occur. If the uterus is not ready for implantation, pregnancy will not begin.

Once a girl is well into **puberty** her **menstrual cycle** begins. She will know this has happened because about every four weeks she will have a period - a few days of bleeding from her vagina. What is actually happening during these events?

1. Each month some eggs start to ripen in the ovaries. After about two weeks one ovum (egg) will be ripe and ready to leave. In the uterus, a special rich lining of little blood vessels, cells and mucus builds up. This is ready to support the developing baby if the ovum is fertilised. When the ovum is ripe, it bursts out from the ovary into the oviduct. This is called **ovulation**.

Ovulation

2. When the ovum is in the oviduct, it could be fertilised by a sperm and begin to grow into a baby. The ovum travels towards the thick lining of the uterus.

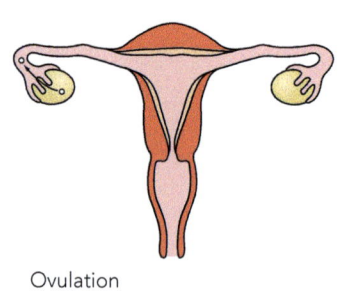

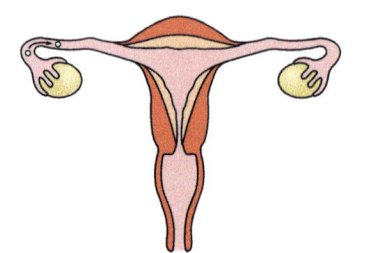

The egg moves along the oviduct

3. If the ovum is not fertilised it dies. The lining of the uterus isn't needed, so about two weeks after ovulation it is lost from the uterus. This lining – cells, mucus and blood – is lost through the vagina as the period, which lasts just a few days. Then the whole cycle starts again.

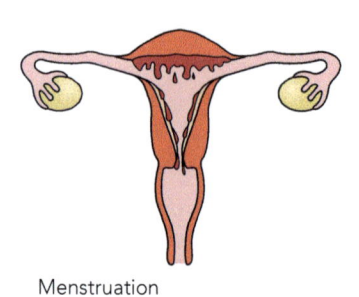

Menstruation

The changes in the female reproductive system during the menstrual cycle

The menstrual cycle starts during puberty. It takes about 28 days (four weeks) from beginning to end, although this varies a lot – particularly when a girl is young and her periods first start. The menstrual cycle carries on (except when a baby is developing) until the ovaries run out of ova. The menopause is when the periods finally stop at about 50 years of age.

The menstrual cycle involves changes in hormone levels in the body. Girls and women may feel tense or irritable at some stages of the cycle, particularly just before a period is due. This is called premenstrual tension (PMT).

Key terms

- menstrual cycle
- ovulation
- puberty

3 Reproduction and growth

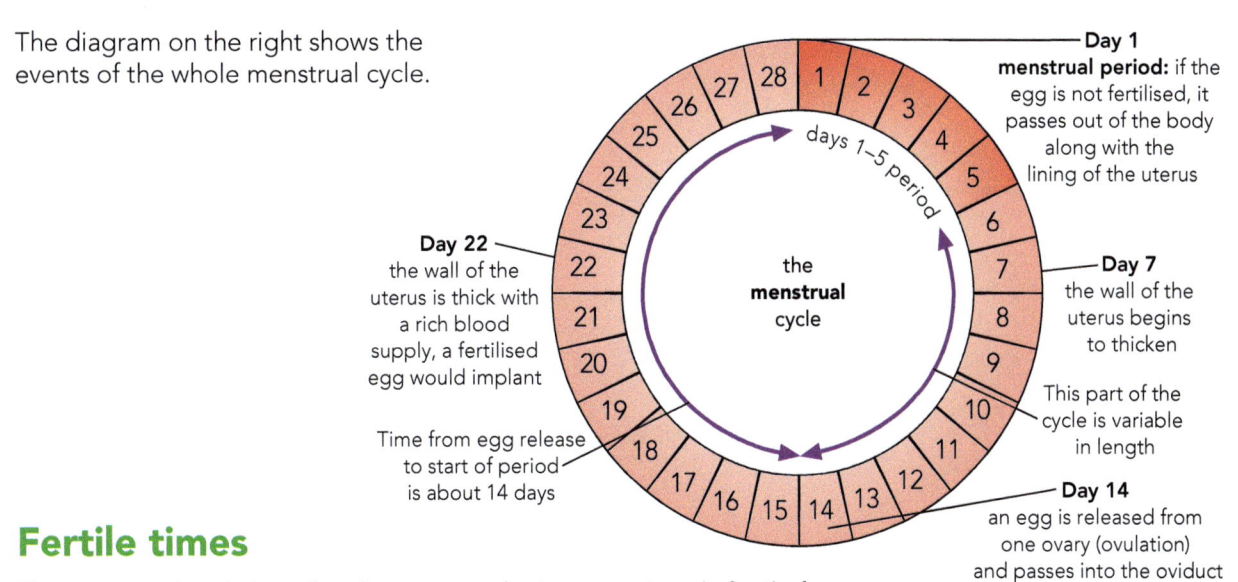

The diagram on the right shows the events of the whole menstrual cycle.

Day 1 — menstrual period: if the egg is not fertilised, it passes out of the body along with the lining of the uterus

Day 7 — the wall of the uterus begins to thicken

This part of the cycle is variable in length

Day 14 — an egg is released from one ovary (ovulation) and passes into the oviduct

Day 22 — the wall of the uterus is thick with a rich blood supply, a fertilised egg would implant

Time from egg release to start of period is about 14 days

Fertile times

The menstrual cycle lasts for about a month. A woman is only fertile for a very short time during this cycle. She can only get pregnant when an ovum (egg) has been released from the ovary in the middle of the cycle. Each ovum only lives for about 24 hours after ovulation. So the ovum must meet a sperm in that short space of time. Sperm can live inside the female body for about three days after they are released. This means that there are about three days each month when sexual intercourse can result in pregnancy. These are the two days before ovulation and the day of ovulation itself.

Practical activity — Predicting periods

Aisyah's periods are usually every 28 days. She always makes a note of the day she starts her period to help her be ready for the next one. Here are some pages from her calendar.

- Predict the day and date of Aisyah's next period.
- Aisyah and her husband want to have a baby. On which days in November should they have sexual intercourse to have the best chance of becoming pregnant?

Summary questions

1. **a)** What is the menstrual cycle? **b)** What controls the menstrual cycle?
   c) What is ovulation?
2. **a)** Why does the lining of the uterus thicken each month? **b)** What is a period?
3. Make a model of the menstrual cycle which can be used to teach women about how their cycle works and when they are fertile. It will need a pointer or some other way of indicating the different days of the cycle.

3.3 The male reproductive system

Learning outcomes

After this topic you should be able to:
- name the main parts of the male reproductive system
- describe the main functions of the male reproductive system.

The special cells (gametes) that take part in reproduction have to join together to form a new life. When they join together it is called **fertilisation**.

The sex cells or gametes

Female sex cells are always bigger than male sex cells, but there are usually many more male gametes than female ones. The male cells have to travel to reach the female cells inside the body of the woman (see topics 3.1 and 3.2). In humans and other animals, the big female sex cell is called an **ovum** (plural ova) or egg. The small male sex cells are called **sperm**. They leave the body of the male and swim towards the egg by lashing their long tails.

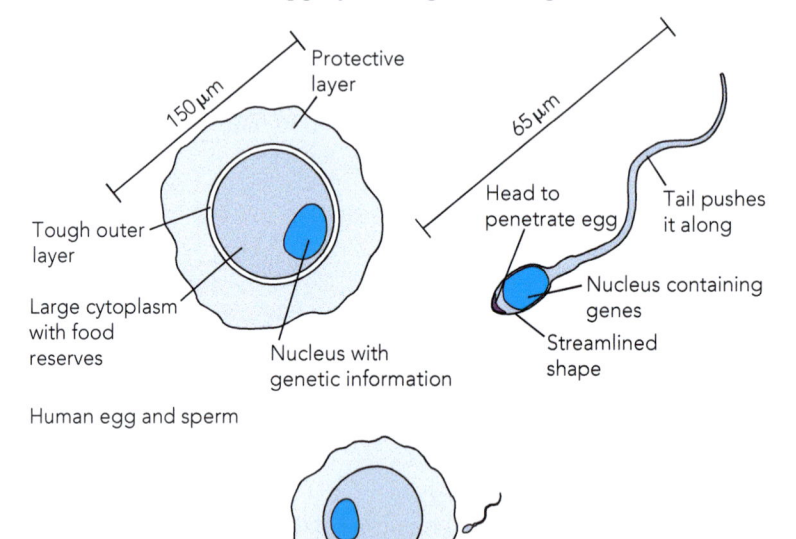

Human egg and sperm

The relative size of the egg and the sperm

Male reproductive organs

Men have **testes** (singular **testis**) which make sperm, the male sex cells. They are held in a bag of skin called the **scrotum**.

The sperm travel up the sperm ducts from the testes and mix with a liquid produced by the glands. The sperm and liquid together are called **semen**. This travels out of the man's body through a tube in the **penis** called the urethra. (The urethra also carries urine away from the body.) Once a boy's body begins making sperm, it will go on for the rest of his life.

During the development of a baby boy the testes are formed in his abdomen. By the time of birth they have usually moved down into the scrotum.

In normal healthy semen there are hundreds of millions of sperm – over 20 million sperm per 1 cm^3 of semen. An average ejaculate contains 3 cm^3 of semen.

3 Reproduction and growth

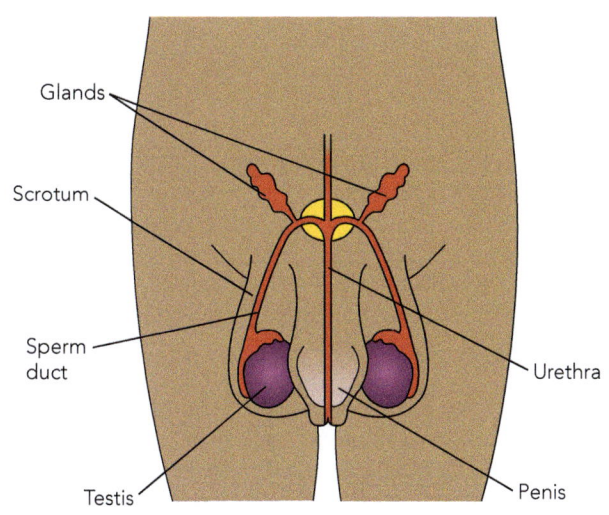

The male reproductive system (labels: Glands, Scrotum, Sperm duct, Testis, Urethra, Penis)

- The testes make sperm. They also make the male sex hormone which controls the changes in a boy's body at puberty.
- The penis fits inside the vagina of the woman. The penis contains special tissue which fills with blood when a man is sexually excited. The sperm leave the penis to go into the body of the woman during ejaculation (see page 58).
- The glands add liquid containing food to the sperm to make semen.
- The scrotum is a bag of skin which holds the testes outside the body of the man. It keeps them at a slightly lower temperature than the rest of the body. This is the right temperature for them to make sperm as fast as possible.
- The **sperm duct** carries the sperm from the testes to the penis.
- The urethra carries the semen out of the penis. A special ring of muscle or sphincter makes it impossible for urine and semen to pass out of the penis at the same time.

Key terms

- fertilisation
- ovum
- penis
- scrotum
- semen
- sperm
- sperm duct
- testes (testis singular)

Summary questions

1. Sort out the following words into two columns headed Female and Male:
   penis, vagina, testes, ovaries, uterus, scrotum, sperm, egg, oviduct, sperm tube, glands

2. a) What is the job of the testes?
   b) State the ways in which sperm differ from eggs.
   c) Suggest why the sperm are so different from the female gamete.

3. Make a table to show the similarities and differences between the male and female reproductive systems.

3.4 Fertilisation and development of the early embryo

Learning outcomes

After this topic you should be able to:
- explain how the egg is fertilised by the sperm
- describe how the fertilised egg moves along the oviduct and implants in the uterus.

All that is needed to make a new human being is an egg, a sperm and somewhere warm and safe for the baby to grow. Ask anyone who has had a baby and they will tell you that this makes it all sound far too simple – but it does give you the basic facts! In human reproduction, a sperm must join with an ovum (egg) inside the body of a woman. Then the baby develops and grows inside her body for about 40 weeks before it is born.

The journey of a sperm

The sperm get inside the woman's body during sexual intercourse. This is also known as 'making love' and 'having sex'. It is a very enjoyable part of a loving relationship between a man and a woman which makes it possible to have a baby.

When the man feels sexually excited, his penis fills with blood and becomes stiff (erect). When the woman feels sexually excited her vagina becomes wider and very moist which makes it easy for her partner to slip his penis into it.

During sex, the man and woman move their bodies against each other which makes them both feel good. When the man is very excited certain muscles contract that pump semen out through his penis. This is known as **ejaculation**. Although only a small amount (about a teaspoonful) of semen is produced each time a man ejaculates, it contains about 500 million sperm.

Sperm meets egg

In sexual intercourse, the semen is pumped into the woman's vagina. Then the sperm can easily swim in the semen up through the cervix, into the uterus and on into the oviducts. Millions of sperm die on the way. When an ovum is passing down one of the oviducts at the time, lots of sperm will gather around it. Finally one sperm will break through the protective layers around the outside of the egg and get in. The tail of the sperm breaks off. The nucleus of the sperm joins with the nucleus of the egg and they fuse. This is **fertilisation**.

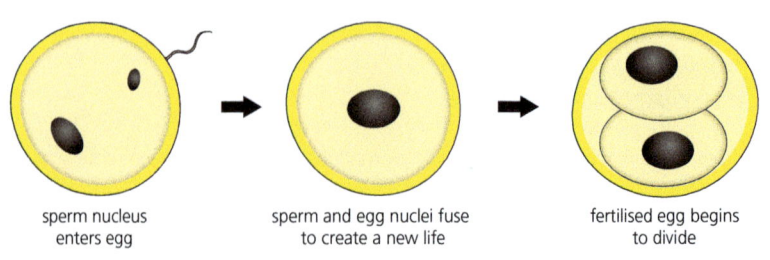

sperm nucleus enters egg → sperm and egg nuclei fuse to create a new life → fertilised egg begins to divide

A new life is created when sperm and egg nuclei fuse

3 Reproduction and growth

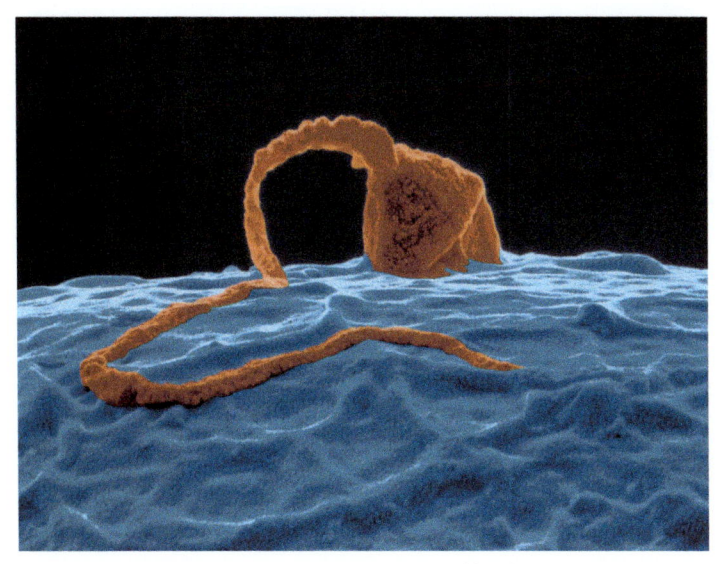

The moment when a sperm gets into an ovum to fertilise it – and a potential new human life is formed

The start of a pregnancy

When fertilisation happens, the sperm and egg form a single new cell. This cell contains all the information needed to grow into a new person. A baby contains millions of cells so a lot of growing and developing has to be done before a baby can be born. The single cell will grow and divide and the new cells will divide again. This starts to happen as the fertilised egg continues to be moved along the oviduct by the beating of the cilia.

When the tiny developing **embryo** reaches the uterus, it settles into its blood-rich lining. This lining has formed during the menstrual cycle, and the embryo starts to attach to it firmly. This is called **implantation**. The cell division that starts after fertilisation will happen time after time for about 40 weeks. The fertilised ovum becomes a complete baby which is ready to be born.

Key terms

- ejaculation
- embryo
- fertilisation
- implantation

Summary questions

1. a) In what ways do eggs and sperm differ from each other?
   b) The sperm do not always meet an ovum. Why not?
   c) Why do you think so many sperm are produced at a time but usually only one ovum?
2. Draw or label a sequence of diagrams showing ovulation, fertilisation, cell division and implantation in the body of a woman.
3. Imagine you are **either** a sperm cell **or** an egg cell. Describe your journey from the testis or the ovary until you implant in the lining of the uterus.

3.5 Pregnancy and birth

Learning outcomes

After this topic you should be able to:

- describe simply the development of the fetus during pregnancy
- explain how the developing fetus gets the nutrients and oxygen it needs and gets rid of waste products during pregnancy
- describe how factors such as alcohol and smoking can affect the growth of the fetus.

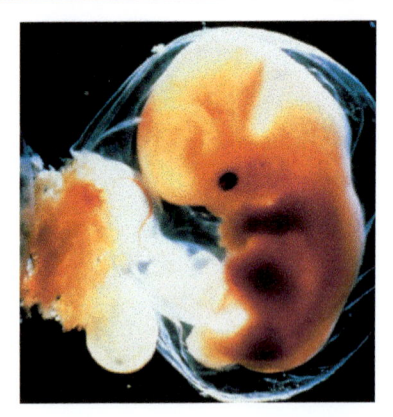

When a woman has a baby growing inside her uterus, she is pregnant. Her periods stop because the uterus no longer needs to prepare for pregnancy each month. However, it has to supply the needs of a growing **fetus**.

Supporting the fetus

As the fertilised ovum divides and grows it forms a ball of cells that develops into an embryo, a tiny human being with a whole life-support system of its own.

The **placenta** is a special organ where blood from the mother and the fetus run very close together. The mother gives food and oxygen to the fetus through the placenta, and takes away carbon dioxide and other waste products. The placenta also protects the fetus from many diseases and harmful substances in the mother's body.

The bag of **amniotic fluid** supports the fetus and cushions it from knocks and bumps. It also makes it easy for the fetus to move about.

By the end of the first 12 weeks of pregnancy, the fetus is formed with all its organs. For the rest of the time it is mainly getting bigger and maturing. By about 28 weeks of pregnancy, it may well survive if it was born. Towards the end of the 40-week pregnancy, its head usually points downwards ready to be born.

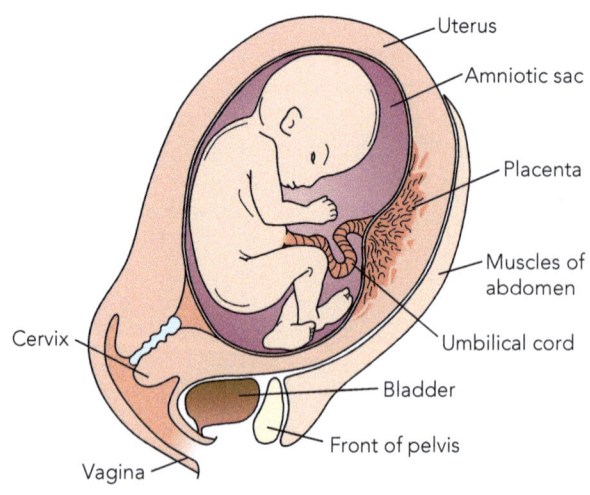

At 5 weeks the embryo is about the size of a red bean

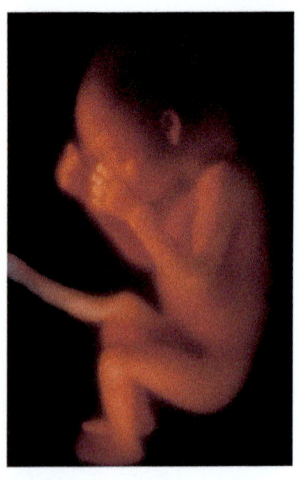

At 19 weeks a human fetus still has a lot of growing and maturing to do before it can survive but it looks a lot like a baby (computer artwork)

The fetus inside the uterus

Keeping the fetus safe

The placenta supplies the growing fetus with food and oxygen and removes carbon dioxide and other waste products. The **umbilical cord** carries blood from the fetus to the placenta and back again.

3 Reproduction and growth

Blood: carries waste products from the fetus to the mother

Umbilical cord

Uterus lining

Carbon dioxide and other waste products diffuse into the mother's blood

Blood: carries oxygen and food to the fetus from the mother

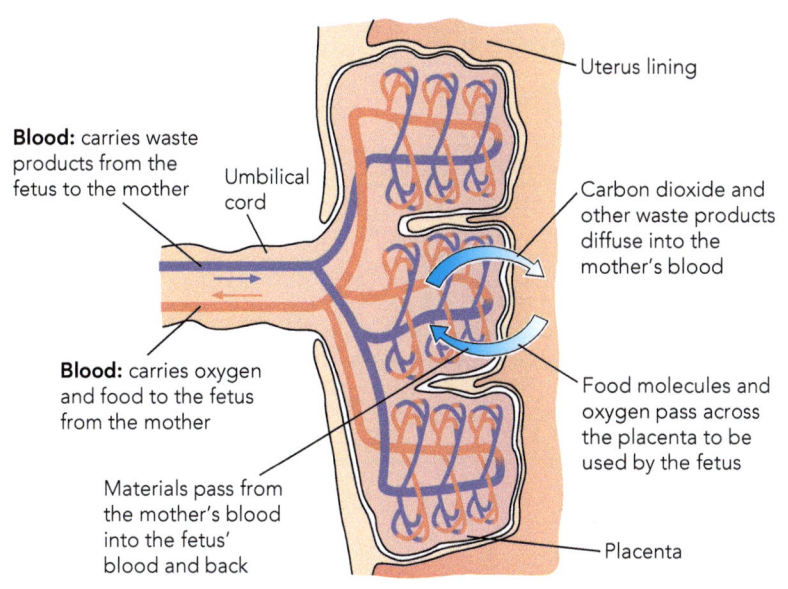

Food molecules and oxygen pass across the placenta to be used by the fetus

Materials pass from the mother's blood into the fetus' blood and back

Placenta

The placenta

A fetus needs many nutrients including protein for growth, calcium for healthy bones and iron to make blood. These nutrients come from the mother's blood so a pregnant woman must eat a healthy diet.

The placenta also keeps many harmful substances away from the developing fetus. However, some things can pass through the placenta and cause damage to the fetus. These include:

- alcohol which can cause brain damage
- drugs – even drugs prescribed by a doctor can damage a developing fetus. Pregnant women must be very careful about taking any medicine
- carbon monoxide from cigarette smoke which means that the fetus gets less oxygen. This can mean the baby is born small, too soon or dead
- viruses such as rubella can cause serious problems in a fetus even though they do not make adult people very ill at all.

No more room...

By the end of a 40-week pregnancy the fetus is getting too big for its mother's body. It no longer has room to move about and the placenta can hardly supply enough food and oxygen. During birth the baby is pushed out of the uterus. This is called labour, a process that can take several hours and is very hard work for the mother.

Key terms

- **amniotic fluid**
- **fetus**
- **placenta**
- **umbilical cord**

Summary questions

1. Write a paragraph describing what you think life is like inside the uterus for a fetus. What can it hear? What might it feel as it gets bigger but the uterus stays the same size?
2. What is the job of **a)** the placenta, **b)** the amniotic fluid and **c)** the umbilical cord?
3. Work in a group. Produce a leaflet or a poster about pregnancy, the placenta and what can harm a developing baby. This poster is to be used with women in your community to help them have healthier pregnancies and babies.

3.6 Growth and the factors that affect growth

Learning outcomes

After this topic you should be able to:
- explain what is meant by growth
- describe how growth changes through life
- explain what is meant by a growth chart.

A newborn baby is very small – around 50 cm long and 3 kg in weight. You were once this tiny but since birth, you have grown a lot. What is more, before you were born you grew from a single fertilised egg cell, only visible under the microscope, into a complete new baby containing millions and millions of cells.

A newborn baby

Practical activity Getting bigger

Take a balloon and measure the circumference (all the way around it). Blow some air into the balloon and measure it again. Now blow more air into the balloon and measure it again.
- What has happened to the balloon?
- Is this the same as growth?
- Think carefully – what do you think we mean when we talk about growth in living things?

Expert tips

Biomass is the mass of biological material – so this includes all the carbohydrates, fats, proteins and other compounds in your body.

In organisms, growth means making more cells. It can also mean cells getting bigger because they make more material. Growth often involves both of these things. A fertilised egg divides and forms more cells and these in turn divide again and again. The cells also use food to get bigger – they gain biomass. In the fetus, this food comes from the mother through the placenta. Once the baby is born, this food comes from what the baby eats.

We measure growth by looking at permanent changes in an organism. In people, we can't actually measure the number of cells. Instead we measure things such as height, weight (although this can change a lot even in a day) and the circumference of the head.

A baby grows very fast in the first few months of its life. A healthy child will grow steadily until it reaches **puberty** in the teenage years. Then growth is fast as the body matures and the child becomes an adult.

Around the world, health care workers and parents check that children are growing well using **growth charts** (see opposite). These are very helpful – they show how an average child will grow and the range for healthy smaller and larger children. However, many healthy children from many different countries will not fit into these ranges. Although the charts are scientific, they are only averages.

3 Reproduction and growth

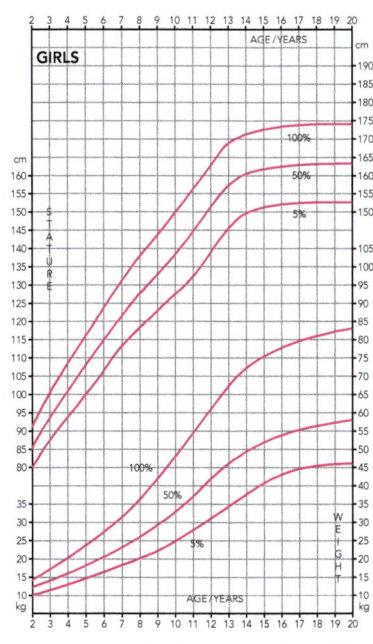

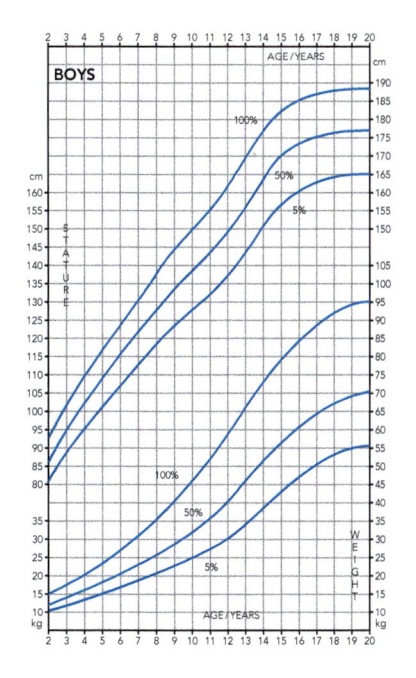

Average growth charts for girls and boys

What affects growth?

Many things will affect how a child grows. A baby needs food and drink, which come together in the form of milk. As a child grows it needs a balanced diet (see page 4), clean water to drink and to be free from infectious diseases.

You have already learnt how different substances can affect the growth of a fetus in the uterus. Cigarette smoke causes a lack of oxygen in the blood of the developing baby. This means that the cells cannot respire properly, so they can't grow and the baby is very small. If the mother drinks alcohol, this may affect the way the brain of the baby grows. When the mother suffers from malnutrition, the fetus will not grow properly either.

You have also learnt the importance of a balanced diet in growth (see page 8). When children do not get enough protein and energy from their food, they will not be able to grow properly. Their bodies will not be able to make new cells, and the cells will not be able to get bigger. Lack of vitamins and minerals can also affect growth.

On the next pages you will learn more about growth and the factors which affect it in our lives.

Key terms

- growth chart
- puberty

Summary questions

1 What is growth?
2 Use the growth charts to answer these questions.
   a) What height should an average boy be at one year old?
   b) What height should an average girl be at 5 years old?
   c) What height should an average boy and an average girl be at 18 years old? Explain the difference.

63

3.7 The changes during adolescence

Learning outcomes

After this topic you should be able to:
- describe how the body changes during puberty in both boys and girls
- explain that the changes are controlled by hormones.

Expert tips

When you are learning about this topic remember that everyone is different; this means they develop differently. We should all be aware of this and realise that there isn't such a thing as being 'normal'.

All of the special organs which are needed for making and growing babies are there at birth, but they need to develop to work properly. The stage at which the body changes from that of a child to that of an adult ready for reproduction is called **puberty**.

Puberty in boys

Puberty in boys usually begins between the ages of 11 and 16. It may happen over a few months or it may take many years to complete. It is different for every single boy but they all end up as an adult male.

During puberty, facial hair (a beard and moustache) starts to grow. Body hair also appears. This varies – some men are very hairy, others are smooth.

The Adam's apple (larynx) in a boy's throat gets larger and his voice becomes deeper. This can happen gradually or very suddenly.

A boy's sex organs (the penis and the testes) grow larger and the skin on them darkens so that they are more obvious. His testes start making sperm and the male sex hormone testosterone. This controls the development of all the other male characteristics. Pubic hair grows around his sex organs and hair grows under his armpits.

The body shape changes as the bones and muscles grow to give broad shoulders and chest with relatively narrow hips. This adult male shape can take a long time to develop.

Boys also grow taller very quickly during puberty.

Puberty in girls

Girls often begin puberty slightly earlier than boys. Their body shape changes and their reproductive organs prepare for pregnancy.

Puberty in girls usually begins between 10 and 15 years old. As in boys, it may happen quite quickly or it may take several years of slower development. Whatever the rate, all girls experience the same basic events.

A girl's breasts develop. They become larger and the nipples are more obvious. The size and shape of the breasts varies from one girl to another.

Her body shape alters as fat develops around her hips, bottom and thighs to give a more curvy 'female' shape. Pubic hair appears and hair grows under her armpits.

3 Reproduction and growth

Inside a girl's body the ovaries begin to release a ripe ovum each month. The ovaries also make the female sex hormone oestrogen which controls all the changes in the girl's body. Her uterus prepares for pregnancy each month, so her monthly period begins.

A girl also grows quickly during puberty and reaches nearly her adult height by the end of it.

Changes for everyone

Puberty affects your brain as well as your body. Many people have emotional changes during puberty. You may become more interested in the opposite sex. You may become moody, and fall out with your family and even your friends more easily.

The sex hormones also affect your skin and many young people get spots during puberty. You also develop a stronger body smell and need to wash more often. It is a time of great changes – but at the end of it you will gradually emerge as an adult.

> **Expert tips**
>
> When you draw the graph for Summary question **2**, make sure you use plenty of space on the graph paper, put the axes the correct way around and use a proper scale on each axis. Plot the points carefully and put a smooth curve through them. Do not continue your line beyond 18 years.

> **Key terms**
>
> - **puberty**

Summary questions

1. Make a table to summarise the changes that happen at puberty. You will need three columns: Changes that happen to females; Changes that happen to males; Changes that happen to everyone.

2. a) Here is a table which shows how Ravi grew from birth to the age of 18.

Age /years	0	1	2	3	4	5	6	7	8	9	10	11	12	13	14	15	16	17	18
Height /cm	50	70	86	96	104	111	116	121	126	131	136	141	145	155	165	172	174	176	177

   Draw a graph to show the changes in Ravi's height with age.
   b) When did Ravi have his growth spurt during puberty?

3. Produce a leaflet or a webpage which can be used by 11- or 12-year-old students to help prepare them for the changes in puberty.

3.8 Drugs affecting reproduction and growth

Learning outcomes

After this topic you should be able to:

- explain how reproduction including the conception of a baby can be affected by drugs
- describe how growth and development can be affected by drugs.

A drug is a chemical which has an effect on your body. You have probably used a number of legal drugs in your life already such as tea, coffee or chocolate. Many drugs are a legal and useful part of our lives. **Pharmaceutical drugs** are medicines that help treat or cure many diseases. Examples include painkillers and antibiotics. Some drugs are illegal and can be harmful, as you will see.

Controlling fertility

In many parts of the world people now choose the size of their families. The **contraceptive pill** contains pharmaceutical drugs that stop ovulation taking place. This means that a woman does not get pregnant. If she and her partner decide they want to have a baby, she stops taking the pill. The woman can choose whether she wants to be fertile or not.

Some women find that they cannot have children because they do not make the right balance of hormones, so they do not release an egg each month. There are drugs that can replace these hormones. These **fertility drugs** may make the woman ovulate and so she may get pregnant and be able to have a child but they do not always work.

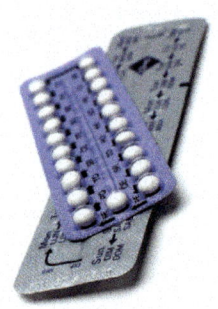

These are pharmaceutical drugs which women can use to control their own fertility

Drugs which affect the fetus

Doctors and scientists now know that there are some drugs which can cross the placenta (see age 61) and affect the fetus as it grows. Often these drugs will stop the growth and development of the baby and cause permanent damage. Alcohol is a drug which is legal in many parts of the world. When a woman drinks alcohol while she is pregnant, the growth and development of her baby may be affected. In some cases the child will develop fetal alcohol syndrome. It will not grow properly and will not be able to learn and behave like most children.

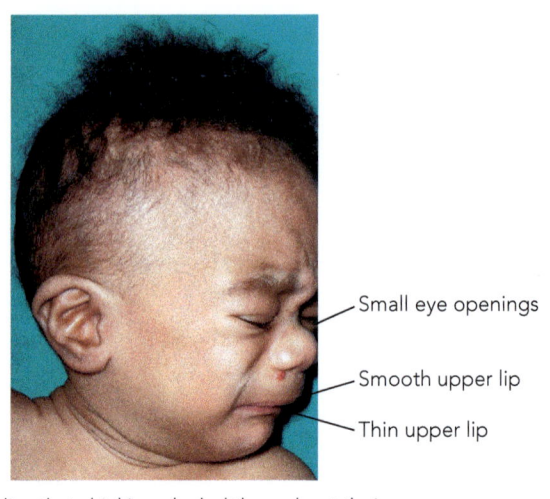

- Small eye openings
- Smooth upper lip
- Thin upper lip

Many women do not realise that drinking alcohol throughout their pregnancy can affect the development of their baby

3 Reproduction and growth

Thalidomide was a pharmaceutical drug given to some pregnant women about 55 years ago. It stopped them feeling sick. People did not know that it also stopped the limbs of the developing baby from growing. This resulted in many children being born without arms or legs before scientists realised what was causing the problem. Many tests are carried out on modern drugs to make sure that they do not harm the developing fetus.

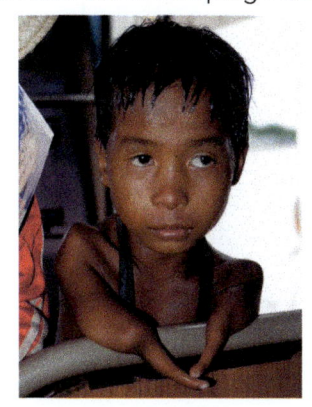

Some drugs such as thalidomide had a terrible affect on the growing fetus

Some women take illegal drugs such as marijuana, heroin and cocaine when they are pregnant. These drugs can cross the placenta. They can damage the development of the brain of the fetus if they are used in early pregnancy. Most drugs affect how well the baby grows and mean it is very small when it is born. Small babies are more likely to get ill and die. A baby may also be born addicted to the drug used by its mother. This can make them very ill indeed.

Drugs which affect the growth of children

There are many widely used pharmaceutical drugs which help babies and children grow healthily. Extra vitamins help prevent deficiency diseases. Antibiotics cure bacterial infections so that children are not ill for weeks and months at a time. Vaccines prevent children getting many serious diseases that would affect their long-term health and growth or even kill them.

Sometimes children do not grow properly because their bodies do not make growth hormones. Drugs can replace the growth hormones so the children grow normally.

Key terms

- **contraceptive pill**
- **fertility drugs**
- **pharmaceutical drugs**

Summary questions

1. Give two examples of drugs which can be used to help people control whether they have children. Explain simply the way in which they work.
2. In many countries, doctors advise women not to drink alcohol if they are pregnant. Why is this a good idea?
3. Work in a group. Design a poster warning women of the dangers of using illegal drugs when they are pregnant.

3.9 Drugs affecting behaviour

Learning outcomes

After this topic you should be able to:
- describe how drugs can affect behaviour
- describe a way of demonstrating the effect of a drug on reaction times.

Tea, coffee and cigarettes all contain legal drugs. Alcoholic drinks are legal in some countries and not in others. There are other drugs which are not legal. The legal and illegal drugs people use for pleasure can affect both their minds and their behaviour.

A drug is any substance taken into the body that modifies or affects the chemical reactions in the body.

Caffeine – an everyday drug

Coffee is drunk in many countries around the world

Coffee and tea are some of the most popular drinks around the world. Yet every time you drink tea or coffee you are taking in a small dose of a drug called **caffeine**. Caffeine makes your body more active – it stimulates it. This is why tea or coffee will help you wake up in the morning and pick you up if you are feeling tired during the day. They also keep you awake at night if you drink too much during the evening. It is legal, socially acceptable and widely enjoyed. But caffeine not only affects your brain and behaviour, it can also affect your heart rate and blood pressure.

Expert tips

There are many different types of drug and they have many different effects on the body. So what is a drug? It is any substance taken into the body that affects chemical reactions within the body.

Normal web | Caffeine web

These webs were spun by the same spider before and after it was given caffeine

Practical activity — Caffeine and reaction times

There are several ways of investigating reaction times. They include letting go of a metre ruler and measuring how far it falls before you catch it again, and standing in a circle holding hands with your class and seeing how fast a hand squeeze travels around the ring.

- Plan a way to measure normal reaction times and the effect of drinking a can of cola drink containing caffeine on the reaction times of a student in your class.

3 Reproduction and growth

Addictive behaviour

When someone becomes addicted to a drug, they cannot manage without it. They need to use more and more to keep feeling the effects. If someone drinks lots of coffee for some time and then uses less, they can feel unwell, with headaches and tiredness. If they continue to avoid the coffee they will soon overcome the addiction and feel normal again, but for most people it is easier just to make another cup!

Caffeine is not seen as a dangerous drug but it easily becomes part of our lives. This shows clearly what can happen when we use other, more damaging drugs. These drugs include alcohol, nicotine and illegal drugs such as heroin and cocaine.

Changing behaviour

Some drugs used for pleasure affect the mind by producing vivid waking dreams. People may think they can fly and fall from high buildings or cliffs.

Alcohol is a commonly used drug and small amounts can make people feel relaxed and more confident. However, larger amounts can make people aggressive and violent, or very sad and depressed. It has a big effect on people's behaviour. Alcohol damages the liver and the brain and can cause death – but as it is addictive, some people keep drinking.

Nicotine in cigarettes can make people feel and behave more calmly but it is very addictive. Some people keep smoking, which can lead to heart disease and lung cancer.

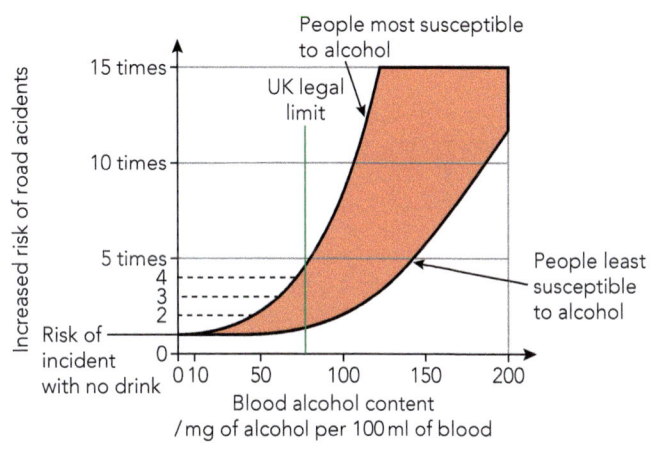

Some people are more affected by alcohol than others – but drinking alcohol always increases the risk of being involved in a car accident. This is why some countries do not allow drivers to drink any alcohol at all

Many drugs increase the risk of diseases such as heart attacks, but some people choose to ignore that risk. Injecting drugs also means people are more likely to get diseases such as **HIV/AIDS** and hepatitis. Addicts may change their behaviour and do anything to get the drugs they crave. They may turn against their families and steal money and other things to pay for their drugs. They can often lose their jobs or drop out of school because they cannot work when they are using drugs. They may stop looking after themselves. The use of addictive drugs often leads to serious health problems and even death.

Key terms

- caffeine
- HIV/AIDS

Summary questions

1. **a)** What is a drug?
   b) List two legal drugs and two illegal drugs.
   c) What does being addicted to a drug mean?

2. **a)** Which part of your body is affected by almost all illegal drugs?
   b) Give three examples of how illegal drugs can affect your behaviour.

3. Plan a short presentation you could give to explain to younger students the way that illegal drugs can affect behaviour and why it is a good idea to avoid using them.

3.10 The impact of disease

Learning outcomes

After this topic you should be able to:
- describe how diseases affect conception, growth, development, behaviour and health
- use secondary sources to find out about diseases which affect the country where you live.

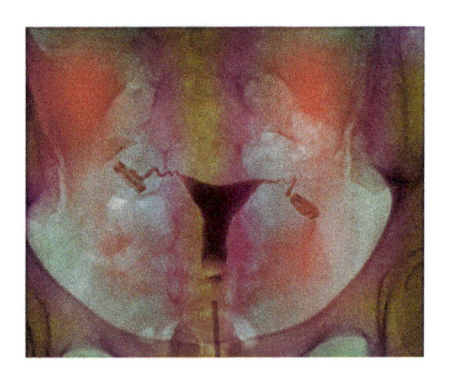

Health – feeling fit and well – is very important. If you have a disease, your health is always affected. There are many different types of disease. As you saw in Stage 7, infectious diseases are caused by micro-organisms such as bacteria and viruses. Deficiency diseases are caused by a lack of the right type of food. Being overweight and unfit increases your risk of getting heart disease or diabetes. Cancers can be caused by many factors – for example, most lung cancers are caused by smoking. Diseases can affect reproduction, growth, development and even the way we behave.

Disease and reproduction

Some diseases make it difficult for people to have children. Sometimes a woman can get an infection in her oviducts. They may become blocked. Work out why this means she cannot easily have children.

If a teenage boy or a man catches mumps it may affect his testes so that he no longer makes fertile sperm. He will be unable to father a child.

Some diseases a woman may catch while she is pregnant may affect her unborn child. Rubella can cause deafness, brain damage and death to the fetus as it does not grow and develop properly. Many **sexually transmitted diseases (STDs)** can be passed to the unborn child and cause great damage and even death. **HIV/AIDS** can be passed from mother to child during birth.

Doctors look inside an oviduct to see if it is blocked by disease

Disease, growth and development

If a child is ill, it will not grow and develop normally. For example, in some parts of the world there is little iodine in the diet, children develop swollen necks as their thyroid glands try to work. They do not grow properly – they are short – and their brain does not develop fully. This is a deficiency disease known as **cretinism**. It can be prevented by adding iodised salt to the diet.

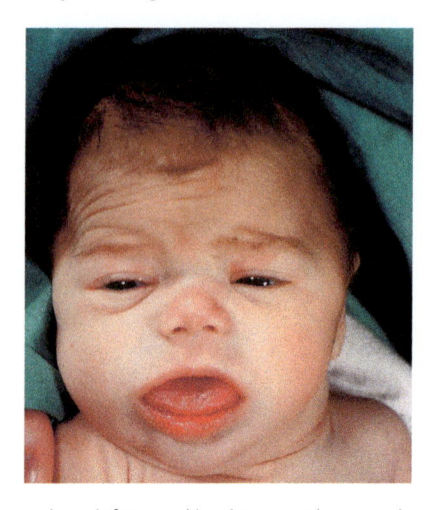

Iodine deficiency like this is easily treated

3 Reproduction and growth

If children do not get the protein they need to grow they will be stunted and short. They will not develop muscles and their internal organ systems will not form fully. They may suffer diseases such as marasmus and kwashiorkor.

Infectious diseases can slow the way a child grows – repeated infections mean they do not have the energy spare for normal growth. Tuberculosis and HIV/AIDS have a long, slow effect on growth.

Key terms

- cretinism
- HIV/AIDS
- sexually transmitted diseases

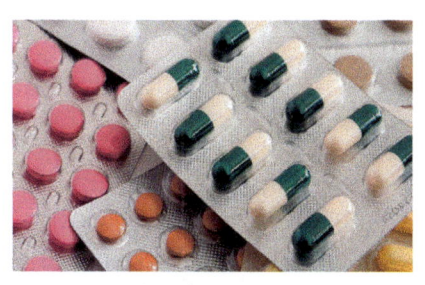

Disease and behaviour

Most diseases affect your behaviour by making you feel unwell. You are tired and lack energy. You may ache or have a sore throat. People stay in bed rather than go to work in the office or the fields when they are ill. Children cannot go to school.

Some diseases mean that people can no longer care for their children or their partner. They need to be looked after all the time.

Some diseases affect the mind rather than the body. They can have a very dramatic effect on the behaviour. People with mental illnesses may be full of energy, or very sad and tired with no energy at all. They may hear voices that tell them to behave in certain ways. If they obey those voices, they may behave in ways that seem strange to people who are healthy.

Drugs can be used to cure diseases. By clearing infections and treating some serious conditions, pharmaceutical drugs such as antibiotics allow people to reproduce, grow and behave as healthily as possible.

Disease affects the body in many different ways.

Medicines such as these can cure many different diseases and allow your body to function healthily

Practical activity   Finding out about local diseases

Different countries have different health problems. Use secondary sources – books, leaflets from the local doctor's surgery, the internet, people at home – to find out which diseases are the most common in **your** country.

Discover as much as you can about three of the most common diseases in your country. Try and choose diseases that affect people in different ways. For each disease explain the way it:

- is spread
- affects people
- can be treated or cured.

Summary questions

1. Explain the ways in which diseases can affect reproduction.
2. Describe two diseases which affect growth and development and suggest ways to prevent or cure them.
3. Make a poster to show what you have found out about the diseases which are most common in your country.

Chapter 3 — End of chapter questions

1 Seven terms to do with human reproduction are listed below. Definitions are also given. Match the letters that represent the terms with the numbers that represent the definitions.

   A mammary glands
   B ovulation
   C umbilical cord
   D menstruation
   E amniotic fluid
   F semen
   G cervix

   1 fluid that surrounds the fetus in the womb
   2 release of an ovum from the ovary
   3 passing of blood and tissue from the lining of the uterus
   4 connection between the uterus and the placenta
   5 fluid that contains sperm
   6 ring of muscle between vagina and uterus
   7 organs that produce milk [7]

2 The diagram shows the male reproductive system.

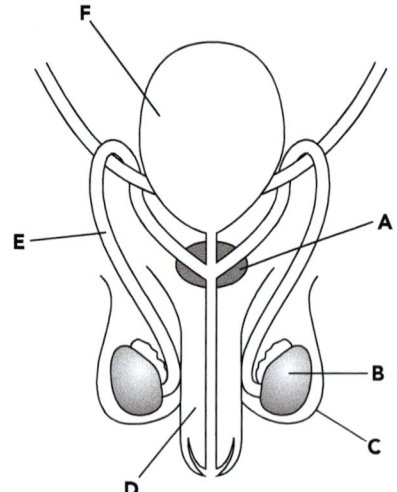

   The following is a list of functions of the system shown in the diagram.
   1 production of sperm
   2 production of seminal fluid
   3 movement of sperm
   4 release of sperm into the vagina

   a Copy and complete the table.

Function	Part of the reproductive system	
	Name	Letter from diagram
1		
2		
3		
4		

   [8]

   b Name the hormone that stimulates the production of sperm. [1]

3 The diagram shows the female reproductive system.

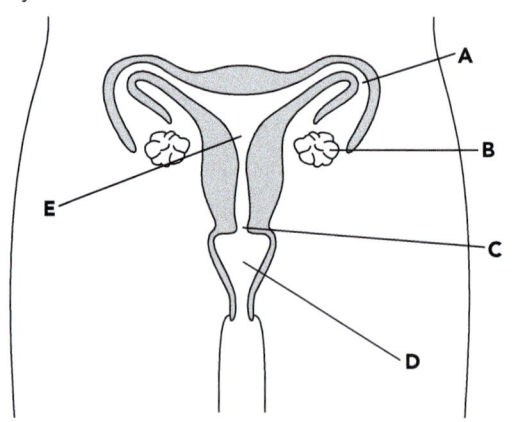

   a State the letters from the diagram that indicate where the following occur.
      i   fertilisation
      ii   ovulation
      iii implantation
      iv   release of sperm [4]
   b Name the structures labelled **A** to **E**. [5]

4 The diagram shows a human ovum and a human sperm just before fertilisation.

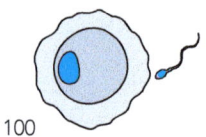

   Magnification × 100

   a Calculate the actual diameter of the ovum. Show your working. [2]
   b Describe the adaptations that enable the sperm to reach the human egg. [3]

72

3 Reproduction and growth

c Describe what happens after the sperm reaches the outside of the protective layer around the ovum. [3]

d Explain why males produce huge numbers of sperm, but females only release one or two eggs each month. [3]

5 The diagram shows the timing of events during a woman's menstrual cycle that lasted for 28 days.

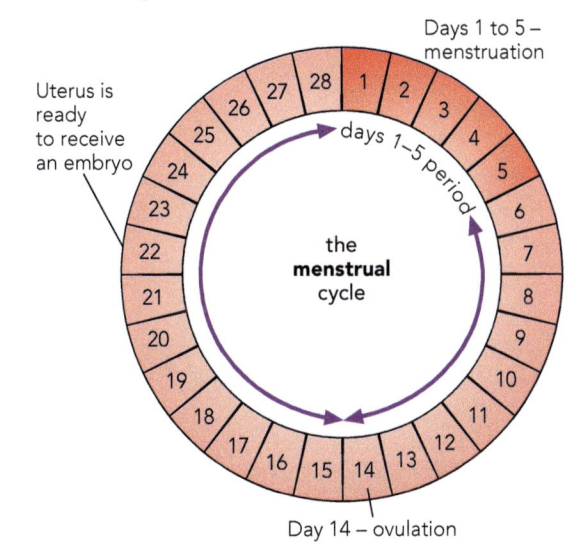

Days 1 to 5 – menstruation

Uterus is ready to receive an embryo

the menstrual cycle

Day 14 – ovulation

a State what happens during menstruation. [2]

b Describe the changes that occur to the uterus between days 6 and 14. [3]

c Sperm can live for up to three days after they are released. A woman's fertile period refers to the days during the cycle when the ovum could be fertilised.

  i On which days in the cycle shown in the diagram could the ovum be fertilised? Explain the way in which you calculated your answer. [3]

  ii Explain why the fertile period may not be on the same days during each cycle. [2]

  iii What name is given to the process by which an embryo enters the lining of the uterus? [1]

d There are a variety of ways in which a couple could avoid fertilisation taking place.

Explain two different ways in which fertilisation may be prevented. [4]

e Explain why girls who have begun to have periods should make sure their diet contains enough iron. [2]

6 a The following is a list of events that occur during human reproduction. They are not in the correct sequence.

  1 the division of the zygote into a two-celled embryo

  2 fertilisation

  3 implantation

  4 the development of the fetus in the womb

  5 birth

  6 production of sperm

  7 release of an ovum from an ovary

  8 ejaculation of sperm

Arrange these events, 1 to 8, in the correct sequence. The first one is 6. [4]

b The fetus is attached to the uterus by the placenta and the umbilical cord. The placenta is often described as the 'life support system' for the fetus.

  i Draw a simple labelled diagram to show the way in which the fetus is attached to the uterus. [6]

  ii Explain in detail the ways in which the placenta keeps the fetus alive and healthy. [5]

7 a Write a definition of the term 'drug'. [2]

b Explain the difference between a pharmaceutical drug and an illegal drug. [3]

c Some people think that smoking just one cigarette can be far more dangerous than drinking one alcoholic drink. Explain why people think that smoking one cigarette can be so dangerous. [2]

73

4 Elements, mixtures and compounds

Science *in context!*

Chemical giants

John Dalton

By the start of the 1800s, science had become more firmly based on evidence from experiments. An English scientist called John Dalton, who taught in Manchester, UK, loved experimenting. He liked to work alone and never trusted the results of other scientists. His careful experiments suggested to him that all matter is made up of tiny particles. He thought that these particles could not be broken down into anything smaller. He called the particles atoms.

John drew up a list of elements – substances that were made of only one type of atom and couldn't be broken down into simpler substances. He thought of atoms as hard, indestructible spheres with each element having atoms of a different mass.

Here is a list of Dalton's elements:

An element was defined as something that couldn't be broken down into any simpler substances. However, this led to some compounds (substances that are made of more than one element) getting onto John's list of elements. At the time, these compounds were very difficult, if not impossible, to split up so he thought they must be elements.

No wonder scientists had trouble making any sense of the chemical elements! Most elements had not yet been discovered and others were actually compounds. It was a bit like trying to do a jigsaw puzzle without the picture, with half the pieces missing and with some pieces from a different jigsaw altogether thrown in.

John Dalton was co-founder of the British Association for the Advancement of Science. When he died in 1844, over 40 000 people attended his funeral in Manchester, UK

4 Elements, mixtures and compounds

Dmitri Mendeleev

Dmitri Mendeleev (1834–1907) was the youngest of 17 children

Chemistry changed forever when a Russian chemist discovered how to sort out the chemical elements in his Periodic Table. It was at the end of the 1860s that the real breakthrough was made by Dmitri Mendeleev.

Dmitri was writing a textbook and wanted to organise the elements properly. So he wrote each element onto its own card to help him sort them out. Dmitri enjoyed playing cards, especially the game patience, and one evening he dosed off while working. He had a dream in which the element cards lined up in rows, just like in a game of patience.

When he woke, he realised that he should put the elements in order of their masses, but then start a new line so that similar elements lined up with each other.

His first table in 1869 had 17 columns, but he revised it two years later to a table with fewer columns. Dmitri called his table the Periodic Table because of the regular repeating pattern of elements.

Chemists still needed persuading that Dmitri had found the code that could make sense of chemistry. His Periodic Table had quite a few gaps left in it. He explained that when new elements were discovered, these spaces would be filled. This failed to convince some of his fellow scientists.

However, we can judge a good theory by its power to make predictions. Sure enough, Dmitri had the perfect model to predict the properties of elements that had not yet been discovered. His predictions closely matched the properties of newly discovered elements and so his Periodic Table became widely accepted.

In this chapter you will find out about changes of state, gas pressure and diffusion. You will also learn about elements, mixtures and compounds, as well as the chemical symbols for the first 20 elements of the Periodic Table.

> **Key points**
>
> - When the particles in a gas collide with the walls of their container, they produce a force that causes gas pressure.
> - Diffusion is when substances mix without us stirring them up. This happens automatically in liquids and gases because their particles are constantly moving around in random motion.
> - Elements are substances that cannot be broken down into any simpler substances.
> - The smallest part of an element that we can still recognise as the element is an atom. Elements are made up of only one type of atom.
> - When atoms bond together they form molecules.
> - If the atoms in a molecule are not all the same type, then we have a compound.
> - There are about 100 elements but millions of compounds.
> - Each chemical element has a symbol (for example, hydrogen's is H, helium's is He).
> - We can show the number and type of each atom in a molecule by its chemical formula (for example, the formula of carbon dioxide is CO_2).
> - The elements have been sorted out into a useful structure called the Periodic Table. This shows us patterns in the properties of elements.

4.1 Revisiting the particle model

Learning outcomes

After this topic you should be able to:
- recall the Stage 7 work you did on solids, liquids and gases, including explaining their properties using the particle theory.

You already know that scientists believe that all matter is made up of particles. You have seen that the arrangement of particles and their movement in **solids**, **liquids** and **gases** is described by the **particle theory**. The particles are too small to see, but using this theory we can explain the properties of materials.

State of matter	General properties
solid	fixed shape cannot be compressed
liquid	no fixed shape can flow very difficult to compress
gas	no fixed shape spreads out to fill its container easily compressed

In a solid the particles are lined up next to each other, touching their nearest neighbours. They are fixed in position but do vibrate.

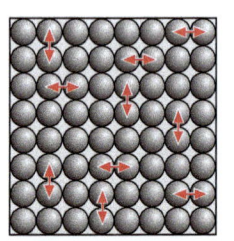

In a liquid the particles are still very close together, but can slip and slide over each other.

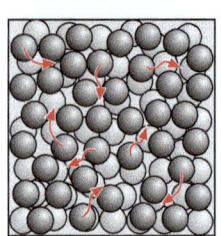

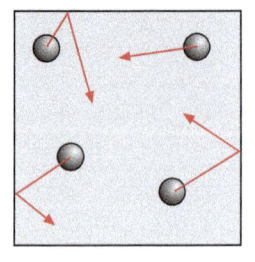

Expert tips

The particles in both a liquid and a gas can move about randomly, but on average, the particles in a gas move a lot more quickly.

In a gas the particles move rapidly around at random and there is lots of space within the gas.

Changes of state

You should also remember the names given to the changes of state shown on page 77.

Key terms

- gas
- liquid
- particle theory
- solid

4 Elements, mixtures and compounds

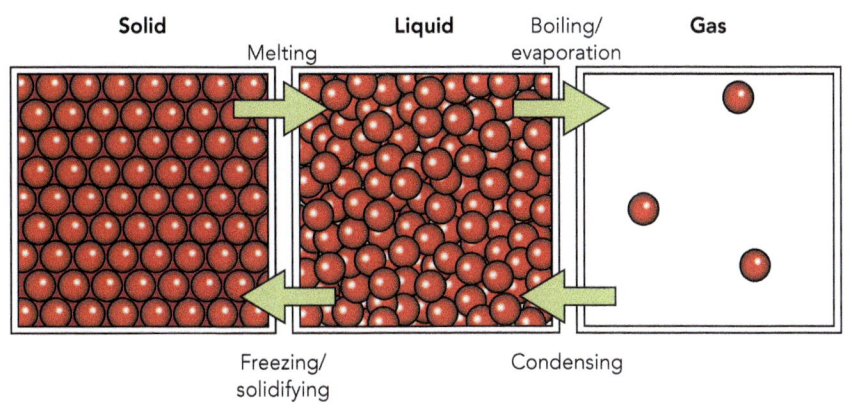

Solid — Melting → **Liquid** — Boiling/evaporation → **Gas**

← Freezing/solidifying   ← Condensing

Learn these changes of state

Practical activity   A closer look at water

Look at an ice cube in a beaker half full of water.
- Draw what you see.
- Why are your observations hard to explain using the particle theory?

Fill a plastic fizzy drinks bottle up to the top with water. Screw on the top so there is no air above the water. Place the bottle in a freezer and leave it until next lesson.
- What happens?
- In what way are your observations related to water pipes bursting when the temperature gets less than 0 °C in winter?

Look at this photo:
- List some advantages of the fact that ice is less dense than liquid water.

Summary questions

1. Using the particle theory, explain why:
   a) liquids flow but solids do not flow
   b) solids have a fixed shape but liquids and gases take up the shape of their containers.
2. Define the following words:
   a) boiling   b) melting   c) condensing   d) freezing
3. Using the particle theory, explain what happens when:
   a) we heat a solid until it melts
   b) we heat a liquid until it boils.

77

4.2 Gas pressure

Learning outcomes

After this topic you should be able to:
- explain what causes gas pressure using the particle theory
- explain the effect of increasing the temperature on the pressure of a gas.

Gases are in the air around us all the time. As their particles can move around very quickly, and at random, they frequently collide with other gas particles and objects.

The particles of a gas in a sealed box will collide with the inside surfaces of the walls of the box. Each collision results in a tiny force on the box. There are millions of particles of gas colliding, even in very small spaces, so each of these tiny forces adds up to cause **gas pressure**.

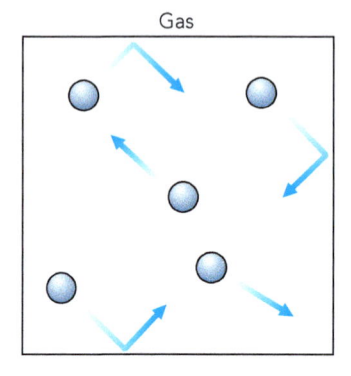

As the particles of gas collide with the walls of the container, they produce a force that causes gas pressure

Atmospheric pressure is a result of the forces produced by air particles colliding constantly with objects.

When you blow up a balloon, you force more and more particles of gas inside the balloon with each breath. This increases the number of collisions per second, so the pressure inside the balloon increases. As the balloon is made of thin rubber, it stretches and inflates.

Practical activity — Exploring gas pressure

Watch your teacher boil some water in the bottom of a can on a tripod (see photo). When plenty of steam is escaping from the top of the can, heating is stopped and a bung seals the can.
- Describe what happens as the can is allowed to cool down.
- Use the particle theory to explain your observations.

4 Elements, mixtures and compounds

The effect of temperature on gas pressure

When we pour hot water onto a sealed gas syringe containing a little air, the plunger moves outwards without us having to pull it.

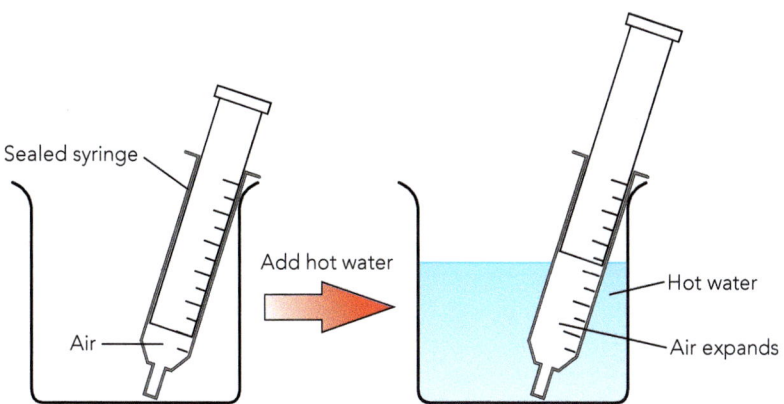

Sealed syringe — Add hot water → Hot water, Air expands, Air

The hot water heats up the gas inside the syringe. The gas particles gain energy and move around more quickly. This means that they collide with the inside walls of the syringe more often. Also, the collisions will be more forceful than those at a lower temperature. Therefore the gas pressure in the syringe increases. This results in the gas inside the syringe expanding because it can push out the plunger. The plunger stops moving out when the gas pressure inside and outside the syringe are equal again.

> **Expert tips**
>
> Gas pressure depends not only on the force caused by particle collisions, but also on the area over which the force is applied. The smaller the area, the larger the pressure for the same force applied.

> **Key terms**
>
> - **gas pressure**

Summary questions

1. What causes gas pressure?
2. Look at the experiment below:

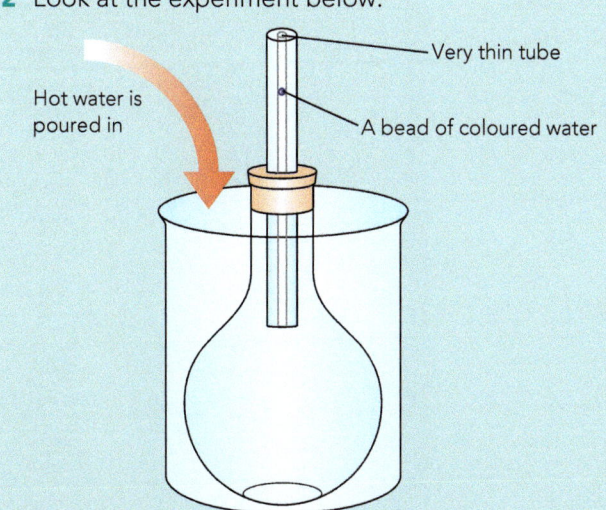

   Very thin tube, A bead of coloured water, Hot water is poured in

   Explain what would happen when the hot water is poured into the beaker. Use the particle theory in your answer.

4.3 Diffusion

Learning outcomes

After this topic you should be able to:
- explain the process of diffusion
- explain why diffusion takes place in liquids and gases but not in solids.

Do you like the smell of freshly baked bread? The spreading of particles from the hot bread, through the air and into your nose is an example of the process called **diffusion**.

Diffusion is the process whereby the particles in liquids and gases spread around, mingling and mixing together with each other (without us having to stir the substances to mix them).

Practical activity — Diffusion through a liquid

Use tweezers to place a few crystals of potassium manganate(VII) into a beaker of water.

⚠ **Do not allow potassium manganate(VII) crystals or its solution to come into contact with your skin.**

Purple colour starts spreading through the water

Potassium manganate(VII) crystals

- Record what you see happen in the next few minutes.

Leave the beaker until next lesson.

- Explain all your observations using the particle theory.

Practical activity — Diffusion of gases

⚠ **Bromine liquid is corrosive and its vapour is toxic so use a fume cupboard in this demonstration.**

Bromine is a dark brown liquid that evaporates easily at room temperature. The gas it gives off is dark orange. The gas is much denser than air.

Your teacher will place a little bromine in the bottom of a gas jar, and then place a second gas jar on top of it.

- What do you think will happen?
- Why is the experiment done in a fume cupboard?
- At the end of the lesson, record your observations and explain them using the particle theory.

4 Elements, mixtures and compounds

Practical activity Applying diffusion

Watch your teacher place the top of a bottle of concentrated ammonia solution next to an open bottle of concentrated hydrochloric acid.

- What happens?

The ammonia and hydrogen chloride react together.

- Explain your observations using the particle theory.

Now watch the demonstration shown below:

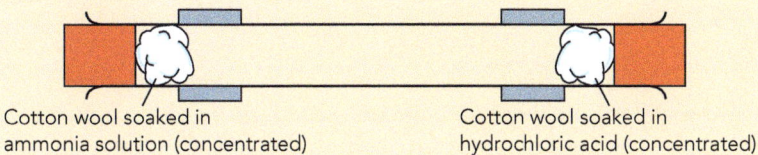

Cotton wool soaked in ammonia solution (concentrated)

Cotton wool soaked in hydrochloric acid (concentrated)

- Describe what happens in the experiment.

The particles of ammonia are lighter than the particles of acid.

- Explain your observations as fully as you can using the particle theory.

⚠ **Concentrated ammonia and hydrochloric acid are corrosive liquids.**

Particles of liquids and gases can diffuse and mix with each other as their particles are in constant random motion.

The particles arising from a dissolved solid can diffuse through a liquid. The tiny particles of the dissolved solid are moved throughout the liquid by the moving particles of the liquid.

We find that smaller, lighter particles diffuse faster than larger, heavier particles.

This is shown inside the long tube in the experiment above. The ammonia particles are lighter than the acid particles so they can diffuse through the air particles in the tube more quickly.

Key terms

- diffusion

Summary questions

1 What is diffusion?

2 **a)** Which you would expect to diffuse faster, A or B?
    A a gas through another gas
    B a liquid through another liquid
  b) Explain your answer to part **a**.

3 Explain why you can smell food cooking in the kitchen from another room.

4 Smoking cigarettes is banned in petrol stations because of the risk of explosions. Explain why naked flames can cause explosions in petrol stations even if they never come into direct contact with any liquid petrol.

81

4.4 Atoms, molecules and elements

Learning outcomes

After this topic you should be able to:
- describe what an atom is
- explain the meaning of the terms 'element' and 'molecule'.

We have used the particle model to explain how substances behave. Now we will look in more detail at these particles. This will help us to explain the difference between substances.

You've probably heard of 'atoms' before. We know that atoms are something to do with the particles that make up solids, liquids and gases. But what are they exactly?

Imagine that you had a magic knife and started chopping up a piece of one of the chemical elements, such as iron. You keep cutting and cutting until the bits of iron are really tiny – smaller than the smallest thing we can see through a normal microscope. Eventually the smallest particle you would get to, that could still be called iron, would be an **atom**. It would be an individual atom of iron.

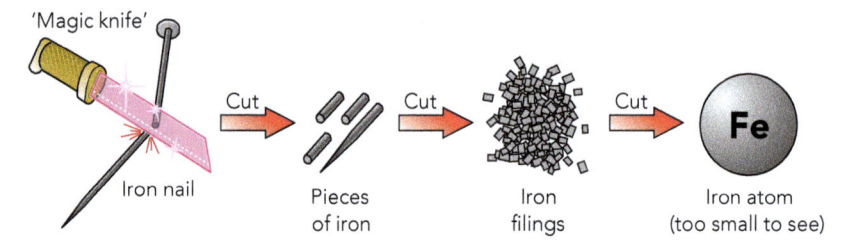

Iron nail → Cut → Pieces of iron → Cut → Iron filings → Cut → Fe Iron atom (too small to see)

Iron is one of a hundred or so different **elements**.

Elements are substances made up of only one type of atom.

It follows that if we do the same imaginary chopping up on each of the known elements, we will arrive at about a hundred different atoms. Each atom differs from others by its size and mass, but we think of them all as spheres. To make it easier to tell them apart, the different atoms are often given different colours when we show them in drawings.

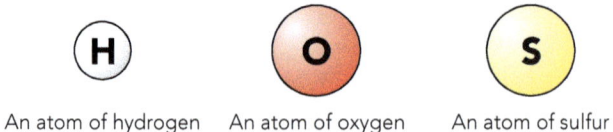

An atom of hydrogen   An atom of oxygen   An atom of sulfur

We also have model kits to show how atoms join (or bond) to each other. One of these kits has coloured plastic balls with holes in them. Each ball has a set number of holes. In the kit you also get plastic sticks (called 'bonds') that fit into the holes and join one ball to another.

Alternatively, you can use polystyrene balls painted different colours for atoms; thin, pointed sticks can be used for the bonds that join the atoms to each other.

4 Elements, mixtures and compounds

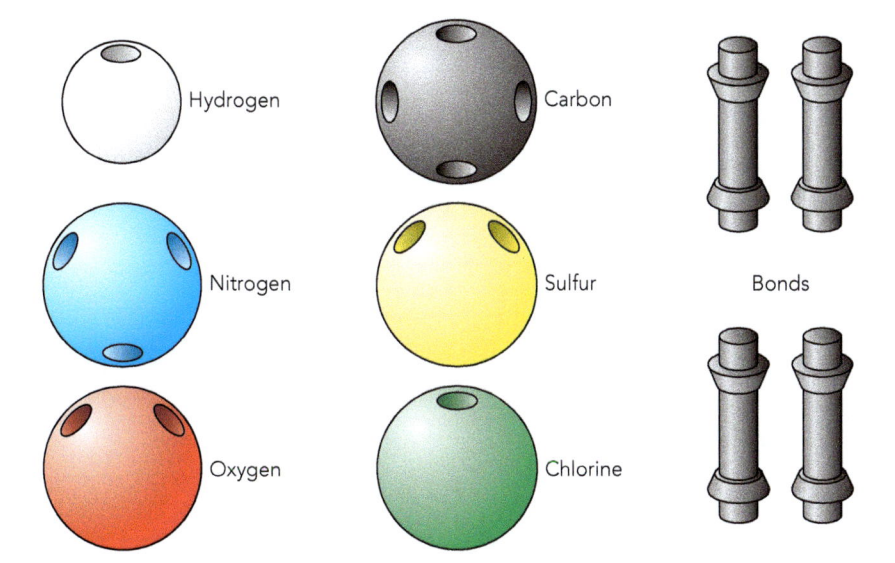

Look at these models below:

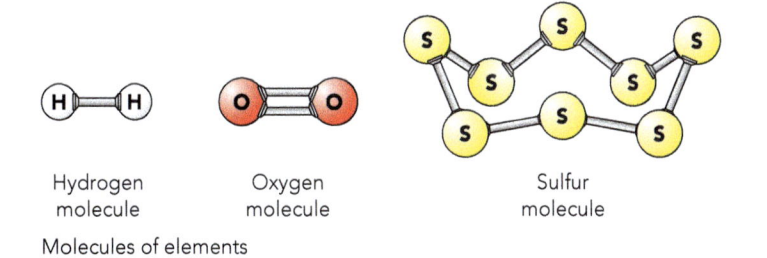

Hydrogen molecule
Oxygen molecule
Sulfur molecule

Molecules of elements

These show how the atoms are joined together to form **molecules**.

Molecules are groups of two or more atoms bonded together.

Notice how each model molecule contains only one type of plastic ball. They contain only one type of atom so they are **molecules of elements**.

Expert tips

'An element is a substance made of only one type of atom.'

But you can also define an element as 'A substance that cannot be broken down chemically into simpler substances'.

Key terms

- **atom**
- **element**
- **molecule**

Summary questions

1. Copy and complete:

   An _____ is a substance made up of only one type of _____.

   It cannot be _____ down into any _____ substances.

2. What is the difference between an atom and a molecule?

3. Atoms are the building blocks of matter. Why do you think there are millions of different substances on Earth if there are only about 100 different types of atoms?

83

4.5 Chemical symbols and formulae

Learning outcomes

After this topic you should be able to:
- list the chemical symbols of the first 20 elements
- interpret chemical formulae.

Chemical symbols

On page 82, did you notice the letters written on the atoms of hydrogen, oxygen, sulfur and iron? Hydrogen had H, oxygen O, sulfur S and iron had the letters Fe. These are called the chemical symbols of these atoms (or of the elements).

To a chemist, the symbol H represents one atom of the element hydrogen. Here are the symbols of the atoms of some common elements:

Atom	Symbol	Atom	Symbol
hydrogen	H	zinc	Zn
carbon	C	iron	Fe
oxygen	O	copper	Cu
chlorine	Cl	helium	He

You can see that the symbol for some atoms is a single capital letter. Others have two letters – a capital followed by a lower case letter. Notice that the symbol for some atoms comes from their Latin name. For example, iron's symbol is Fe, which comes from its Latin name, *ferrum*.

You need to know the symbols of the first 20 elements. Some also appear in the table above.

Atom	Symbol	Atom	Symbol
1. hydrogen	H	11. sodium	Na
2. helium	He	12. magnesium	Mg
3. lithium	Li	13. aluminium	Al
4. beryllium	Be	14. silicon	Si
5. boron	B	15. phosphorus	P
6. carbon	C	16. sulfur	S
7. nitrogen	N	17. chlorine	Cl
8. oxygen	O	18. argon	Ar
9. fluorine	F	19. potassium	K
10. neon	Ne	20. calcium	Ca

Key terms

- **chemical formula**

Practical activity — Researching the first 20 elements

Your task is to describe each of the first 20 elements in one informative sentence.

For example, 'Hydrogen is a highly flammable, colourless gas with a very low density.'

4 Elements, mixtures and compounds

Find a way to help you memorise the first 20 chemical elements in order.

Beryllium    Boron 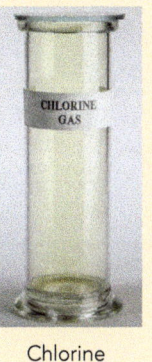   Chlorine    Phosphorus    Silicon

Chemical formulae

You have already seen how we use models to represent atoms and molecules. The molecules on page 83 were made up of the same type of atom. However, a water molecule contains two types of atom – hydrogen and oxygen.

Scientists use their own short-hand way of showing a molecule. Rather than draw a molecule, they use its **chemical formula**.

It shows us how many of each type of atom there are in a molecule. The formula does this by using the symbols of atoms and subscript numbers.

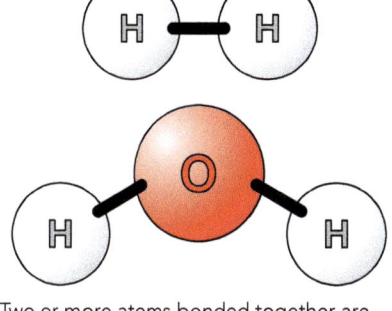

Two or more atoms bonded together are called molecules. These are molecules of H_2 and H_2O

Look at the table below:

Name of molecule	hydrogen sulfide	chlorine	methane
Diagram of molecule	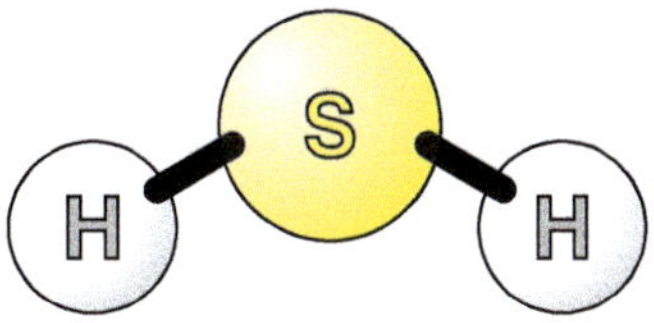	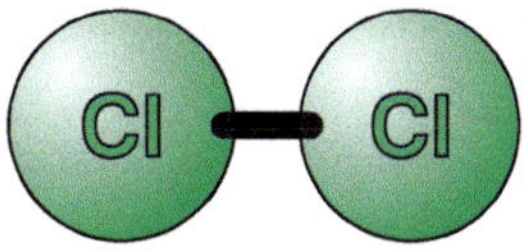	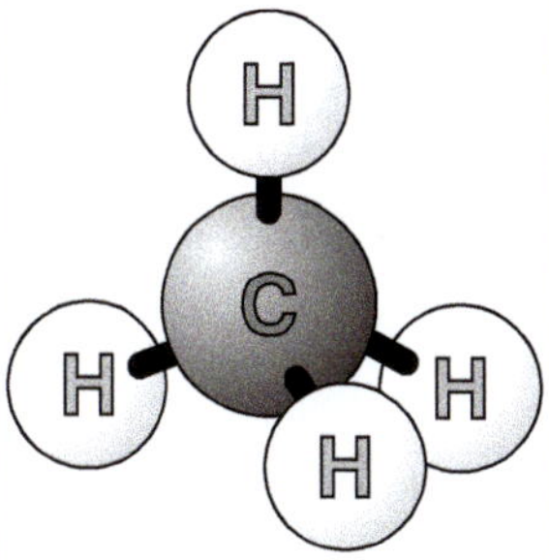
Chemical formula	H_2S	Cl_2	CH_4

Summary questions

1. Give some rules for writing the chemical symbol for an atom.
    a) Find the names of all the elements whose symbols start with the letter 'H'.
    b) If you discovered a new element, what would you call it and what symbol would you give it?
2. a) Draw the molecule whose chemical formula is NH_3.
    b) How many atoms are there in NH_3?
    c) Explain why NH_3 is not a chemical element.

85

4.6 Introducing the Periodic Table

Learning outcomes

After this topic you should be able to:
- recognise why the Periodic Table is important to scientists
- use secondary sources to find information
- spot patterns in data.

The chemical elements

Trying to make sense of the many millions of different substances on Earth sounds like a very difficult job. Fortunately, not many of these substances are elements. We only have around 100 different elements to find out about. Even this is a large number. However, many of the elements have things in common, so studying them is made a lot easier!

Practical activity Detailing the elements

Your teacher will give each group about five elements to find out about.

You will need to use books, DVDs, CD-ROMs or the internet.

- Find out for each of your elements:
  a) its symbol
  b) its state at 20 °C
  c) whether it is described as a metal, a non-metal or a metalloid (semi-metal)
  d) whether it is magnetic or not
  e) its appearance
  f) any other interesting information.

We will be looking for patterns in the information gathered by the whole class.

To help us find patterns, record the information on the sides of a cube made from card.

- Record each piece of information on a different side of the cube for each element.
- Write the word 'metal' in blue, 'non-metal' in red and 'metalloid' in green.

Use a large capital S for solids, an L for liquids and a G for gases.

This information will be used in the next activity.

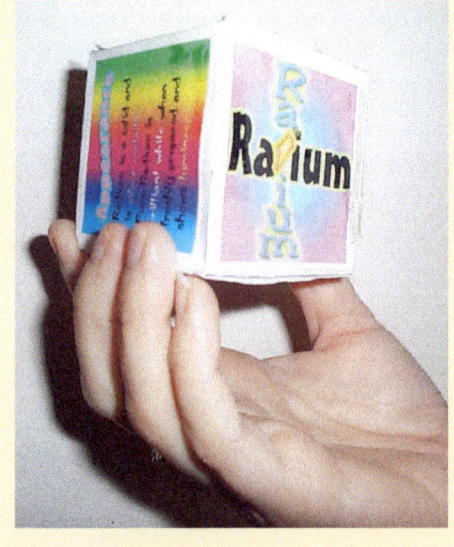

The Periodic Table

In 1869 a Russian chemist called Dmitri Mendeleev arranged the elements in order of atomic mass (see page 75). He started with the lightest atoms, getting heavier. He made some adjustments so that similar elements lined up in vertical columns. The columns are called groups. He called the arrangement the **Periodic Table**. Periodic means 'repeated at regular intervals'.

4 Elements, mixtures and compounds

This shows the main sections of the Periodic Table

Practical activity — Sorting out the elements

Clear a space on the floor and place your cubes in the positions they would be in the Periodic Table.

Turn all the cubes to show metal, non-metal or metalloid.

- What do you notice? Are there more metals or non-metals?
- Describe which part of the Periodic Table contains metals and which contains non-metals. Where are the metalloids (or semi-metals) found?

Now turn the cubes to show the state of the elements at 20 °C (S, L or G).

- What can you say about the numbers of solids, liquids and gases?

Now show which elements are magnetic and which are non-magnetic.

- What do you notice?
- Summarise any generalisations you can make about the chemical elements or about the Periodic Table.

Get your own copy of the Periodic Table to stick in your book. Use colour coding and a key to show your findings.

Key terms

- Periodic Table

Summary questions

1. Copy and complete:
   The elements can be sorted out into _____, non-metals and a few _____. The Periodic _____ shows elements with _____ properties in the same column. The columns are called _____.

2. What does the word 'periodic' mean in the term 'Periodic Table'?

3. Why are the chemical symbols for elements useful when scientists from different countries communicate with each other?

4.7 Elements and compounds

Learning outcomes

After this topic you should be able to:
- define the word 'compound'
- distinguish between elements and compounds
- use a range of equipment correctly
- discuss and control risks to yourself and others.

You have seen models of molecules made of different types of atom on page 85. These molecules of water, H$_2$O, hydrogen sulfide, H$_2$S, and methane, CH$_4$, are examples of substances that we call **compounds**.

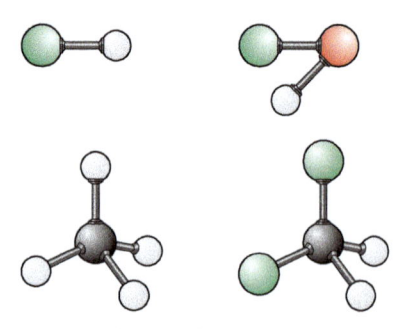

All these models show small molecules of compounds

A compound is a substance made up of two or more different types of atom.

Now we will look at a mixture of elements before they react together. Then we will compare the mixture with the compound formed in the reaction.

Practical activity — Investigating iron and sulfur

Collect some iron filings on a piece of paper.

Then collect a spatula of sulfur on another piece of paper.
- Describe each element.

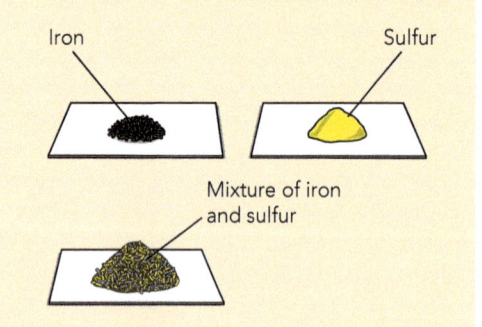

Now thoroughly mix the iron and sulfur together.
- What shows us that no new compound has formed?

Next heat the **mixture of elements** in an ignition tube with a loose plug of mineral wool in the opening.

⚠ Do this in a fume cupboard or a well-ventilated laboratory.

⚠ The mineral wool is to reduce the chance of sulfur vapour igniting and forming toxic sulfur dioxide gas.

Focus your heating on the bottom of the tube. When you see the first signs of a reaction, stop heating and see if the reaction continues.
- What observation tells us when the reaction starts?
- Describe the product formed.

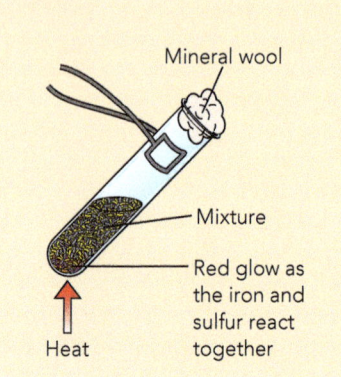

4 Elements, mixtures and compounds

Practical activity — Comparing a mixture and a compound

Look at a sample of iron sulfide and compare it with a mixture of iron and sulfur.
- What differences do you notice?

Use a magnet wrapped in cling-film to test the compound and the mixture.

Add iron sulfide to some water in a beaker and stir. Compare this by doing the same thing with the mixture of iron and sulfur.
- What happens in each test?

Watch your teacher add some dilute hydrochloric acid to the compound and the mixture in a fume cupboard.
- What differences do you notice between the reactions?

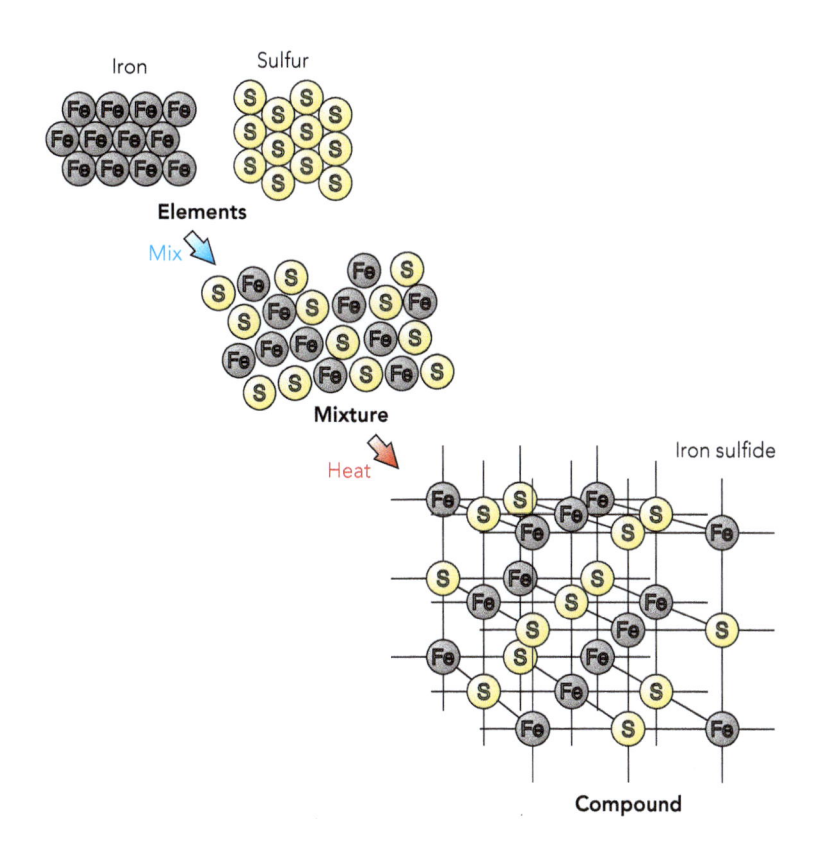

Key terms
- compound

Summary questions

1. Define the word 'compound'.
2. Name two differences between a mixture of iron and sulfur and a sample of the compound of iron and sulfur (called iron sulfide).
3. Write a word equation for the reaction of iron when heated with sulfur.

4.8 Forming compounds from elements

Learning outcomes

After this topic you should be able to:
- distinguish between mixtures and compounds
- carry out a reaction to make a compound from its elements
- represent chemical reactions by word equations.

Differences between mixtures and compounds

The proportions of iron and sulfur atoms in any sample of the compound iron sulfide will always be the same. The ratio in this case is 1 : 1 and that's why its formula is FeS.

However, the proportions in a mixture can vary. We could mix one part iron with two parts sulfur, or three parts iron with one part sulfur, and so on.

Any compound always has fixed proportions of its elements (as shown by its chemical formula).

Below is a table summarising the differences between compounds and mixtures of elements.

Compounds	Mixtures of elements
Have a fixed composition (there will always be the same proportions of elements in any particular compound).	Have no fixed composition (the proportions vary depending on the amount of each element mixed together).
Need chemical reactions to separate the elements in them.	The elements can be separated again more easily (by physical means using the differences in properties of each element in the mixture, such as their solubility in water, boiling point, magnetic or not).
There are chemical bonds between atoms of the different elements in the compound.	There are no chemical bonds between atoms of the different elements in a mixture of elements.

Making compounds

We can make some compounds by reacting two elements together. The compound is totally different from either of the two elements that combined.

For example, sodium is a very reactive element. It is a metal that we have to store under oil to keep it away from oxygen and water vapour in the air. Chlorine is a very dangerous, toxic gas. Yet when these two elements react together, they make a compound that we sprinkle on food – sodium chloride (common salt). We can show this reaction by the **word equation**:

sodium + chlorine → sodium chloride

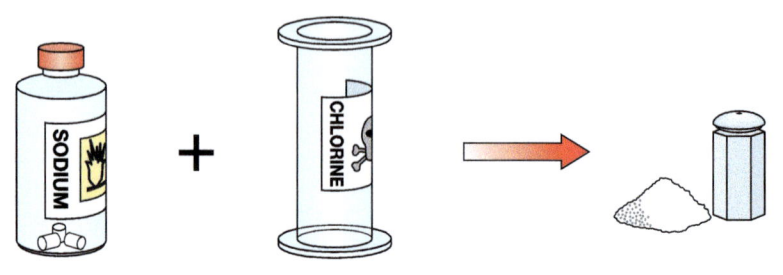

Key terms
- products
- reactants

The substances we start with before the reaction are called **reactants**. The substances formed in reactions are called **products**.

4 Elements, mixtures and compounds

Other non-metals, such as sulfur, oxygen and bromine, also react with other elements to form compounds:
- Sulfur makes compounds called sulfides, for example magnesium sulfide.
- Oxygen makes oxides, and bromine makes bromides.

Practical activity   Combining elements

Watch your teacher demonstrate the following chemical reactions:

hydrogen + oxygen   sulfur + oxygen   magnesium + oxygen   zinc + sulfur

⚠️ **The reactions of sulfur + oxygen and zinc + sulfur must be carried out in a fume cupboard.**
- Record your results in a table that describes the reactants and the products, and also what happens as the elements react.
- Write a word equation for each reaction.
- What were the signs that chemical reactions had taken place?

In chemical reactions, atoms get re-arranged. Look at the reaction of hydrogen and oxygen shown using the models on the right:

The word equation is:

hydrogen + oxygen → water (hydrogen oxide)

Practical activity   Making copper sulfide

Collect 3 g of copper wire and wind it into a spiral.

Collect 1.5 g of sulfur on a piece of paper.
- What do the elements look like?

Now mix the copper and sulfur together in a boiling tube, with the sulfur covering the copper.
- Do you think a compound has been formed? Explain your answer.

Heat the mixture of elements in the boiling tube with a loose piece of mineral wool in its mouth. (The mineral wool is to reduce the chance of sulfur vapour igniting and forming toxic sulfur dioxide gas.)

⚠️ **Do this in a fume cupboard (or watch your teacher demonstrate it).**
- What do you see happen when the reaction starts?
- What does the product look like?
- Write a word equation for the reaction between copper and sulfur.

Summary questions

1. List three differences between a compound and a mixture.
2. Name the elements that make up: a) phosphorus bromide   b) NH_3.
3. Write word equations for the reactions between:
    a) hydrogen and chlorine   b) potassium and chlorine   c) zinc and sulfur.

4.9 Investigating elements, mixtures and compounds

Learning outcomes

After this topic you should be able to:
- plan a method to separate a mixture of compounds
- carry out your plan safely
- classify samples as elements, mixtures or compounds.

Think of the differences between a mixture and a compound (see page 90). One difference is the ease with which we can separate the components of a mixture compared with separating the elements that make up a compound.

The different substances in a mixture will each have different properties. We can often use these differences to separate them.

This coffee filter is separating a mixture. Can you explain how it works?

In the following investigation you will be given a mixture of compounds to separate.

Practical activity — Separating mixtures of compounds

You will be given one of the following mixtures of compounds:
- sand and sugar
- sand and salt
- powdered chalk and copper sulfate.

Your task is to plan a method to separate each of the mixtures into samples of the pure compounds.

(Hint: Think about differences in solubility between the two compounds in each mixture.)

Make sure your plan is safe. Include details of any risks and how you will deal with them in your plan.

⚠ **Let your teacher check your plan before you start your practical work.**

Classifying elements, mixtures and compounds

In this chapter, we have dealt with many compounds made up of two elements. Examples are iron sulfide, copper sulfide and magnesium oxide. These 'two-element' compounds all have two words in their name, and end with the letters '-ide'.

Another common ending to the names of compounds is '-ate', as in copper sulfate. This ending indicates a 'three-element' compound, in which one of the elements is oxygen. The name

4 Elements, mixtures and compounds

'copper sulfate' gives you a clue as to the other two elements it is made up of. Copper sulfate contains copper and sulfur as well as oxygen. This is shown in its chemical formula, $CuSO_4$.

> **Expert tips**
>
> Elements **always** have one-word names, such as hydrogen, carbon and sodium.
>
> Many compounds have two-word names, such as zinc oxide, **but** there are plenty of exceptions. These exceptions are often where we use common names for everyday compounds. Examples are the compounds water and salt (although their chemical names are hydrogen oxide and sodium chloride).

> **Practical activity**   Element, mixture or compound?
>
> Your teacher will provide you with samples of substances (or photos of them) for you to classify as elements, mixtures or compounds.
>
> Each sample will have some information, such as its chemical formula.
> - Explain your decision for each classification you made. If you cannot decide for any sample, state why.

The chlorine in the gas jar is made up of Cl_2 molecules. The gas jar is made of glass which contains silica – a giant structure of mainly silicon and oxygen atoms linked together by strong bonds. The air around the gas jar is made up mainly of oxygen (21%) and nitrogen (78%).
- Classify chlorine, silica and air as a mixture, an element or a compound

> **Summary questions**
>
> 1 A compound is made up of the elements zinc, sulfur and oxygen. What is its chemical name?
>
> 2 What is the chemical name and formula of water?
>
> 3 a) You are given a mixture of iron and sulfur.
>
>   Is this A, B or C?
>   A a mixture of elements
>   B a mixture of compounds
>   C a mixture of an element and a compound
>
>   b) Neither iron nor sulfur dissolve in water, but sulfur does dissolve in a flammable liquid called xylene. Use this information to explain a method to separate the iron and sulfur from the mixture.

93

Chapter 4 — End of chapter questions

1. A group of students is investigating diffusion.

    In Test 1, they plan to time how long it takes a coloured gas to diffuse throughout a gas jar of air.

    In Test 2, they plan to fill the gas jar with water and time how long it takes a coloured ink to diffuse throughout the water.

    a. What measuring instrument will they need to judge which test is quicker? [1]

    b. i Predict whether diffusion happens more quickly in Test 1 or Test 2. [1]

    ii Explain your answer to part **i** using the particle theory. [2]

2. When bromine gas diffuses through a vacuum, the orange colour spreads through a flask almost instantly. When the same flask is full of air, it takes an hour for the orange colour to spread evenly throughout the flask.

    Explain these observations. [2]

3. Copy and complete:

    Some elements can react together to form _____ .

    For example, oxygen reacts to form _____ and chlorine forms _____ .

    We can describe these chemical reactions by _____ equations. For example,

    iron + _____ → _____ bromide [6]

4. To answer this question, use the information below:

    H forms 1 bond. Br forms 1 bond. F forms 1 bond. O forms 2 bonds. S forms 2 bonds. B forms 3 bonds. C forms 4 bonds. P can form 5 bonds.

    a. Draw a 'ball and stick' diagram to show these molecules:

    i HOBr [1]

    ii PBr_5 [1]

    iii BF_3 [1]

    iv C_2H_6 [1]

    v S_8 [1]

    b. Which of the molecules in part **a**:

    i is **not** a molecule of a compound? Explain your answer. [2]

    ii is a molecule of a compound containing atoms of three different elements? [1]

    iii contain hydrogen atoms? [2]

    c. Draw a table showing the number of atoms in each molecule listed in part **a**. [6]

5. Look at this list:

    CF_4 P_4 O_3
    HI   He N_2H_4

    a. Which are elements and which are compounds? [2]

    b. How many atoms are in each of the molecules? [6]

6. Give the chemical symbol for:

    a. helium [1]

    b. sodium [1]

    c. argon. [1]

7. Write a word equation to describe the reaction between:

    a. zinc and oxygen [1]

    b. potassium and chlorine [1]

    c. copper and sulfur [1]

    d. iron and bromine [1]

    e. aluminium and iodine. [1]

8. Look at the molecule below:

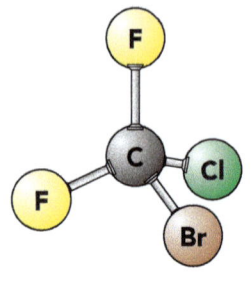

    What is the chemical formula of the compound? [1]

4 Elements, mixtures and compounds

9 Look at the boxes below:

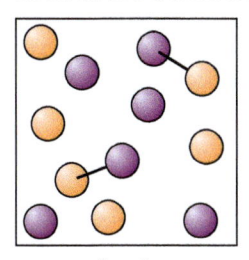

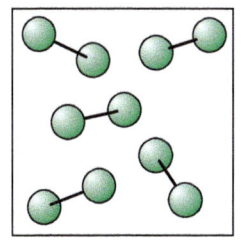

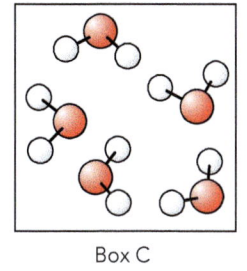

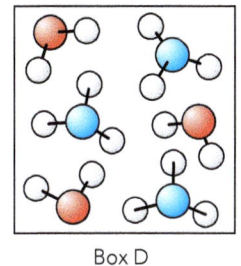

Box A Box B Box C Box D

a Which boxes contain mixtures? [2]
b Which box contains only one element? [1]
c Which box contains a mixture of different compounds? [1]
d Which box shows a chemical reaction in progress? [1]
e Which box contains some ammonia, NH_3? [1]

10 Read this information:

Sodium, aluminium and zinc are elements that conduct electricity.

Iodine and sulfur are elements that do not conduct electricity.

When zinc and sulfur are heated together, they react vigorously to form a new substance called zinc sulfide.

a Use only the information given above to:
  i name two metals [2]
  ii name two non-metals [2]
  iii give the name of a compound. [1]
b i Write a word equation for the reaction of zinc with sulfur. [1]
  ii Why is the reaction between zinc and sulfur carried out in a fume cupboard? [2]
  iii Write the name of the compound formed when magnesium reacts with sulfur. [1]

11 The diagrams below show the different arrangement of atoms in six substances.

Each atom is represented by a circle labelled with its chemical symbol.

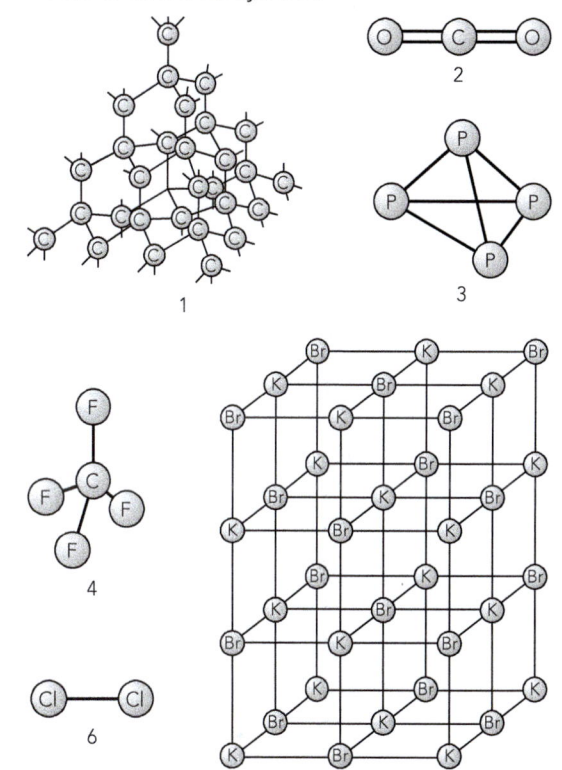

a i Which of the diagrams represent the structures of elements? Write down the correct numbers. [1]
  ii Explain your answer to part **i**. [1]
b Give the formula of two of the compounds represented in the diagrams. [2]
c Give the name of the substance labelled 5. [1]
d Give the names of the chemical elements whose atoms can be represented by the following symbols:
  i C
  ii Cl
  iii Cu [3]

5 Metals, non-metals and corrosion

Science in context!

Interesting elements

Hydrogen – the low density (but very flammable) element

Have you seen the airships that sometimes fly over big sporting events? They take those spectacular overhead pictures for TV. Modern airships are filled with a gas called helium (a very unreactive gas) and they are a very safe way to travel. However, this was not true of the giant airships built in the 1930s.

A modern airship, filled with helium gas

Airships are really huge balloons fitted with engines that drive propellers. The Germans were the masters of airship technology. After the First World War in 1918, they continued developing airships for passenger flights. Their biggest airship was the Graf Zeppelin which was like a luxury, flying hotel. It flew right around the world (although it did take three weeks).

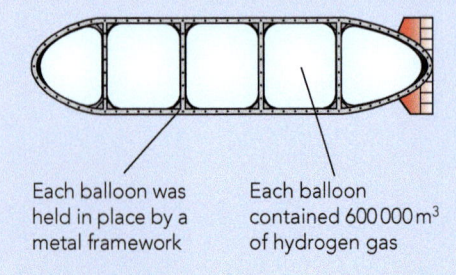

Each balloon was held in place by a metal framework

Each balloon contained 600 000 m³ of hydrogen gas

Rather than being filled with helium, the airships were at that time filled with the lightest of all gases, hydrogen. Britain also built two large passenger airships – named the R100 and the R101. But on 4 October 1930, the R101 crashed in France. It was on its way to India and 48 people died.

After that experience, travel by airship was left to the Germans. However, disaster struck in 1937. Their newest and most advanced airship, called the Hindenburg, crashed as it came in to land in New Jersey, US. It was a stormy day but crowds had still gathered to see the great airship arrive after flying over the Atlantic. They couldn't believe their eyes as it burst into flames on landing. In about 30 seconds the airship was totally destroyed.

The huge volume of hydrogen gas burned fiercely as it reacted with the oxygen in the air:

hydrogen + oxygen → water (hydrogen oxide)

Thirty-six people died at the airfield. Remarkably, 62 others survived, although some died later of their injuries.

Hydrogen was just too dangerous to use in airships. The Hindenburg marked the end of giant airships.

5 Metals, non-metals and corrosion

Humphry Davy – the element hunter!

Humphry Davy was a brilliant chemist. However, the long hours he spent working in the laboratory with gases would eventually kill him.

Davy was born on 17 December 1778, in Cornwall, UK.

Sir Humphry Davy (1778–1829)

Davy's reputation as a scientist grew as he studied the effects of gases on the body. In 1801 the Royal Institution in London invited him to be one of their public lecturers.

It was the invention of the first battery that helped Davy become famous. He could generate his own electricity using the first cells. He made huge batteries and could really impress his audiences with sparks, bangs and flashes.

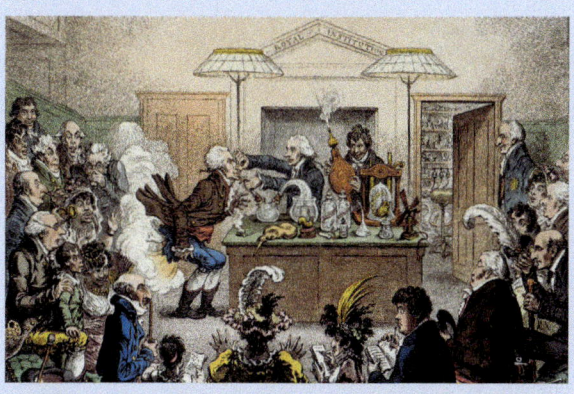

A cartoonist of the day illustrates a lecture by Sir Humphry Davy

However, his greatest success came when he tried passing electricity through molten compounds. In 1807 he discovered **potassium** by passing electricity through molten potash (potassium carbonate). The silvery blobs of metal were amazing. When Davy dropped a piece in water it 'skimmed about excitedly with a hissing sound, and soon burned with a lovely lavender light'. He also discovered **sodium** in the same year by passing elecricity through molten sodium chloride.

He went on to use his batteries the following year to isolate **magnesium**, **calcium**, **strontium** and **barium**. He also discovered **boron** using potassium to displace it from one of its compounds. However, he died in 1829 after years of ill health, most probably caused by inhaling many gases in his research.

In this chapter you will find out about the differences between metals and non-metals. You will also look at some chemical reactions which are not beneficial and learn about representing reactions using word equations.

Key points

- The chemical elements can be classified as metals or non-metals (with a few semi-metals or metalloids).
- In general, metal elements are good conductors of heat and electricity, have high melting points and are dense, shiny, hard, ductile and malleable.
- In general, non-metallic solid elements are poor conductors of heat and electricity, have low melting points and are dull and brittle.
- Rusting is an unwanted oxidation reaction of iron.
- Iron needs air (oxygen) and water in order to rust.
- We can protect iron from rusting by various methods that stop air and water getting to the iron.
- Many other metals will also corrode or tarnish over time.

5.1 Metals, non-metals and the Periodic Table

Learning outcomes

After this topic you should be able to:

- recall the Stage 7 work you did on some of the properties of metals and non-metals
- locate metals and non-metals in the Periodic Table.

You have studied metals and non-metals before in Stage 7. You found out that metals are good conductors of heat and electricity.

Power cables contain aluminium metal to transfer electrical energy over large distances

On the other hand, non-metals are insulators. They do not let heat or electricity pass through them. The exception is carbon in the form of graphite, which is a good conductor.

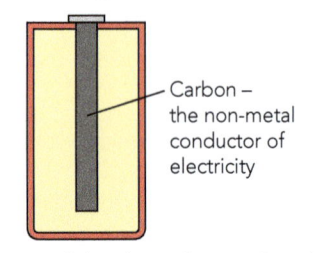

Carbon – the non-metal conductor of electricity

Graphite is used to make one of the electrodes in a dry-cell battery

More about the Periodic Table

On page 87 we saw how the chemical elements are arranged in the Periodic Table. There are eight main groups in the Periodic Table. These are shown numbered on the next page.

- Group 1 and 2 elements (starting at the top with Li and Be) are all metals.
- Group 7 and 0 elements (starting at the top with F and He) are all non-metals.

However, the elements in the middle groups start with non-metals at the top, but finish with metals at the bottom.

We can draw a 'staircase' (shown by the bold line in the Periodic Table on the next page) to divide the metals and non-metal elements. A number of the elements near this dividing line have some metallic properties and some non-metallic properties. We call these elements **semi-metals** or **metalloids**.

Key terms

- **metalloid**
- **semi-metal**

5 Metals, non-metals and corrosion

Look at the elements in Group 4 below:
- C – carbon is a non-metal.
- Si – silicon is a semi-metal or metalloid.
- Ge – germanium is a semi-metal or metalloid.
- Sn – tin is a metal.
- Pb – lead is a metal.

The elements get more metallic as we go down a group.

Expert tips

There are many more metallic elements than non-metallic elements on Earth.

Metals, non-metals and semi-metals (metalloids) in the Periodic Table

The elements between element 57 (La) and element 72 (Hf) and all the elements beyond element 86 (Rn) are not shown in the version of the Periodic Table shown above. The heaviest elements are all radioactive and unstable. Ever-heavier atoms are still being made in laboratories. At present scientists are trying to make atoms of elements beyond number 115. Like all these heaviest atoms they can only exist for a fraction of a second. They then decay to form smaller atoms.

Summary questions

1. Which of the following is the best estimation of the number of metallic elements in the Periodic Table?
   - A 25%
   - B 50%
   - C 75%
   - D 90%

2. a) Sort the following elements into a table showing metals, semi-metals and non-metals:

   sodium   phosphorus   iodine   silicon   calcium   vanadium

   b) What is another word that means the same as 'semi-metal'?

3. Predict which one of the following elements is the best thermal conductor (best conductor of heat):

   sulfur   argon   potassium   helium

99

5.2 Properties of metals and non-metals

Learning outcomes

After this topic you should be able to:
- list the general properties of metals and non-metals
- plan an investigation to test properties.

In Stage 7 you tested electrical conductivity and thermal conductivity using the apparatus below:

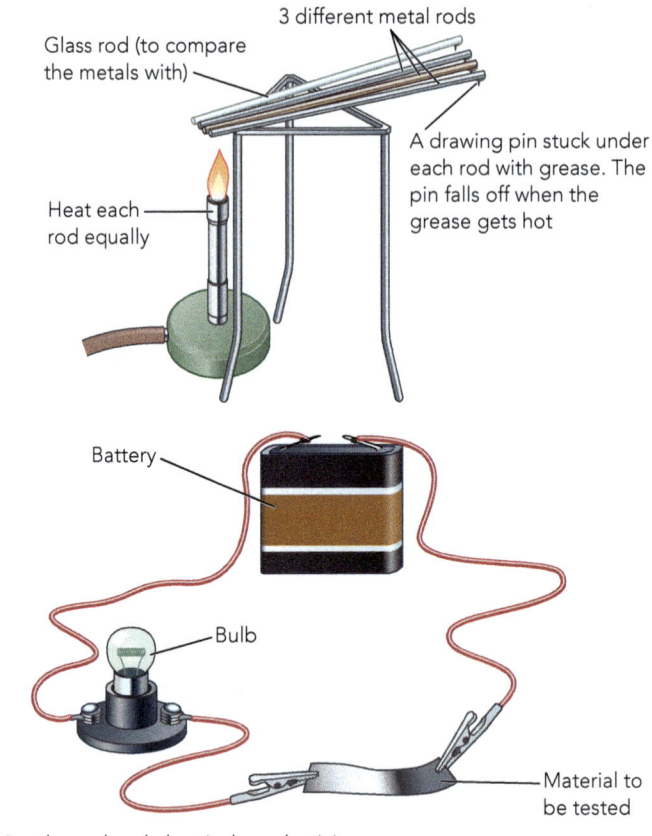

Testing thermal and electrical conductivity

Try some tests of your own in the following activity.

Practical activity — Planning property tests

Hardness
A harder material can scratch the surface of a softer material.
- Describe a way to arrange some samples in order of hardness.

Density
- Given equal-sized cubes of different materials, describe a way to put the materials in order of density.

Flexibility
- Given strips of materials, describe a way to put them in order of flexibility.

Melting points
Use a database to compare the melting points of metals and non-metals on a graph.

Tensile strength
Plan an investigation to compare the strength of metal wires.

⚠ Before carrying out any of your tests, your plan must be checked by your teacher.

5 Metals, non-metals and corrosion

The spider diagrams below summarise the general properties of metal and non-metal elements:

Properties of metals

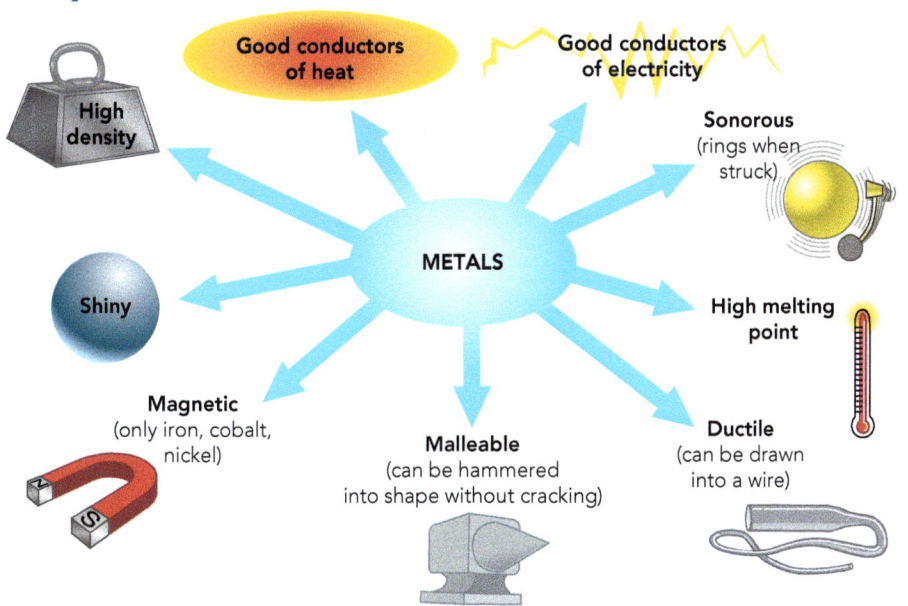

Good conductors of heat
Good conductors of electricity
High density
Sonorous (rings when struck)
Shiny
METALS
High melting point
Magnetic (only iron, cobalt, nickel)
Malleable (can be hammered into shape without cracking)
Ductile (can be drawn into a wire)

Properties of non-metals

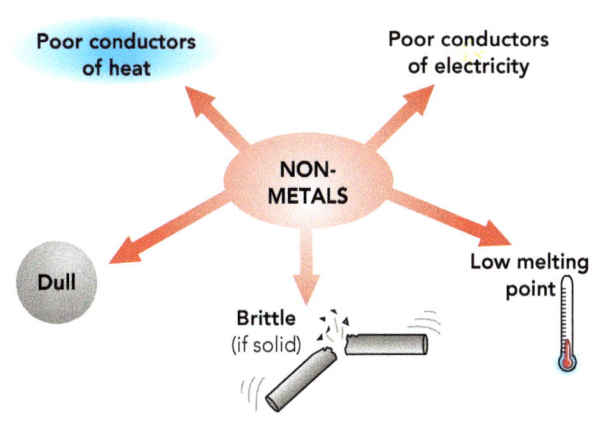

Poor conductors of heat
Poor conductors of electricity
NON-METALS
Dull
Brittle (if solid)
Low melting point

Expert tips

These are the **general** properties of metallic and non-metallic elements – there are exceptions, such as metals with low melting points (e.g. mercury) and non-metals with high melting points (e.g. carbon).

Summary questions

1. Which of the following properties are typical of metals and which are typical of non-metals?
   high density, poor thermal conductivity, dull, ductile, good electrical conductivity, brittle

2. Which word describes a metal that:
   a) can be hammered into shapes without smashing?
   b) can be drawn out into wires?
   c) makes a ringing sound when struck with a hard object?

3. An element melts at 115 °C and has a density of 1.96 g/cm³.
   a) Is this element more likely to be a metal or a non-metal?
   b) What test could you carry out to confirm your answer to part **a**?

101

5.3 Exceptional elements

Learning outcomes

After this topic you should be able to:
- recognise that some elements have unexpected properties
- interpret data from secondary sources.

In the previous topic we saw the general properties of metallic and non-metallic elements. There are some elements that are classified as metals or non-metals but have some surprising properties.

The alkali metals

In Group 1 of the Periodic Table, we find an unusual group of metals.
- Li – lithium
- Na – sodium
- K – potassium
- Rb – rubidium
- Cs – caesium

Whereas most metals are hard and dense, the alkali metals are soft and have low densities. In fact, these metals can be cut into smaller pieces with a knife.

This piece of sodium metal is being cut with a knife

Look at the densities of lithium, sodium and potassium compared with three more typical metals in the table below.

Alkali metal	Density / g/cm³	More typical metal	Density / g/cm³
lithium	0.53	iron	7.87
sodium	0.97	copper	8.93
potassium	0.86	zinc	7.14

Any substance with a density of less than 1.0 g/cm³ will float in water. So lithium, sodium and potassium all float in water. They also react very vigorously with water, unlike most metals.

Most metals also have high melting points. In the following activity you can research how the melting points of the alkali metals compare with some typical metals.

Practical activity Comparing melting points

Use a database to complete a table like the one above to compare the melting points of lithium, sodium and potassium with the three typical metals, iron, copper and zinc.
- What can you conclude by comparing the two sets of melting points?

Now look up the melting points of rubidium and caesium.
- Draw a bar chart to display the melting points of the alkali metals going down the group.
- What pattern do you see going down Group 1?

5 Metals, non-metals and corrosion

Mercury

Mercury (Hg) is another unusual metal. It exists as a liquid at room temperature.

Practical activity   Data on mercury

Predict the melting point of mercury by looking at the melting points of other elements near mercury (Hg) in the Periodic Table.

Use a database to find the melting point of mercury.
- Compare the melting point of mercury with those of more typical metals. What do you find?

Predict the density of mercury by looking at the densities of other elements near mercury (Hg) in the Periodic Table.

Now look up the density of mercury.
- Compare the density of mercury with those of typical metals. What do you find?

Mercury – the liquid metal

Carbon

The non-metal carbon has two common forms – graphite and diamond. These two forms have some remarkable properties. Unlike other non-metallic elements, diamond and graphite have very high melting points. Diamond melts at 3550 °C and graphite actually sublimes (turns directly from a solid to a gas without melting) at 3720 °C.

Graphite is a good thermal and electrical conductor, unlike other non-metals, and diamond is the one of the hardest known substances.

Graphite

Diamond

Summary questions

1. **a)** In what ways are the alkali metals similar to other metals?
   b) In what ways do the alkali metals differ from other metals?
2. **a)** Give one use of mercury that relies on its low melting point.
   b) Find a use for diamond that relies on its incredible hardness.
3. Most metals have silvery surfaces when freshly cut or when sanded down. Name two metals that do not have this silvery appearance.

5.4 Elements from compounds

Learning outcomes

After this topic you should be able to:
- explain how to break down some simple compounds into their elements
- carry out an experiment to break down a compound
- test predictions against evidence collected.

We have seen in the previous chapter that all the atoms in an element are the same type. So we can't break elements down into simpler substances in a chemical reaction.

However, compounds contain atoms of different types. So we should be able to break down compounds into simpler substances, including elements.

We can break down some compounds by heating them up. We say that they **decompose**. The reaction is called thermal decomposition.

Some compounds are broken down by passing electricity through the compound once it is melted or dissolved in water.

The breakdown of a compound by electricity is called **electrolysis**.

In the following demonstration you can see water broken down into its elements by electrolysis.

Practical activity — Breaking down water

Watch your teacher break down water into its elements.
- Predict which elements will be collected.

Let the experiment continue until there is enough of each gas to test.
- What are the results of the gas tests?
- Which gas was there more of? By how much? Explain these results.
- Write a word equation to show the chemical change brought about by electrolysis.

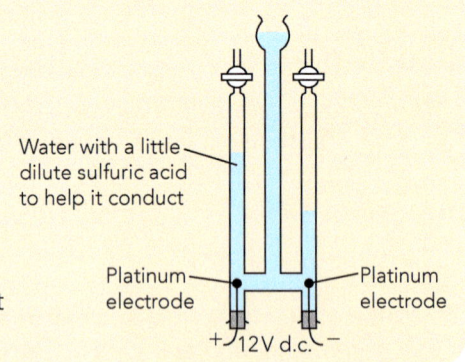

Obtaining copper from its compounds

Many metals are extracted from their compounds found in rocks using electrolysis. Copper is purified using electrolysis. Copper can be obtained from copper sulfate solution. You can try this on a small scale in the next experiment.

Practical activity — Breaking down copper sulfate solution

Set up the circuit shown below:
- Which electrode (the positive or negative) does the copper metal collect on?

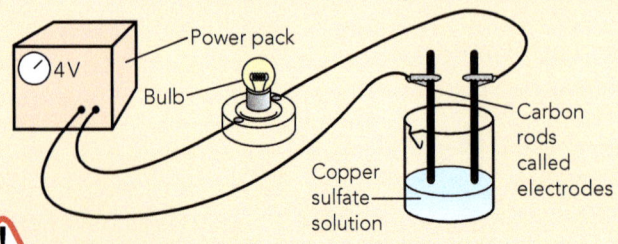

⚠ Make sure you wear eye protection.

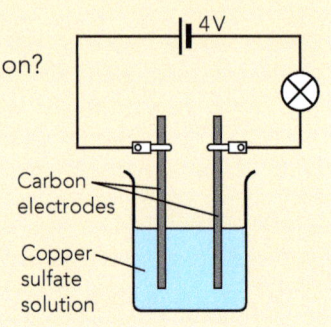

5 Metals, non-metals and corrosion

Obtaining chlorine from salt

The chemical name for common salt is sodium chloride. What elements is sodium chloride made from?

In the next experiment you can obtain chlorine gas from a solution of salt.

Practical activity: Breaking down sodium chloride solution

⚠ Chlorine gas is toxic, so do this experiment in a fume cupboard or a well-ventilated laboratory. Turn the source of electricity off as soon as possible.

⚠ Make sure you wear eye protection.

Set up the circuit shown below:

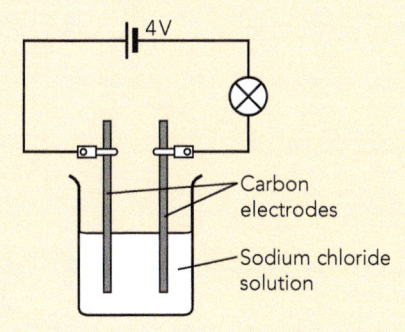

Diagram: 4V battery connected to a bulb and two carbon electrodes dipped in sodium chloride solution.

Test the gas given off from the positive electrode with damp blue litmus paper.
- Describe what happens at the electrodes.
- Find out which gas is given off from the negative electrode.
- Find out how this experiment would need to be changed in industry to get sodium metal from a sample of sodium chloride.

Expert tips
You do not need to know the details of how electrolysis takes place at this level – just that it can be used to break down compounds into elements.

Key terms
- decompose
- electrolysis

Summary questions

1. Write a word equation for the breakdown of sodium chloride into its elements by electrolysis.
2. Draw a circuit you could use to obtain copper from a solution of copper sulfate.
3. What does the electrolysis of water (with a little acid added) tell us about the chemical formula of water?
4. Do some research to find out how the compound aluminium oxide is broken down by electrolysis.
   a) What is the useful product made in the process?
   b) Draw a diagram of the cell used to carry out the electrolysis.

5.5 Making and testing hydrogen

Learning outcomes

After this topic you should be able to:
- describe how to make a sample of hydrogen gas
- describe some properties of hydrogen
- use a general equation and a word equation to describe a chemical reaction
- use a range of equipment safely.

Hydrogen is the first element in the Periodic Table. It is a non-metallic element, with the lowest density of all the chemical elements. It is also highly flammable (see page 96).

Practical activity — Making and testing hydrogen

⚠️ **Make sure you wear eye protection.**

Add a small piece of magnesium ribbon to a 2 cm depth of dilute sulfuric acid in a test tube.
- What do you see?

Hold a boiling tube upside down over the mouth of the first tube.

Hydrogen is less dense than air so it will displace air from the boiling tube.

Test the gas collected in the boiling tube with a lighted splint.
- What happens?

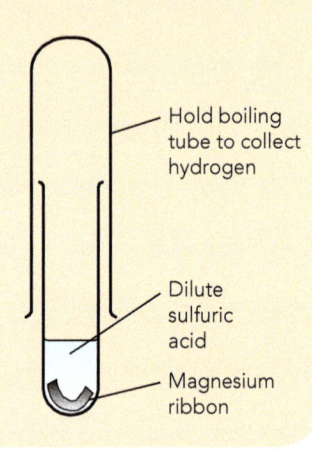

Labels: Hold boiling tube to collect hydrogen; Dilute sulfuric acid; Magnesium ribbon

You hear a popping sound in a positive test for hydrogen gas. The lighted splint causes the hydrogen gas in the boiling tube to react with oxygen gas in the air. Water is the product made – you won't see it because it is present as steam due to the heat of the reaction:

$$\text{hydrogen} + \text{oxygen} \rightarrow \text{water}$$

What is the chemical name for water?

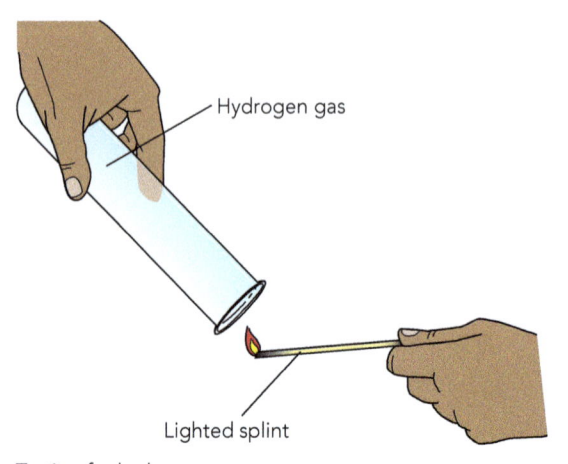

Testing for hydrogen gas (Hydrogen gas; Lighted splint)

5 Metals, non-metals and corrosion

> **Practical activity** — Investigating other metals and acids
>
> ⚠️ **Make sure you wear eye protection.**
>
> Now repeat the experiment on the opposite page but use dilute hydrochloric acid instead of sulfuric acid.
>
> Compare the result with the reaction between magnesium and dilute sulfuric acid.
>
> You can also change the metal to see if you can still make hydrogen gas.
>
> Instead of magnesium, try iron, zinc and copper in turn with dilute hydrochloric acid.
>
> Compare the results with the reaction between magnesium and dilute hydrochloric acid.
>
> - Which metal would you **not** use to make hydrogen gas?

If there is a reaction between a metal and any dilute acid, the gas given off will always be hydrogen. Look at the formulae of the three acids that are commonly used in schools:

Acid	Formula
hydrochloric acid	HCl
sulfuric acid	H_2SO_4
nitric acid	HNO_3

Can you see the element that each acid contains? All acids contain hydrogen. It is released as a gas (H_2) when some metals react with the acid. The metal has to be reasonably reactive for the reaction to work. Copper is not reactive enough.

We can write a **general equation** for those metals that do react with dilute acids:

metal + acid → a salt + hydrogen

So for magnesium and dilute sulfuric acid the word equation is:

magnesium + sulfuric acid → magnesium sulfate + hydrogen

The salt made in this reaction is magnesium sulfate. It dissolves in the water present in the dilute acid so we do not see it forming. We will look in more detail at salts at the start of chapter 6.

Magnesium reacting with dilute sulfuric acid

> **Key terms**
>
> - general equation

> **Summary questions**
>
> 1. Give three facts you have learned about hydrogen gas.
> 2. Write a word equation for the reaction that causes the 'pop' in the test for hydrogen.
> 3. a) Write the general equation for the reaction of a metal with a dilute acid.
>   b) Name a metal that does not follow this general equation and will **not** react with dilute acid.
>   c) Zinc metal reacts with dilute sulfuric acid. Write a word equation for this reaction.

5.6 Rusting

Learning outcomes

After this topic you should be able to:
- explain why rusting is an unwanted chemical reaction
- state the conditions needed for iron to rust
- use a range of equipment correctly.

Key terms

- **corrosion**
- **rusting**

The **rusting** of iron and steel (which contains a very high proportion of iron) is a form of **corrosion**. Corrosion is the 'eating away' of a material by a chemical reaction.

Rusting costs a huge amount of money each year so it is an unwanted chemical reaction. It spoils the appearance of objects and can weaken their structures. Therefore chemists need to understand exactly what causes rusting in order to stop it happening.

There is a high cost to pay in replacing rusty objects

In the following activity you can find out what causes the rusting of iron. Have you any ideas before you start? You can carry out a survey to find out where rusting is most likely to take place and how old the rusting objects are.

5 Metals, non-metals and corrosion

Practical activity — What makes iron rust?

Set up the experiment below to see if air, water or both air and water are needed for rusting:

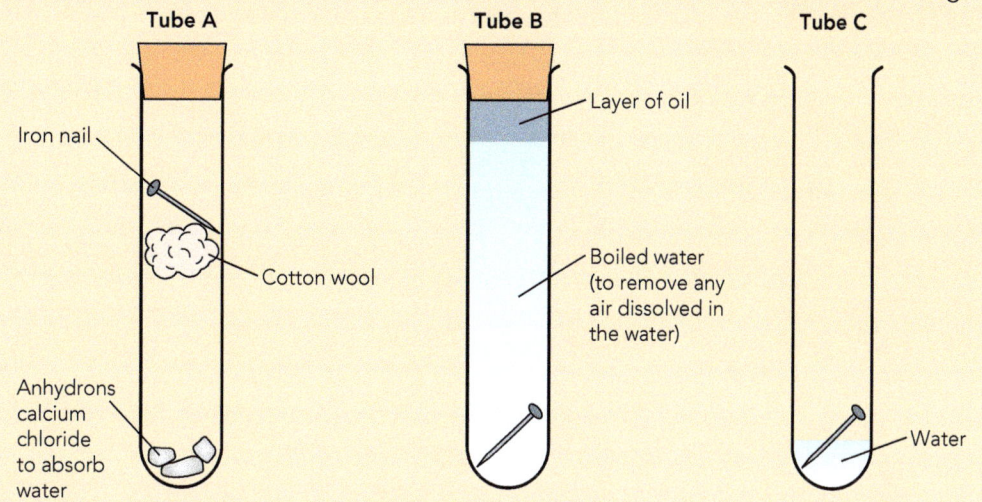

Tube A — Iron nail, Cotton wool, Anhydrous calcium chloride to absorb water

Tube B — Layer of oil, Boiled water (to remove any air dissolved in the water)

Tube C — Water

In tube A we have **air only**. Normal air will have some water vapour in it. So anhydrous calcium chloride is put in tube A – it is a solid that absorbs water vapour from the air.

In tube B we have **water only**. The water has been boiled to drive off the dissolved air in the water. The layer of oil and the bung stop any more air coming into contact with and dissolving in the water while the test is taking place.

In tube C the iron nail is in contact with air and water.

- Leave the experiment for a few days, then record your observations in a table.
- Which tube(s) show signs of rust?
- What are the conditions needed for iron to rust?

Experiments show us that:

iron needs both air (oxygen) and water in order to rust

When iron rusts, it reacts with oxygen (the reactive gas in the air) and water. In the chemical reaction, a form of hydrated iron oxide is formed. Hydrated iron oxide is iron oxide with water bound in its structure. This compound is sometimes referred to as iron hydroxide.

Rust is a crumbly substance that flakes away exposing fresh iron to attack. The iron can corrode completely. This presents us with problems because iron, often in the form of steel, is the most widely used metal in the construction and car industries.

Rust flakes away easily exposing fresh iron to air and water

Summary questions

1. What does the word 'corrosion' mean?
2. In the experiment 'What makes iron rust?', explain why:
    a) tube A has anhydrous calcium chloride in the tube
    b) tube B has water that has been boiled in it.
3. What is needed for iron to rust?

5.7 Investigating rusting

Learning outcomes

After this topic you should be able to:
- use a word equation to describe rusting
- plan an investigation into the factors that affect the rate of rusting
- make predictions based on your scientific knowledge.

We can represent the chemical reaction taking place when iron objects rust with a word equation:

iron + oxygen + water → hydrated iron oxide
(rust)

This is an example of an **oxidation** reaction. During this oxidation, oxygen is a reactant and an oxide is the product. We say that iron has been oxidised in the reaction.

The following experiment demonstrates that oxygen is used up during the process of rusting.

Practical activity — Oxygen and rusting

Place some damp iron wool in a boiling tube and clamp it upside down in a beaker of water.

Leave the experiment for at least a week.

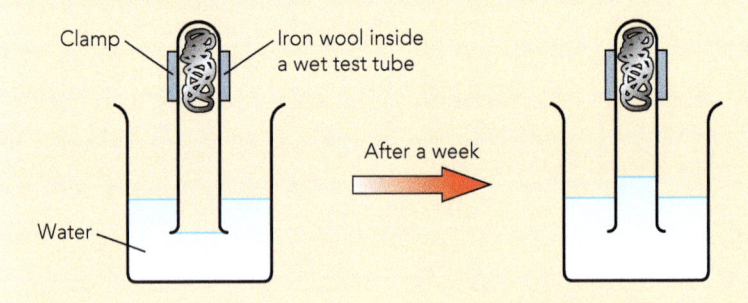

- Explain why the level of the water rises in the tube.
- Measure roughly the fraction of air that has been used up in the experiment.

When the above experiment is carried out carefully with very accurate measurements taken, we find that:
- 21% of the air is used up in the rusting reaction
- the mass of the rust (hydrated iron oxide) is greater than the mass of the iron at the start of the experiment.

The missing 21% corresponds to the percentage of oxygen in the air.

The extra mass in the product of the reaction comes from:
- oxygen atoms (from oxygen gas, O_2) bonding to iron making iron oxide, and
- water molecules, H_2O, bonded into the structure of iron oxide.

5 Metals, non-metals and corrosion

Factors affecting rusting

Chemists have found that iron rusts more quickly in moist tropical areas near the sea. It is worth investigating which factors might be at work in these places. For example, the humidity is high. This means that there is a high percentage of water vapour in the air. So one idea would be:

- the more water molecules in a given volume of air, the faster they will react with the iron.

Your task in the next two investigations is to plan if two other factors might also affect the rate of rusting.

- As rusting happens faster near the coast, does salt affect the rate of rusting?
- As it is hot in the tropics, does temperature affect the rate of rusting?

Practical activity   Does salt affect rusting?

If salt does affect rusting, does the amount of salt in a given volume of water matter?

Plan an investigation to find out if salt affects the rate of rusting.

Which variables will you:

- choose to change in each test (the independent variable)?
- observe or measure to judge the effect of changing the independent variable (the dependent variable)?
- keep constant to make it a fair test (the control variables)?

Make a list of apparatus and materials you will need to set up this investigation.

- Describe a 'control experiment' you could set up.

⚠ **Do not start any practical work until your teacher has checked your plan.**

Practical activity   Does temperature affect rusting?

Plan an investigation to find out if temperature affects the rate of rusting.

Predict what you would expect to happen, explaining why using the particle theory.

(Hint: For particles to react together they must collide with each other with enough energy.)

⚠ **Do not start any practical work until your teacher has checked your plan.**

Key terms

- oxidation

Summary questions

1. Write a word equation to describe what happens when iron rusts.
2. Why is rusting described as an oxidation reaction?
3. State three factors that affect the rate of rusting of iron objects.

5.8 Preventing rust

Learning outcomes

After this topic you should be able to:

- describe ways in which iron can be protected against rusting.

We can protect iron and steel from rusting by keeping the metal away from air and water.

The fencing around this tennis court has a plastic coating around the steel wire so no air or water can cause rusting. As the plastic is also softer than wire, it reduces the risk of injury if you can't stop yourself running into the fence during a game

A barrier on the surface of the iron can be made by:

- covering with oil or grease
- painting
- coating in plastic
- coating in tin
- coating in zinc (or attaching bars of a metal more reactive than iron, e.g. magnesium).

Tin cans are really steel cans that have been coated with a very thin layer of tin. The layer of tin keeps air and water from the iron. It is applied to the iron by **electroplating**. This is the protection of the surface of one metal by coating it with a thin layer of another metal applied by electrolysis.

However, if the tin gets scratched, the steel beneath will start to rust.

A better way to protect iron and steel is to coat them with a more reactive metal, such as zinc, instead of the less reactive tin. Protecting iron with a thin layer of zinc is called **galvanising**. Zinc is more reactive than iron. So the air and water will attack the zinc rather than the iron. Rubbish bins are often made from galvanised steel because they are likely to get knocked about when they get emptied. Even when the layer of zinc gets damaged, it still protects the exposed steel underneath.

5 Metals, non-metals and corrosion

These bins have been galvanised as protection against rust. The zinc on their surfaces protects the iron or steel beneath, even when they get dented

Magnesium is used as bars bolted onto iron in extreme conditions, for example in the sea or in underground pipes. Like galvanising, this protection of iron by a more reactive metal is called **sacrificial protection**.

Ships have magnesium blocks attached to their hulls

Adding nickel and chromium to molten steel forms a rustproof alloy called **stainless steel**. As this is expensive, we still use cheaper – but less effective – methods such as painting, for large-scale protection.

Expert tips

Alloys are **mixtures** of a metal with other elements. They are not compounds.

Practical activity — Protect your bike

Look at a bicycle or a photo of a bicycle:
- List the different ways in which we protect it from rusting.
- Explain why particular methods are used in different places on the bicycle.

Key terms

- electroplating
- galvanising
- sacrificial protection
- stainless steel

Summary questions

1. Think of at least three methods that we can use to protect iron from rusting. Explain the way each method works.
2. Take each way of preventing rust that you have listed in question **1** and name an object protected by that method. Explain why each object is protected in that particular way.
3. If a large proportion of the metal in steel sinks is iron, why don't steel sinks rust?

5.9 Corrosion of other metals

Learning outcomes

After this topic you should be able to:
- explain why metals tarnish differently
- interpret data from secondary sources of information
- present findings and conclusions.

Despite the problems of rusting, iron is the most widely used metal in the world. You have seen how iron (and steel, which is made up mainly of iron) can be protected against rusting. Most iron extracted from compounds found in rocks is turned into steel.

Steel is usually over 95% iron with carbon present in varying amounts. The amount of carbon determines the strength and hardness of the steel. You can also add other metals to make alloy steels.

Molten iron is obtained from iron oxide in a blast furnace

In the following activity you can find out more about the uses of iron and steel.

Practical activity — The uses of iron and steel

Using books, CD-ROMs, DVDs and the internet, find out about the uses of iron and steel. Include data on the different types of steel and how changing its properties enables different uses. Try to find data on the composition of steels used in different industries.

Choose your own method to present your findings to the rest of the class.

5 Metals, non-metals and corrosion

Tarnished metals

As well as iron, other metals also react with substances in the air. Their surfaces can lose their shiny appearance. We say the metal surface has become **tarnished**.

Metals react with oxygen and other substances in air at different rates. Some do not react at all. Some, such as lithium and potassium, react quickly whereas others, such as copper, react slowly. Gold is so unreactive that it doesn't react with the gases in air at all. This is why gold objects made thousands of years ago still reflect light as brightly today.

Platinum metal, like gold, is used for jewellery because it does not tarnish

Often the metal will form a dull coating of the metal oxide as it reacts with oxygen gas in the air. However, other gases in the air can also get involved in tarnishing. These gases include water vapour, carbon dioxide and pollutant gases (such as sulfur dioxide). Even nitrogen, which is not a reactive gas, will react with atoms at the surface of highly reactive metals.

This copper roof has turned green because the metal has reacted with gases in the air (including carbon dioxide gas in this case) and has become tarnished

Practical activity   The strange case of aluminium

Aluminium is quite a reactive metal but has many outdoor uses.

Using books, CD-ROMs, DVDs and the internet, find out about the uses of aluminium and why it does not tarnish or corrode as we might expect.

Key terms

- tarnished

Summary questions

1. What happens to a metal when it becomes tarnished?
2. a) Name the most likely gas in the air that will cause a metal to tarnish.
   b) Name two other gases that might be involved in the tarnishing process.
3. The surface of magnesium ribbon when rubbed with sandpaper becomes shiny. Explain why.

Chapter 5 — End of chapter questions

1 The numbers in this Periodic Table represent different elements.

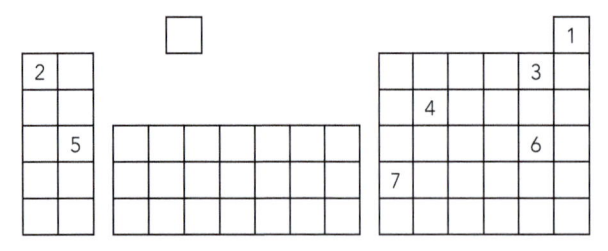

   a Which two elements are in the same group? [1]
   b Which elements are metals? [3]
   c Which group is element 7 in? [1]
   d Which element is a semi-metal (or metalloid)? [1]
   e Which element is called an alkali metal? [1]
   f Which group is element 1 in? [1]

2 Look at this outline of the areas in the Periodic Table:

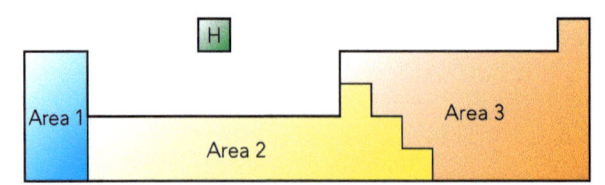

   a What does the symbol H stand for? [1]
   b In which areas of the Periodic Table would you find:
      i metallic elements? [2]
      ii non-metals, such as nitrogen and phosphorus? [1]
      iii very reactive metals, such as sodium and potassium? [1]
      iv less reactive metals, such as iron and zinc? [1]
   c Why is sodium chloride not found in the Periodic Table? [1]
   d What is the significance of the line between Area 2 and Area 3 in the Periodic Table? [1]

3 a Make a Venn diagram for these substances like the one shown below:

iron; gold; carbon; chlorine; water; salt; oxygen; sulfur; copper sulfide; silicon; sodium; magnesium; zinc; iodine; germanium

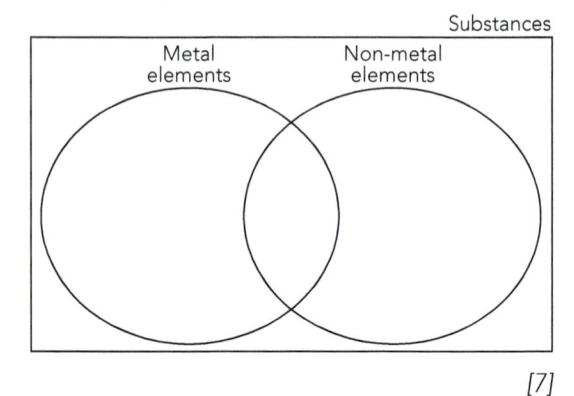

[7]

   b What type of substances do we find in the area of overlap between the metal and non-metal elements? [1]
   c What type of substances do we find in the area outside the sets of metal and non-metal elements? [1]

4 Read this information:

Magnesium, calcium and barium are elements that are good conductors of heat and electricity whereas sulfur and phosphorus are elements that are classed as insulators.

When the elements magnesium and sulfur are heated together, they react vigorously to form a new substance called magnesium sulfide.

   a Using only the information given above:
      i state the names of two metallic elements [2]
      ii state the names of two non-metallic elements [2]
      iii state the name of a substance that would not be listed in the Periodic Table. Explain your answer. [2]
   b i Write a word equation to show the reaction between magnesium and sulfur. [1]

5 Metals, non-metals and corrosion

  ii Explain a safety precaution that should be taken when carrying out the reaction between magnesium and sulfur. *[2]*

  iii Name the product formed when magnesium reacts with sulfur. *[1]*

5 The rusting of iron costs society many millions of dollars every year.

The experiment below shows an investigation into the factors that are needed for iron to rust.

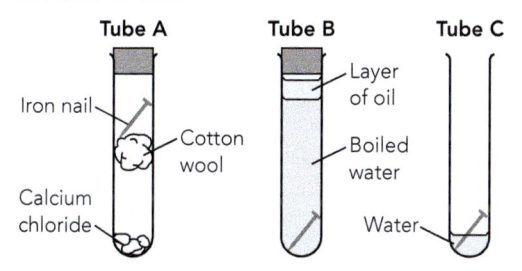

a Which test tube shows an iron nail in contact with:
  i only water? *[1]*
  ii water and air? *[1]*
  iii only air? *[1]*

b Why is the water in tube **B** boiled? *[1]*

c Explain why the nail in tube **A** is suspended on cotton wool above the calcium chloride in the bottom of the tube. *[1]*

d What will be the conclusion drawn from this experiment? *[2]*

6 Look at the experiment below:

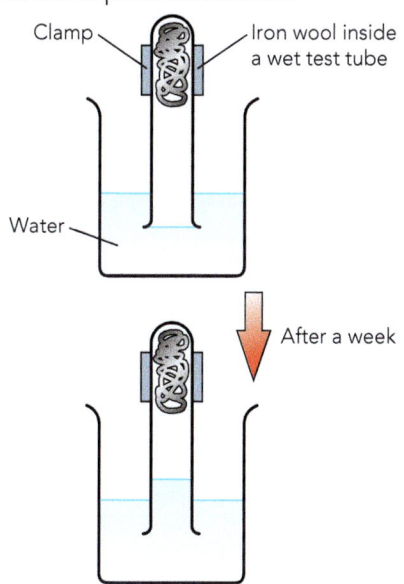

a Name the reactive gas in the air that helps cause rusting. *[1]*

b What is the maximum percentage of the air inside the test tube that can be used up in the reaction? *[1]*

c Write a word equation to represent iron rusting. *[2]*

7 Car owners who live near the coast often complain that their cars have more problems with rust than those in other places.

Which chemical compound causes their cars to rust more quickly? *[1]*

8 Name the method used to prevent rusting in order to protect:
  a a bicycle chain
  b a food can
  c an underground pipe. *[3]*

9 Steels are alloys of iron. Stainless steel is used to make cutlery.

Why is it used instead of cheaper types of steel? *[1]*

10 The hull of a giant oil tanker has blocks of magnesium metal bolted to it. This prevents the ship from rusting.

  a What do we call this type of protection? *[1]*

  b Explain the way in which this type of protection against rusting works. *[2]*

11 A student sets up the experiment shown below:

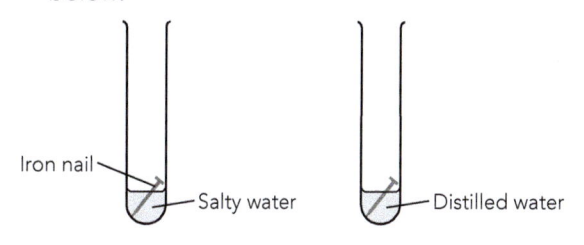

The test tubes are left for 2 days.

What would you expect to see and what would you conclude from this experiment? *[2]*

117

6 Chemical reactions

Science *in context!*

Chemistry in the kitchen

Cooking could really be called 'kitchen chemistry'.

It's all about:
- making and separating mixtures (physical changes)
- making new substances (chemical reactions, also known as chemical changes).

In cooking, we often mix oil-based ingredients with water. Emulsifiers help us achieve these mixtures. Egg yolk is an excellent emulsifying agent, stopping the oil and water from separating out into layers.

But the chemical reactions start when you turn on the heat! That's when we start changing one substance into another.

In cooking, these changes are not possible to reverse – a sure sign that a chemical reaction has taken place.

We cook foods to:
- kill bacteria in the high temperatures
- improve the texture, flavour and taste
- make them easier to digest.

We can cook food in many ways, including microwaving, baking, boiling, steaming, grilling and frying

Cooking potatoes

Ask people what their favourite food is and many will reply chips or French fries. But doctors are warning people that too much of this type of 'fast food' is creating health problems. More people than ever are obese and at risk from heart disease, strokes and diabetes.

However, potatoes are a good source of carbohydrates. They provide us with the energy we need. Potatoes contain plenty of starch. Starch is a natural polymer, meaning it consists of very long molecules made of lots of small molecules joined together. Starch is made up of lots of sugar (glucose) molecules.

We need to cook potatoes before we eat them to help us get at the starch. The starch is stored inside potato cells. Cooking helps to break down the tough cell walls and release the starch. Then we can digest the large starch molecules, breaking them down into glucose molecules.

Plant oils are used to fry potatoes. Doctors would prefer us to boil our potatoes. Frying in oil means you can cook at a higher temperature. This is because plant oils have much higher boiling points than water. Like all chemical reactions, the rate of reaction will increase as we raise the temperature.

Also, people like the taste better because of the flavour added by the oil. The crispy coating and the soft potato in the middle is another attraction. However, the fried potatoes will absorb some of the oil. This increases the energy input of the potato significantly. That's what causes the link to be made with obesity. If you don't exercise enough to use the extra energy, your body will store it as fat.

French fries are very popular in fast-food outlets

6 Chemical reactions

Cooking meat and eggs

Meat and eggs are rich sources of proteins. We need these to build muscle and to help repair our bodies. To understand what happens when we cook them, you need to know a little bit about the structure of protein molecules.

Proteins are natural polymers made from many amino acid molecules. The long protein molecules are held in shape by forces within and between their long chains. When we cook meat or eggs, their protein molecules start moving around more vigorously. Once the temperature gets high enough, the protein molecules lose their original shape. These protein molecules cannot change back again.

In cooked meat, the proteins separate from each other and it becomes tender. In an egg, the proteins in the egg white are coiled up and floating around in a watery solution. When fried or boiled, the proteins 'uncurl' and start forming bonds between each other. The water in the egg white gets trapped between the open structure that builds up.

The longer you heat the egg, the more bonds form between the chains. Then less water can be trapped. That's why overcooking makes the egg white more rubbery!

Overcooking eggs makes the white of the egg have a rubbery texture

Meat is a good source of protein. Cooking changes the shape of the protein molecules

In this chapter you will find out about some common compounds including chlorides, sulfates, oxides, hydroxides and carbonates. You will also get more practice in using word equations to describe chemical reactions.

Key points

- a metal + acid → a salt + hydrogen
- A salt is a compound formed when all or some of the hydrogen in an acid is replaced by a metal.
- base + acid → a salt + water
- When elements burn in air, they react with the oxygen and produce compounds called oxides. These reactions are called combustion reactions. They are examples of oxidation.
- carbonate + acid → a salt + water + carbon dioxide
- We can identify some metals using the characteristic coloured flames produced when their compounds are heated. These are called flame tests.
- reactive metal + water → metal hydroxide + hydrogen

6.1 Preparing a chloride

Learning outcomes

After this topic you should be able to:

- write word equations for the reactions of metals with acids
- prepare crystals of a metal chloride
- discuss and control risks to yourself and others in experiments.

The reaction between a metal and a dilute acid produces hydrogen gas (the bubbles we see as the reaction takes place). On page 106 we used this reaction to collect and test the hydrogen gas given off.

Although not all metals react with dilute acid, in general we say that:

a metal + acid → a salt + hydrogen

A salt is a compound formed when all or some of the hydrogen in an acid is replaced by a metal.

So in the reaction between magnesium and sulfuric acid, we get a salt called magnesium sulfate formed.

- Sulfuric acid makes salts called **sulfates**.
- Hydrochloric acid makes salts called **chlorides**.
- Nitric acid makes salts called **nitrates**.

This is summarised in the table below:

Acid	Salts made	Formula ends in	Example
hydrochloric acid	chlorides	…Cl	magnesium chloride, $MgCl_2$
sulfuric acid	sulfates	…SO_4	sodium sulfate, Na_2SO_4
nitric acid	nitrates	…NO_3	potassium nitrate, KNO_3

Look at the examples of the names of salts in the table.

Can you see that a salt gets the first word in its name from a metal and the second word from an acid?

Salts are crystalline compounds. Their particles line up in regular patterns with water molecules bonded into their structures. Here are some examples of crystals of salts.

Crystals of zinc sulfate. Which metal and acid would you use to make this salt?

6 Chemical reactions

Crystals of iron chloride. Which metal and acid would you use to make this salt?

We can get crystals of a salt from the solution left after the metal plus acid reaction. The best crystals are made by letting the water evaporate slowly, once the first crystals appear as the solution is heated in an evaporating dish.

Key terms

- **chlorides**
- **salt**
- **saturated solution**

Practical activity — Preparing a sample of magnesium chloride

Now you can prepare some crystals of the salt called magnesium chloride, $MgCl_2$.

⚠️ **Eye protection must be worn.**

1. Place 15 cm³ of dilute hydrochloric acid in a small beaker.
2. Add magnesium powder slowly until no more will react and you have some magnesium left undissolved in the solution.
3. Filter off the unreacted magnesium powder, collecting the solution in an evaporating dish.
4. Heat the solution in the evaporating dish on a water bath until you see the first signs of crystals on the inside of the dish just above the solution. At this point we have a **saturated solution**. We say we have reached the point of crystallisation.
5. Leave the solution at room temperature until next lesson so that the rest of the water evaporates off slowly and large crystals form.

- What gas is given off in the reaction?
- Give two ways in which you could tell that the reaction was complete and all the acid was used up.

Summary questions

1. In general, what is formed when an acid reacts with a metal?
2. Write down and complete the word equations for the following reactions:
   a) zinc + hydrochloric acid →
   b) iron + sulfuric acid →
3. Describe a method to get a good sample of salt crystals from a salt solution.

121

6.2 Preparing a sulfate

Learning outcomes

After this topic you should be able to:
- prepare a sample of copper sulfate crystals
- use word equations to describe neutralisation reactions
- use a range of equipment correctly.

We can make many metal **sulfates** using the method on the previous page. You simply use dilute sulfuric acid instead of dilute hydrochloric acid. For example:

zinc + sulfuric acid → zinc sulfate + hydrogen

However, we cannot make copper sulfate using this method because copper metal does not react with dilute acid. Instead, we can use copper oxide, which is a base. Here we have the general equation for a **neutralisation** reaction:

base + acid → a salt + water

For example:

copper oxide + sulfuric acid → copper sulfate + water

Practical activity — Preparing copper sulfate crystals

Now you can try out the reaction between copper oxide and dilute sulfuric acid and prepare a sample of copper sulfate crystals.

⚠️ **Eye protection must be worn.**

1. Pour 25 cm^3 of sulfuric acid into a small beaker. Then add a spatula of black copper oxide.

2. Stir with a glass rod. Warm gently on a tripod and gauze, without letting the mixture boil. Add more copper oxide, one spatula at a time until no more will dissolve.

3. Allow the beaker to cool and filter off the excess copper oxide from the solution.

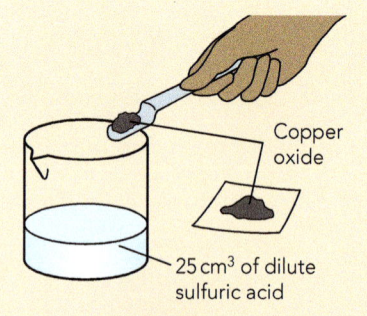

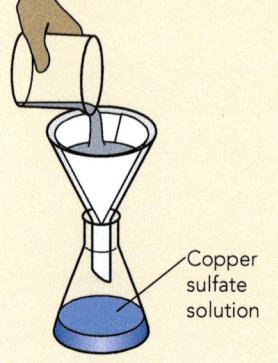

6 Chemical reactions

4 Pour the solution into an evaporating dish. Heat it on a water bath as shown on the right.

Stop heating when you see a few small crystals appear around the edge of the solution.

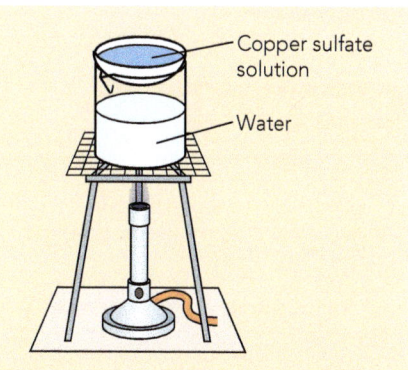

5 Leave the remaining water to evaporate from the solution at room temperature for a few days.
   - Draw a diagram to show the shape of your copper sulfate crystals.
   - Draw the steps shown in this method as scientific diagrams, e.g. like the diagram on page 128. These should be 2-dimensional, 'flat' diagrams.

Copper sulfate can form large crystals under the right conditions

Expert tips

Metals that are very unreactive, or very reactive, cannot be added to acids to make salts. The reaction will not happen with metals such as copper or silver. The reaction would be explosive with metals such as sodium or potassium.

Key terms

- **neutralisation**
- **sulfates**

Summary questions

The questions below refer to the experiment 'Preparing copper sulfate crystals'.

1 a) State one observation that tells us a reaction took place.
  b) What do we call this type of reaction?
  c) Write a word equation for the reaction.

2 a) What do you see when **excess** copper oxide has been added?
  b) State the technique used to remove the excess copper oxide.

3 Why is the solution of copper sulfate left for several days at the end of the experiment?

6.3 Preparing oxides

Learning outcomes

After this topic you should be able to:
- prepare samples of oxides
- use word equations to describe the combustion of elements
- assess the risks to yourself and others when burning substances.

You already know that the reactive gas in the air is oxygen. When elements burn in air, they react with the oxygen and produce compounds called **oxides**.

For example:

magnesium + oxygen → magnesium oxide

sulfur + oxygen → sulfur dioxide

These reactions are called **combustion** reactions. They are examples of oxidation.

If we burn elements in oxygen gas, instead of air, the combustion reactions are much more vigorous.

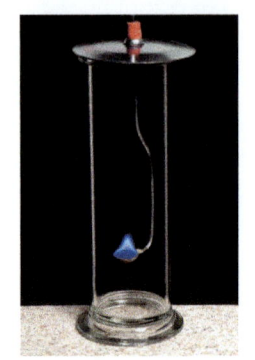

Sulfur reacting with pure oxygen

Sodium reacting with pure oxygen

Key terms
- combustion
- oxides

Practical activity Combustion of carbon

Collect a 2 cm depth of carbon powder (charcoal) in a test tube.

Using test tube holders, heat the carbon gently at first, then more strongly. You will see the carbon glow red when it is reacting with oxygen in the air. A colourless gas is also formed.

⚠️ **Do not point the test tube at anyone during heating. Eye protection must be worn.**

Using a glass dropping pipette, collect some of the gas in the test tube and bubble it into a little limewater. Do this several times.

Remember that limewater turns cloudy white when carbon dioxide gas is bubbled into it.
- What do you see happen?
- Write a word equation for the reaction when carbon is heated in air.

Practical activity Combustion of iron

Hold some iron wool in a pair of tongs and place it in a blue Bunsen burner flame. What do you see happen?

Write a word equation for the combustion of iron.

⚠️ **Eye protection must be worn. Take care with hot metal.**

6 Chemical reactions

A closer look at combustion

Practical activity   How much magnesium oxide forms?

You will need to weigh some magnesium ribbon before it is heated in a crucible. You also need to weigh the empty crucible and its lid.

- Enter your results in a table like the one below:

	Mass / g
Mass of **magnesium** ribbon before heating	
Mass of empty crucible and its lid (a)	
Mass of crucible, lid and magnesium oxide after heating (b)	
Mass of **magnesium oxide** formed (b − a)	

Set up the apparatus as shown:

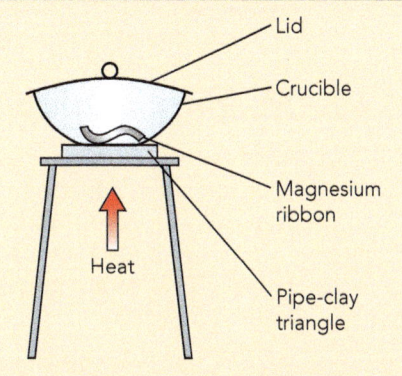

⚠️ **Do not look at burning magnesium directly. Take care with the hot crucible and its lid.**

Start heating the crucible.

Use a pair of tongs to occasionally lift the lid of the crucible slightly for a short length of time. This lets in some more oxygen for the magnesium to react with. Try not to let any white smoke (which is magnesium oxide) escape.

When the reaction has finished, let the crucible and its contents cool down. Weigh the crucible, lid and its contents after the reaction. (Use a pair of tongs to transfer the crucible and lid to the balance.)

- Complete your table of results.
- What colour is magnesium oxide?
- Which weighed more – the magnesium or the magnesium oxide?
- Explain the results of your experiment.
- Describe any ways in which you made your experiment as safe as possible.

Summary questions

1 What is another word for combustion?
2 Why can combustion reactions be described as examples of oxidation?
3 Write a word equation for the combustion of:
   a) copper
   b) magnesium.

125

6.4 Preparing metal hydroxides

Learning outcomes

After this topic you should be able to:
- prepare samples of hydroxides
- use a word equation to describe a precipitation reaction.

Expert tips

When you see brackets in a chemical formula, all the atoms inside the brackets are multiplied by the subscript number outside the brackets. For example, $Al(OH)_3$ has 1 aluminium atom, 3 oxygen atoms and 3 hydrogen atoms.

Metal **hydroxides**, such as copper hydroxide, are bases. They react with acids to form a salt and water. Some of these hydroxides are soluble in water. They form alkaline solutions when they dissolve in water. Group 1 metal hydroxides are all soluble. Examples are lithium hydroxide, LiOH, sodium hydroxide, NaOH, and potassium hydroxide, KOH.

Other metal hydroxides are slightly soluble in water. These include magnesium hydroxide, $Mg(OH)_2$, and calcium hydroxide, $Ca(OH)_2$. (Calcium hydroxide is also known as slaked lime when it is solid, and its solution is known as limewater.)

However, many metal hydroxides are insoluble. The insoluble hydroxides include copper hydroxide, $Cu(OH)_2$, zinc hydroxide, $Zn(OH)_2$, and aluminium hydroxide, $Al(OH)_3$.

Making insoluble hydroxides

We can use soluble metal hydroxides, such as sodium hydroxide (also known as caustic soda), to make insoluble metal hydroxides. For example, if you want to make copper hydroxide, add sodium hydroxide solution to a solution of a copper salt, such as copper nitrate. Nitrates are good salts to choose because **all** nitrates are soluble in water.

When sodium hydroxide and copper nitrate solutions mix, solid copper hydroxide will appear in the solution. We call the copper hydroxide a precipitate and the reaction is **precipitation**. The word equation is:

copper nitrate + sodium hydroxide → copper hydroxide + sodium nitrate
solution   solution   precipitate (solid)   solution

The copper hydroxide appears as a light blue solid, suspended in the solution. The sodium nitrate is soluble in water so it stays dissolved in the solution.

Copper hydroxide precipitate is light blue

6 Chemical reactions

> **Practical activity** — Making hydroxides by precipitation reactions
>
> ⚠ **Make sure you wear eye protection.**
>
> Add a little sodium hydroxide solution to solutions of the following salts in separate test tubes:
> – aluminium nitrate
> – iron(II) nitrate
> – iron(III) nitrate
> – calcium nitrate
> – copper(II) nitrate
> – magnesium nitrate.
> - Record the colour of the hydroxide precipitates formed.

Precipitates of iron(II) hydroxide and iron(III) hydroxide

Expert tips

You can use the colours of hydroxide precipitates to identify the metal in unknown compounds.

Key terms

- **hydroxides**
- **precipitation**

Summary questions

1. What is a precipitation reaction?
2. Write out and complete the word equations for the following:
   a) zinc nitrate + sodium hydroxide →
   b) magnesium nitrate + sodium hydroxide →
3. Which practical technique can be used to separate a precipitate from the solution it was formed in?

127

6.5 Carbonates plus acid

Learning outcomes

After this topic you should be able to:
- write the general equation for carbonates reacting with acids
- write word equations for the reaction of specific carbonates with acids
- identify trends and patterns in reactions.

What happens when you open a can of cola that has been shaken? Why do you think this happens?

Do you know which gas puts that 'fizz' in a fizzy drink? Fizzy drinks are also known as 'carbonated' drinks. The name comes from the carbon dioxide gas dissolved in the drink.

Practical activity — Making carbon dioxide

⚠ Make sure you wear eye protection.

Set up the apparatus as shown below:

3-D drawing — Marble chips, Hydrochloric acid, Limewater

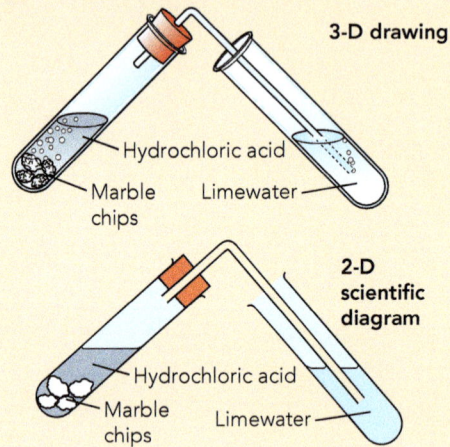

2-D scientific diagram — Marble chips, Hydrochloric acid, Limewater

- What observation tells us that the marble chips and acid react together?
- What happens to the limewater?
- What do you observe when the reaction has finished?

Now collect some carbon dioxide gas or watch your teacher do the experiment below:

3-D drawing — Dropping funnel, Dilute hydrochloric acid, Marble chips, Carbon dioxide gas

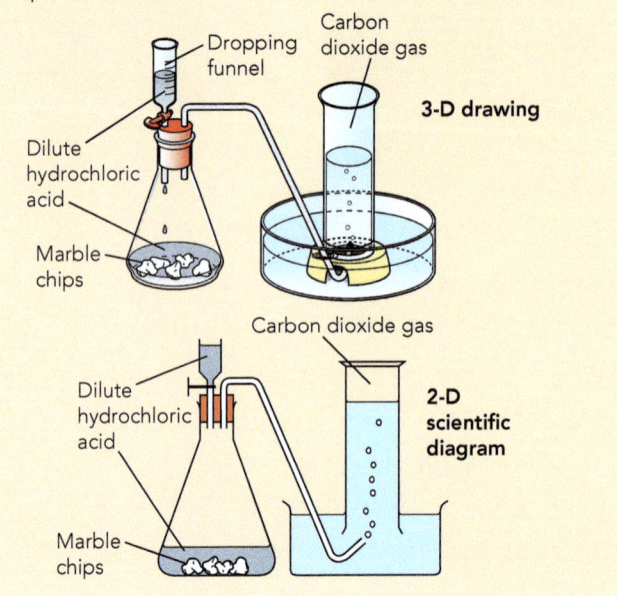

2-D scientific diagram — Dilute hydrochloric acid, Marble chips, Carbon dioxide gas

128

6 Chemical reactions

Marble chips, chalk and limestone are made up mainly of calcium carbonate. There are lots of other **carbonates**. Examples include lead carbonate, zinc carbonate and iron carbonate.

But do **all** carbonates react with any acid to produce carbon dioxide gas?

You can investigate this question in the next activity:

Practical activity — Investigating carbonates and acid

⚠️ **Make sure you wear eye protection.**

You will be given a range of different carbonates and different acids to test.

Think about these questions as you observe each carbonate react with an acid.
- Is a gas given off? If so, which gas is it?
- Describe a test to identify this gas.

After your investigation, answer this question:
- In what ways are the reactions similar and in what ways do they differ?

We always get carbon dioxide gas given off when we react a carbonate with an acid. A salt and water are also formed. The general equation is:

> carbonate + acid → a salt + water + carbon dioxide

For example:
copper carbonate + sulfuric acid → copper sulfate + water + carbon dioxide

Expert tips

When drawing a 2-D scientific diagram, imagine slicing the apparatus in half, lengthways. Then think of pressing the cut edges down on a flat sponge soaked in ink. The 2-D scientific image could then be stamped onto a piece of paper!

Key terms

- **carbonates**

Summary questions

1 Copy and complete:
All carbonates react with _____ to produce a _____, _____ dioxide gas and _____ . We can test for this gas by bubbling it into _____ which turns _____ .

2 Write a word equation for the reaction of the following carbonates with dilute acids:
a) zinc carbonate + sulfuric acid
b) sodium carbonate + hydrochloric acid
c) magnesium carbonate + nitric acid

6.6 Flame tests

Learning outcomes

After this topic you should be able to:
- recognise that flame tests can be used to identify some metals in a compound
- carry out a flame test safely.

On page 126 we saw how precipitation reactions with sodium hydroxide solution can help to identify some metals.

We can also identify some metals using the characteristic coloured flames produced when their compounds are heated. These are called **flame tests**.

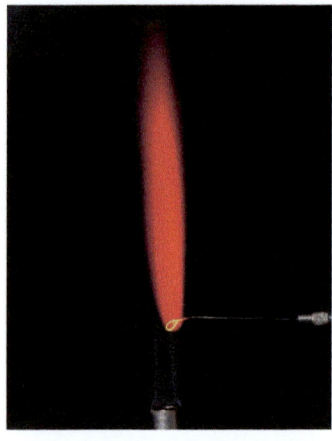

The flame test for lithium

The flame test for potassium

The flame test for copper

The flame test for sodium

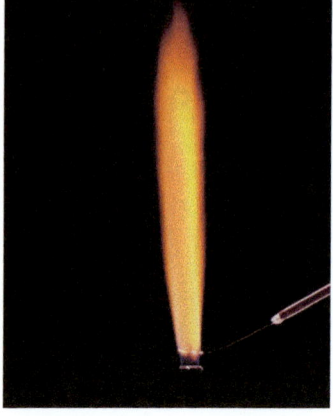

The flame test for calcium

Key terms
- **flame test**

130

6 Chemical reactions

Practical activity — Flame tests for metals in compounds

You can test a salt of each of the following metals in this experiment:

potassium   lithium   calcium   copper   sodium

⚠️ **Eye protection must be worn.**

Take the colour out of a Bunsen flame by opening the air-hole slightly.

Dip a piece of nichrome wire into dilute hydrochloric acid on a watch glass, then heat the wire to clean it.

Repeat this cleaning process until the wire has no effect on the flame.

Put the loop at the end of the clean wire into some water.

Then dip it into one of the unknown salts.

Hold the wire in the edge of the flame.
- Record the colour.

Clean the wire again and test the other metal salts.

Here is a table which shows the flame tests for some common metals (but not all metals give the flame a colour):

Metal in compound tested	Colour of flame
lithium	crimson red
potassium	lilac
copper	blue-green
sodium	yellow-orange
calcium	brick red

Practical activity — Testing for metals

Your teacher will give you five unknown compounds, labelled A to E.

Your task is to carry out flame tests to identify the metal in each unknown compound.

⚠️ **Eye protection must be worn.**

Summary questions

1. Make a set of instructions for carrying out a flame test.
2. Why do scientists find flame tests useful?
3. a) An unknown compound gave a blue-green colour in a flame test. What information does this give you about the compound tested?
   b) A student carried out a flame test on an unknown white solid which resulted in a lilac flame. The student concluded that the substance was potassium. Why was the student's conclusion incorrect?

6.7 Reactions with water

Learning outcomes

After this topic you should be able to:

- describe what happens when a range of metals and non-metals are added to water
- use word equations to describe reactions of water with some elements
- discuss risks involved in the demonstration of some metals with water or steam.

Most elements do not react vigorously with water. However, there is a great range in reactivity between different elements, as we saw when looking at metals tarnishing on page 115.

Practical activity — Elements in cold water

Clean the surface of a strip of magnesium ribbon with sandpaper.

Wind the ribbon into a coil and place it in the apparatus shown below.

Repeat this with a piece of copper foil.

Set up two further sets of apparatus using a piece of charcoal (carbon) in one and a lump of sulfur in the other.

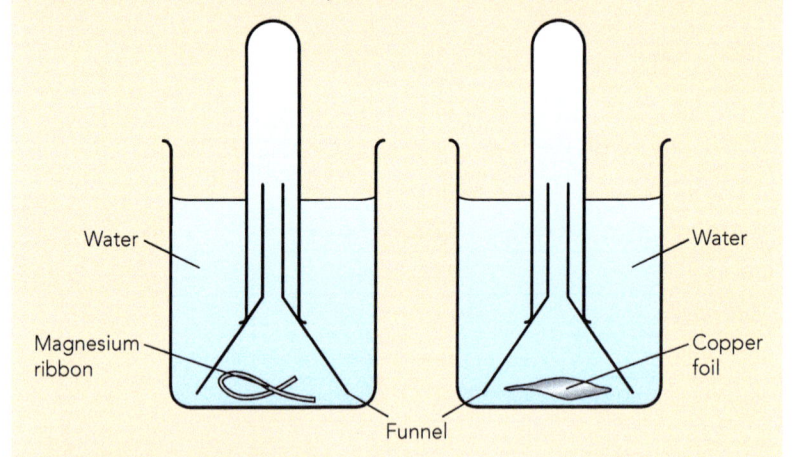

Leave the apparatus for a week.

- What do you observe after a week? Which elements show no sign of a reaction?

Test any gas collected with a lighted splint.

- Which gas was produced? Which metal produced the gas?
- Where did this gas come from?

There is no sign of a reaction between water and copper metal or with the non-metals carbon or sulfur.

The reaction between magnesium and water is very slow. We can make it go faster by reacting hot magnesium with steam.

6 Chemical reactions

Practical activity — Magnesium and steam

Watch your teacher demonstrate the reaction on the right:
- Describe what happens as the magnesium reacts with the steam.
- Which gas burns off at the end of the tube?

The white solid left in the test tube is magnesium oxide (MgO).
- Write a word equation for the reaction.

⚠️ **Eye protection must be worn. This demonstration should be carried out behind a safety screen.**

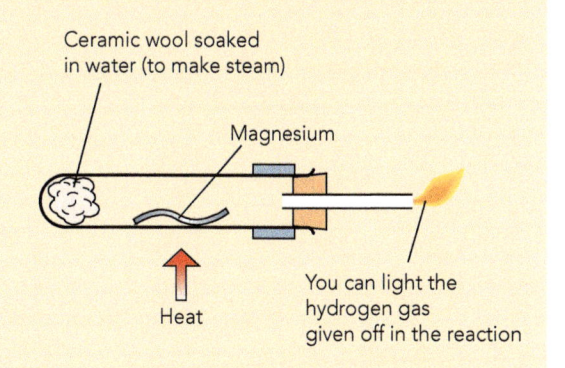

Ceramic wool soaked in water (to make steam)
Magnesium
Heat
You can light the hydrogen gas given off in the reaction

Other metals that react very slowly with cold water but more readily with steam are iron and zinc.

For example:

  zinc + steam → zinc oxide + hydrogen

Practical activity — Sodium and lithium with water

Watch your teacher demonstrate the reactions of lithium and sodium with water.
- Why are the lithium and sodium stored under oil in their jars?
- Record in detail your observations for each reaction.
- What safety precautions did your teacher take when using these metals and demonstrating their reactions? What is the hazard warning sign on each jar of the metals? Why?
- In what ways were the reactions similar?
- In what ways were the reactions different?

⚠️ **Eye protection must be worn. This demonstration should be carried out behind a safety screen.**

The general equation for a reactive metal with water is:

  reactive metal + water → metal hydroxide + hydrogen

For example:

  lithium + water → lithium hydroxide + hydrogen

Summary questions

1. Which one of the following metals does not react with water?
   sodium   zinc   magnesium   copper
2. Iron reacts with steam in a similar way to zinc. Write a word equation for the reaction of iron and steam.
3. Write a word equation for the reaction of sodium with water.

133

Chapter 6 — End of chapter questions

1. A student added a piece of magnesium ribbon to dilute sulfuric acid.
   a. List three ways by which she could tell that a chemical reaction was taking place. [3]
   b. Write down the general equation that describes the reaction between a metal and an acid. [2]
   c. Write the word equation for the reaction between magnesium and dilute sulfuric acid. [1]

2. Copy and complete these word equations:
   a. _____ + hydrochloric acid ↓
      zinc _____ + hydrogen [2]
   b. manganese oxide + _____ ↓
      _____ sulfate + _____ [3]

3. Write down the reactants that could be used to safely prepare the following salts:
   a. calcium chloride [2]
   b. sodium nitrate [2]
   c. potassium sulfate [2]
   d. zinc nitrate [2]
   e. iron chloride [2]
   f. copper nitrate [2]

4. a. Write a word equation for the reaction between nickel carbonate and sulfuric acid. [1]
   b. How could you positively identify the gas given off in the reaction in part a? [1]
   c. Nickel carbonate is insoluble in water. Write a 'step-by-step' method for preparing crystals of the salt formed by the reaction in part a. [4]

5. A group of students wanted to prepare a sample of crystals from the reaction between barium carbonate ($BaCO_3$) and dilute hydrochloric acid.
   a. Give two ways by which they could tell when all the acid had reacted. [2]
   b. Write down the general equation that describes the reaction between a carbonate and an acid. [2]
   c. Write the word equation for the reaction between barium carbonate and dilute hydrochloric acid. [1]

6. Washing soda contains sodium carbonate.
   a. Which gas is given off when sodium carbonate reacts with dilute hydrochloric acid? [1]
   b. Describe a positive test for the gas in part a. [2]
   c. Draw a diagram of the apparatus you could use to conduct the test in part b. [3]

7. Copy and complete the following word equations:
   a. copper + _____ → copper oxide [1]
   b. _____ + _____ → sulfur dioxide [2]
   c. sodium + oxygen → _____ [1]
   d. calcium nitrate + sodium _____ ↓
      _____ hydroxide + _____ [3]

134

6 Chemical reactions

8 A teacher demonstrated the reaction of sodium with water in a large trough.
   a Describe what you would see in the reaction. [3]
   b Name the products of the reaction. [2]

   The teacher then showed the class the reaction of magnesium ribbon with steam in the apparatus shown below:

   Ceramic wool soaked in water (to make steam)
   Magnesium
   Heat
   You can light the hydrogen gas given off in the reaction

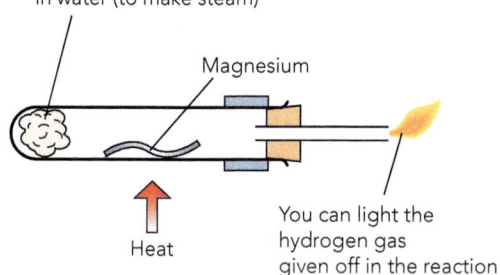

   c Write a word equation for this reaction. [3]

9 a What is 'a salt'? [2]
   b Why is copper metal never used to make a copper salt? [1]
   c Why is sodium metal never used to make sodium salts? [1]
   d What are the salts made from the following acids called?
      i sulfuric acid [1]
      ii nitric acid [1]
      iii hydrochloric acid [1]
   e What change of state is involved in preparing crystals of a salt from one of its solutions? [1]

10 Two groups of students made a salt from the reaction between copper oxide and dilute hydrochloric acid.
   a What do we call this type of reaction? [1]
   b Copper oxide was added to the dilute hydrochloric acid until the copper oxide was in excess. State the technique used by the groups to remove the excess copper oxide. [1]
   c The first group heated the solution of the salt on a water bath until all the water had evaporated. The second group stopped heating the solution when the solution became saturated. Which group collected the best sample of salt crystals? Explain your answer. [2]
   d Name the salt made. [1]
   e Name the other product formed in the reaction. [1]

11 An insoluble compound, lead hydroxide, was made by adding sodium hydroxide solution to lead nitrate solution.
   a What do we call this type of reaction? [1]
   b Write a word equation for this reaction. [2]
   c Describe a method to separate lead hydroxide from the reaction mixture. [1]

135

7 Light

Science *in* context! An illuminating story

How do you see things? Sight is probably our most important sense and even the very first scientists wondered how it worked. It was obvious that it was something to do with our eyes, after all if you close your eyes you stop being able to see. The scientists were unsure if we could see because something was coming out of our eyes or something was going in to them. There are hundreds of scientists that have developed our understanding; this brief introduction can only mention a few of them.

Early ideas

One early idea was that our eyes gave out rays that sought out objects to let us see them. A Greek scientist named Empedocles proposed that our eyes send out these rays. We now call this idea the 'emission theory'. You should be able to think of several problems with this idea, for example why can't we see in a dark cave? Despite these problems the idea lasted for quite a while.

Later Greeks would still use the idea of rays and even discovered important laws about reflection but they mostly stuck with the idea that Empedocles suggested.

Empodocles' ideas lasted for over a thousand years before experiments proved him wrong

Discovering and describing rays

Abū 'Alī al-Ḥasan ibn al-Ḥasan ibn al-Haytham (known as Alhazen in Europe) was a Muslim scientist imprisoned for failing to build a dam on the Nile. During his imprisonment from 1011 to 1021 he wrote his Book of Optics. In this he described how light must enter our eyes for us to see the light. He also made great improvements in our ideas about reflection and refraction by carrying out experiments with lenses and mirrors. After his release from prison he continued with his work and it was eventually translated into Latin allowing European scientists to look at his ideas.

Hundreds of years later European scientists continued to develop optical theory. Isaac Newton studied light intensively and made important discoveries which he described in his book 'Optiks' in 1704. Newton described light as a stream of particles that could be separated out by refraction. Other scientists were developing optical instruments allowing us to study the world in more and more detail. Telescopes and microscopes became available because of the improved manufacturing of lenses and mirrors.

Alhazen's ideas eventually led to modern optics

7 Light

Electromagnetic waves

Even before Newton there were several scientists that thought that light behaved like a wave but it took a while before Newton's model was replaced. The modern model of light is that it is a form of electromagnetic energy; electrical and magnetic waves travelling at very high speed. James Clerk Maxwell produced a mathematical description of these electromagnetic waves in 1862. His theory also suggested that there would be other electromagnetic waves. Experiments soon proved him to be right. There is a whole set of waves that we cannot see including radio waves and X-rays that scientists soon detected.

The story of light still isn't finished; some experiments show that light really does behave like a stream of particles instead of a simple wave.

In this chapter you will learn about the nature of light and how we see things. You will explore reflection and some other ways light travels, including how colours are formed.

Maxwell's equations for light are still used today but work continues to improve our understanding of light

Key points

- Light is a form of energy that travels very quickly in straight lines we call rays.
- We see objects when light from them enters our eyes.
- Light can be reflected, transmitted or absorbed when it hits a surface.
- Light sources produce light. We see other objects when they reflect the light that came from a light source.
- When light is reflected it follows the law of reflection.
- Light rays are refracted and change direction when they move from one material to another.
- White light is composed of a spectrum of colours that can be separated by a process called dispersion.
- Simple colours can be mixed to produce new colours.
- Lenses are used in our eyes, in cameras and in other optical equipment to focus light rays.

7.1 Rays of light

Learning outcomes

After this topic you should be able to:
- describe how light travels from place to place
- trace the path of a simple ray.

Light is a form of energy. It is released by **light sources** and travels very quickly from place to place. In fact, light travels faster than anything else can; a speed of 300 000 000 m/s.

Producing and detecting light

The Sun is the most obvious source of light. Nuclear reactions deep inside the Sun's core release massive amounts of heat and light. There are many other possible sources of light, for example:

- The filament in a lamp is so hot that it glows with a white light.
- A fire will produce an orange-coloured light.
- The chemical reactions in fireflies give off a green glow.

Most objects do not give out their own light. They only reflect the light given out by light sources.

Detecting light

We can only see light when it enters our eyes. The light passes into our eyes and causes a chemical reaction at the back surface. The chemical reaction produces a signal that reaches our brains.

We see light sources directly as they give out light but we see other objects when light reflects off them into our eyes.

There are other ways to detect light. Light sensors capture the energy and transform it into electrical signals that can be measured. These allow us to measure the brightness or energy content of the light accurately.

We can see most objects because they reflect light and the reflected light enters our eyes

Light rays

A ray box is used in a range of scientific experiments. It is just a lamp with some attachments to produce 'rays' of light. These rays travel in straight lines. Light always travels in straight lines.

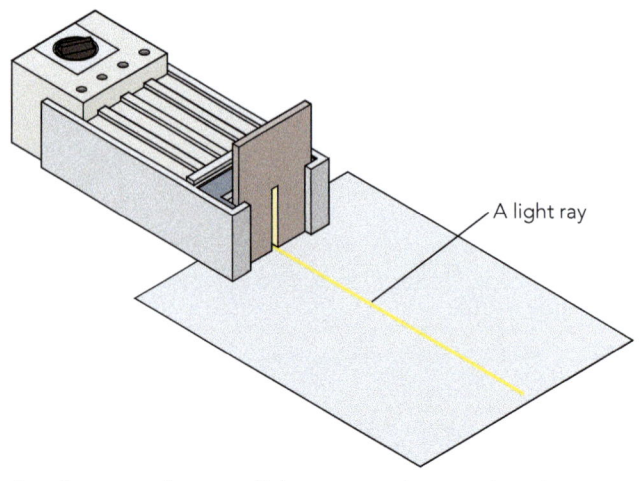

A ray box uses a lamp as a light source and can produce clear rays of light

7 Light

Practical activity — Investigating ray boxes and rays

Use a ray box to confirm that light rays travel in straight lines. Place the ray box on a sheet of paper and then use a single slit in front of the lamp to produce a narrow ray. Mark the path of the ray by drawing two or three dots with a sharp pencil. When you remove the ray box you should be able to use a ruler to show that the ray was travelling in a straight line.

You can use multiple slits and trace all of the rays to make sure that they all travel in straight lines.

⚠ **The lamp in a ray box can become very hot – do not touch it.**

Lasers also produce light rays. We can use smoke or dust to scatter the laser light so that we can see the path in which the ray travels. Because the light from lasers is very intense (bright) it can blind you. Never try to look into a laser beam.

This laser beam is travelling in a straight line into the upper atmosphere. We can only see the beam because some of the light is being reflected into our eyes

Expert tips

Light rays always travel in straight lines so make sure that you use a pencil and ruler to draw them.

Key terms

- **light source**

Summary questions

1. Which of the following are light sources?
   a star   television   the Moon   eyes   a candle   mirror
2. Make a list of at least ten light sources.
3. Describe the sequence of events that enables you to see an object that does not produce its own light.

7.2 Transmitting, absorbing and reflecting

Learning outcomes

After this topic you should be able to:
- describe the behaviour of light when it reaches an object
- investigate how shadows are formed and the factors that affect their size
- identify patterns in results.

The behaviour of light rays

When a light ray reaches a surface three things can happen:

1. The light can be **absorbed**: The energy of the light is transformed into heat in the object, warming it up slightly.
2. The light can be **reflected**. The ray 'bounces off' leaving the object and carrying on. Some materials reflect nearly all the light that hits them, others only reflect a little of the light and absorb the rest.
3. The light can be **transmitted**. The ray passes through the object and carries the energy with it.

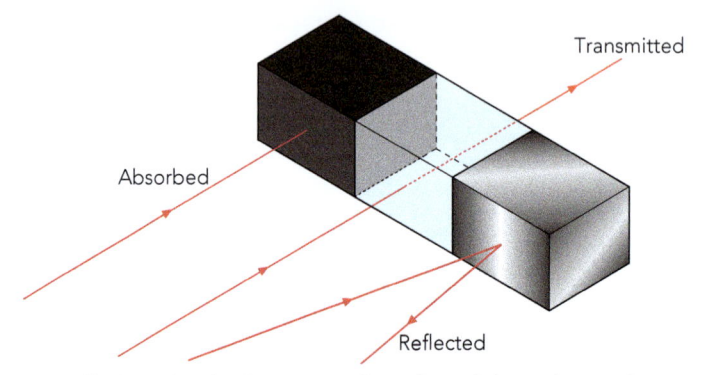

The ray of light is absorbed, transmitted or reflected depending on the properties of the material

Experimenting with shadows

In Student book 7 you saw that a solar eclipse was caused by the Moon blocking out the light from the Sun. The Moon is opaque – light cannot pass through it. This means that the light does not reach the Earth and a shadow is formed on the Earth's surface.

Shadows are caused when an object blocks out the light from a light source. This creates dark areas that are not illuminated (lit up) by the light source. Other areas are illuminated because they do receive the light.

Expert tips

Shadows are strong evidence that light rays travel in straight lines.

Sharp shadows

If the source of light is small then the shadow will have sharp edges. None of the light from the light source can reach the screen but lots of the light can reach the other areas. This gives clear edges to the shadow.

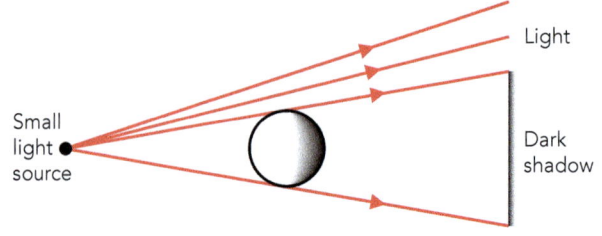

The shadows are clear from this small light source

140

7 Light

Blurred shadows

When there is a large light source, the edges of the shadows can become blurred. This is because light from some parts of the light source can still reach the screen while some of the light is blocked. This means that some areas are in partial light.

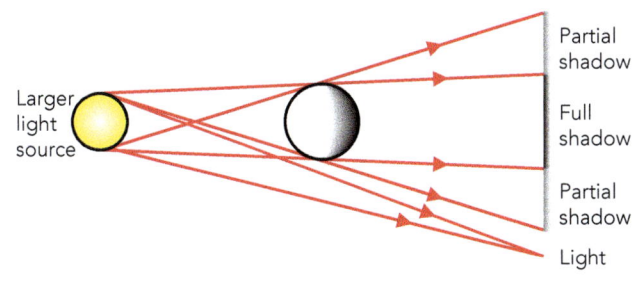

The shadows are more blurred here because the rays of light are coming from a larger source

Practical activity — Investigating the size of shadows

Is there a connection between the size of a shadow and the distance between the object and a screen? Use a light source, object and screen to produce a shadow. Adjust the distance between the screen and object and record how the size of the shadow changes. You can choose to measure the shadow height or width.

Screen distance / cm	Shadow size / cm

Make sure that you keep the distance between the lamp and the object constant.
- Record your data in a clear table.
- Plot a graph to show the relationship.

What is the relationship between the size of the shadow and the distance between the object and screen?

Key terms
- absorb
- reflect
- transmit

Summary questions

1. Put the following materials into three categories; those that are good at reflecting light, those that are good at transmitting light and those that are good at absorbing light.

   glass   white paper   water   black paper   gold   Perspex   silver

2. Design an investigation to find out if the size of a shadow depends on the distance between the screen and the object. Which factors need to be controlled carefully in the experiment to make it fair?

141

7.3 Reflection of light

Learning outcomes

After this topic you should be able to:
- state the law of reflection
- explain why images can be seen in some surfaces but not in others.

When light reaches a surface it can be absorbed, transmitted or reflected. If the light is reflected, the ray leaves the object and keeps on travelling.

Reflection

Reflection can happen from any object or surface. For visible light, metallic surfaces are the best reflectors but even darkly coloured objects reflect some light.

The law of reflection

There is a law of physics that governs the way light reflects from objects. This is called the **law of reflection**. This is easiest to see with a flat (plane) mirror.

Practical activity   Angles of reflection

Draw a straight line onto a piece of paper. This line is where you will place the edge of the mirror.

Draw a line at right angles to the first line. We call this line a **normal**.

Place the edge of a plane mirror onto the paper along the first line you drew.

Shine a ray of light (an incident ray) into the mirror so that it hits the point where the normal meets the mirror.

The angle between this incident ray and the normal is called the **angle of incidence**.

The light ray reflects from the mirror. The angle between the reflected ray and the normal is called the **angle of reflection**.

You should see that the angle of incidence and the angle of reflection are always the same size.

⚠ The lamp in the ray box can become very hot.

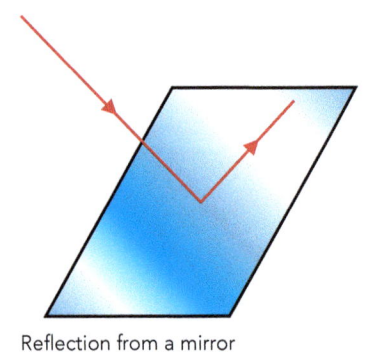

Reflection from a mirror

We can say:

The angle of reflection is equal to the angle of incidence.

The law of reflection works for all reflections.

Images

When we look into a mirror we see an **image** of the real object. The very flat surface of the mirror reflects the rays coming from an object in the same direction as each other and we see a clear image. We can see clear images in other smooth surfaces such as sheets of glass or a calm pond.

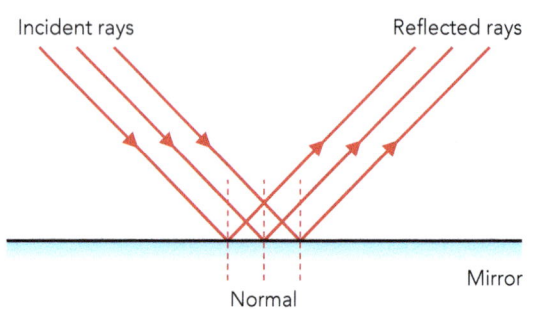

The smooth surface of a mirror means that all of the reflected rays travel in the same direction. This will produce a clear image

7 Light

Can you see the difference between the object and its reflection?

Key terms
- angle of incidence
- angle of reflection
- image
- law of reflection
- normal

Practical activity — Investigating the law of reflection

Use a ray box and mirror to confirm the law of reflection with the technique described opposite. Shine a light ray into the mirror at a range of different incident angles and use a protractor to measure the angles of incidence and reflection.
- Use a pencil to record the path of the rays by drawing two dots at points on the ray and then joining them with a straight line using a ruler.
- Make sure that you measure all angles from the normal.

⚠ **The lamp in the ray box can become very hot.**

Summary questions

1. This diagram shows a ray of light reflecting off a flat mirror.
   a) Which letter represents the angle of incidence and which represents the angle of reflection?
   b) Calculate the missing angles w, y and z.

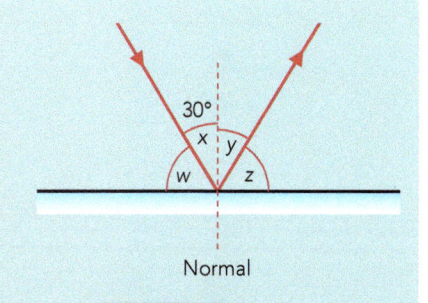

2. A periscope is used to see over objects. It uses two mirrors. Copy and complete this diagram showing how the ray of light reaches the eye.

143

7.4 Refraction

Learning outcomes

After this topic you should be able to:
- describe the behaviour of light as it moves from one transparent material to another
- measure the angle of refraction accurately.

Expert tips

Refraction happens at boundaries so always draw diagrams showing the light rays changing direction at the boundary.

Look at this photo of a straw in a glass of water. The straw appears to be broken but it isn't. The light coming from the bottom half of the straw is changing direction as it travels because of the boundary between the water and the air.

The rays of light coming from the straw are refracted at the boundaries between materials

Changing direction

Light can change direction when it moves from one transparent material to another. This process is called **refraction**. Refraction happens at the boundary between materials. For example, when light moves from air into a glass block or when light moves from air into water. The change in direction always happens at the boundary between the materials.

- The angle at which the ray hits the boundary is called the angle of incidence.
- The angle at which the ray leaves the boundary is called the **angle of refraction**.
- As with reflection, the angles are always measured from a line at right angles to the boundary. This is the normal.

Expert tips

Remember to always measure angles from the normal.

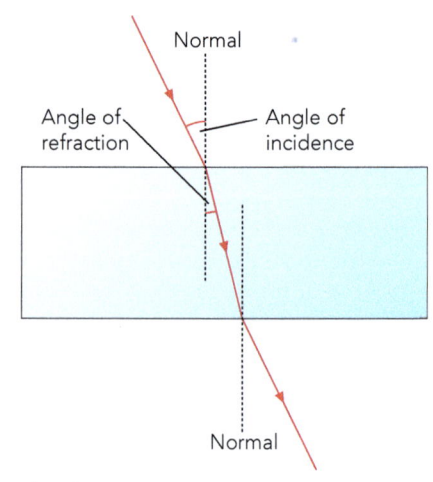

This diagram shows the angle of incidence and refraction

Investigating refraction

We can investigate refraction in a similar way to reflection. This is done by shining rays of light into a glass block and measuring the angles of incidence and refraction.

7 Light

Practical activity — Investigating refraction

Use a ray box to shine a ray of light into a glass block. You should notice that the path of the ray changes if it hits the surface at an angle. You can mark the paths of the rays as they enter and leave the block using a pencil and then measure the angles of incidence and refraction.

- Now shine the ray in at the angles shown in the table and record the angles of incidence and refraction.

Angle of incidence/°	Angle of refraction/°
20	
40	
60	
80	

- Remember to measure all of your angles from the normal.

Is there a simple relationship between the angle of incidence and the angle of refraction?

What happens when the incident ray travels along the normal?

⚠ The lamp in the ray box can become very hot.

Explaining refraction

Refraction happens because the light changes speed as it moves between materials. When light slows down at a boundary the light changes direction towards the normal and the angle of refraction is less than the angle of incidence. The opposite happens when light speeds up. The light changes direction away from the normal.

Key terms
- **angle of refraction**
- **refraction**

Summary questions

1 Choose the correct words to complete the two different sentences describing the way in which light rays are refracted:

   a) When a ray of light moves from *glass* to *air* between two materials it *speeds up / slows down* and refracts *towards/away* from the normal.

   b) When a ray of light moves from *air* to *glass* between two materials it *speeds up / slows down* and refracts *towards/away* from the normal.

2 This diagram shows a ray of light moving from air into a glass block. Copy and complete it to show the full path of the ray of light.

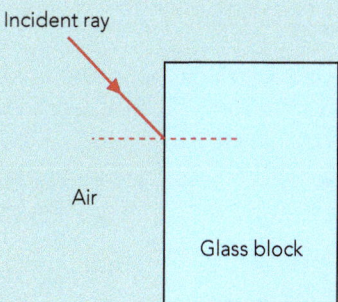

145

7.5 Dispersion and the spectrum

Learning outcomes

After this topic you should be able to:
- describe how a beam of white light can be split into its component colours
- state the order of the colours in the spectrum.

So far we have only looked at what happens to white light when it is reflected or refracted. But white light is not a single colour. White light is a combination of a wide range of colours.

Splitting white light

The component colours in white light can be separated using refraction. Each colour refracts a slightly different amount and so the colours spread out slightly. This effect is called **dispersion**. We can see the effect clearly when we use a triangular glass block called a prism to disperse white light.

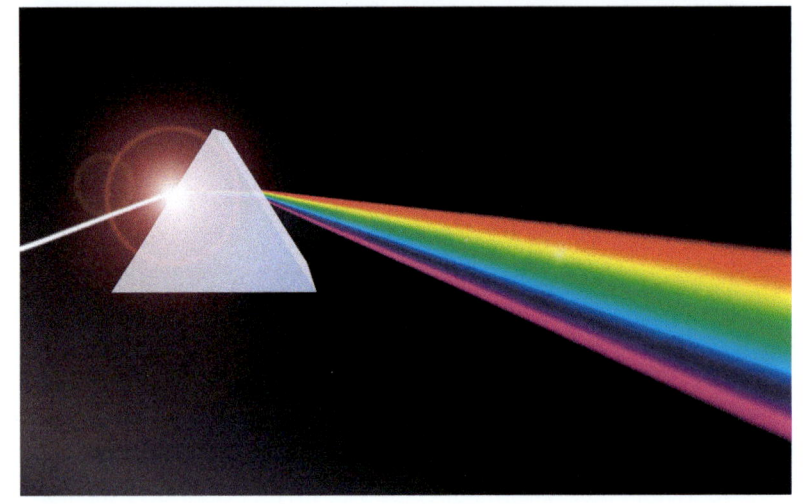

This prism is being used to disperse light. The light refracts twice and this helps to spread out the colours so that they can be seen more easily

Violet light is refracted more than red light and so the colours separate out from each other.

Isaac Newton investigated light and colour. When he used prisms to disperse white light he said that there were seven colours being produced:

red, orange, yellow, green, blue, indigo and violet.

We now know that there is a continuous range of colours produced that we call a **spectrum**.

Practical activity — Dispersing

Use a ray box and prism to separate out the colours of white light into a spectrum. You will have to position the prism carefully to see all of the colours clearly.
- Which colour is refracted the most and which colour is refracted the least?
- How many separate colours can you see in the spectrum?

⚠️ The lamp in the ray box can get very hot.

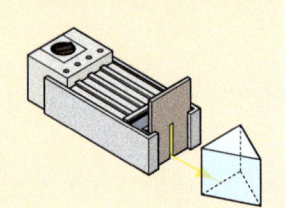

7 Light

In rainbows

This rainbow is produced by diffraction of light from the Sun

Dispersion does not only happen in glass prisms, it can happen whenever light is refracted.

Rainbows are formed as the light from the Sun passes through tiny droplets of water. These droplets act like tiny prisms. The colours of the spectrum are separated out and this produces the rainbow effect. The colours in a rainbow do not match exactly the colours produced the prism shown in the photo. The Sun does not produce pure white light.

Diamonds disperse light more than glass. The white light refracts and reflects at the cut surfaces. This disperses the colours and makes diamonds glitter with different colours.

This diamond is splitting the white light and producing a range of colours

Key terms

- **dispersion**
- **spectrum**

Summary questions

1 What would happen if you tried to use a prism to disperse a beam that contained only green light?

2 This diagram shows two prisms being used to investigate dispersion. The first prism separates out the colours, the second recombines them. Copy and complete the diagram labelling the colours of light including the final colour.

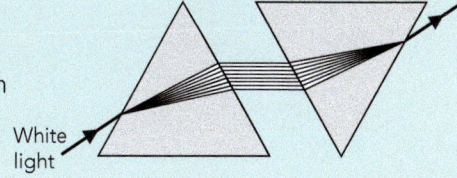

White light

147

7.6 Investigating colour

Learning outcomes

After this topic you should be able to:
- describe the appearance of coloured objects when they are illuminated by coloured light
- explain what happens when different colours of paint are mixed.

White light is a mixture of many different colours. Most surfaces will not reflect all of these colours. Some of the colours will be absorbed.

Reflecting colours

The colour an object appears depends on which colours of light the object reflects and the colour of light shining upon the object.

- A white object appears white in white light because it reflects equally all colours shone onto it.
- A totally black surface does not reflect any of the colours in white light, it absorbs them all.
- A red surface reflects only the red parts of the spectrum and absorbs all of the others.

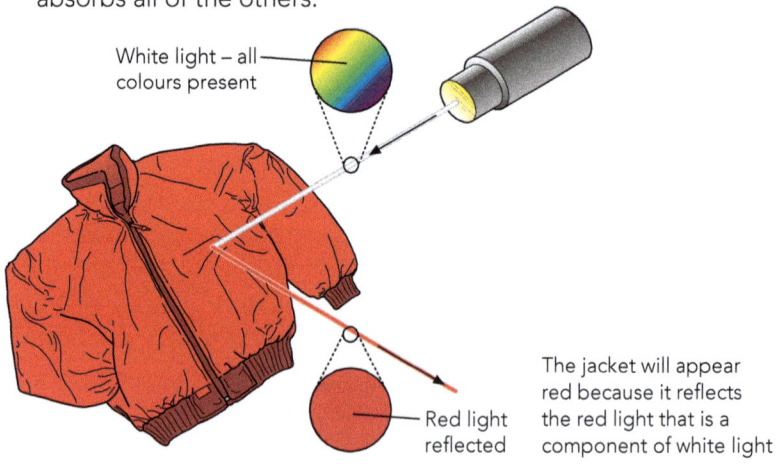

White light – all colours present

Red light reflected

The jacket will appear red because it reflects the red light that is a component of white light

When you shine blue light onto a red object then the object will not reflect any of the light. This means it will look black.

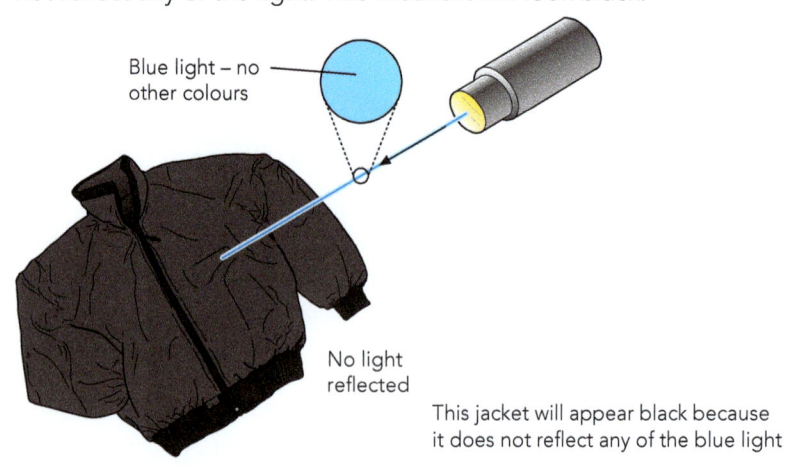

Blue light – no other colours

No light reflected

This jacket will appear black because it does not reflect any of the blue light

Colour combinations

The spectrum contains a wide range of colours but we can sense many more colours. Some surfaces can reflect several parts of the spectrum while absorbing most others. A pink object looks pink because it reflects more than one colour of light. Our eyes detect this mixture of colour and we see the mixture as pink.

7 Light

Mixing paints

Paints work by absorbing some colours while reflecting others. Pure red paint will absorb all of the colours of the spectrum and only reflect red. When another colour of paint is mixed in with the red paint then a new colour can be produced:

- When red paint is mixed with blue paint the result is a purple colour.
- When red paint is mixed with yellow paint orange colours are produced.

Making new colours of paint by mixing them is called **subtractive colour** because you are **subtracting** colours (stopping them being reflected) when the paints mix.

The colours in this picture are reproduced from only three colours of ink (cyan, magenta and yellow) mixed in different combinations

A better set of colours

In printing, only three colours, magenta, cyan and yellow, are used to produce all of the other colours. When these three colours are mixed in different proportions thousands of other colours are possible.

Key terms

- **subtractive colour**

Practical activity — Mixing colours

You have been given two sets of paints or inks:

- Set 1: red, blue and yellow
- Set 2: cyan, magenta and yellow.

These three can be mixed in different amounts to produce many other colours. You may not mix paints between the two sets. See if you can mix the paints to make the colours listed:

- green, pink, black, orange, purple.
- Which set of paints was able to produce the best range of colours?
- Can you use the colours in Set 2 to make the red and blue colours in Set 1?

Summary questions

1. Copy and complete this explanation about a green dress.
   A green dress illuminated by white light will appear _____.
   A green dress illuminated by a green light will appear _____. It is _____ the green light.
   A green dress illuminated by red light will appear _____. It is _____ the red light.

2. Complete this table to show what colours of paint are created.

Paint colours mixed	Colour produced
red and yellow	
blue and yellow	
red, yellow and blue	
yellow and magenta	
yellow, magenta and cyan	

7.7 Coloured light and filters

Learning outcomes

After this topic you should be able to:
- explain why coloured filters can change the colour of light in terms of absorption and transmission
- describe how coloured light can combine to produce new colours.

When light passes through normal glass all of the colours are transmitted. The colour of the light is unchanged. Some materials will allow certain colours to pass through but absorb other colours. This causes the colour of the light to change. We can use these materials as **colour filters**.

These coloured filters for a camera will only allow certain colours to pass through them

Absorbing and transmitting

When white light is passed through a red filter only the red part of the spectrum is transmitted. This means that all of the other colours are absorbed.
- A green filter only allows green light to pass through.
- A blue filter only allows blue light to pass through.

Some filters allow several colours to pass through.
- A cyan filter lets green and blue light pass through.

Practical activity Filtering light

Use coloured filters to test what happens when light passes through them. Shine the light though a filter and onto a white screen (a piece of paper).

Try using more than one filter at a time (e.g. a red one and a blue one).

Filters in series

When you use more than one filter, you can prevent all of the light passing through. For example, if you use a blue filter followed by a red filter then no light can pass all of the way through.

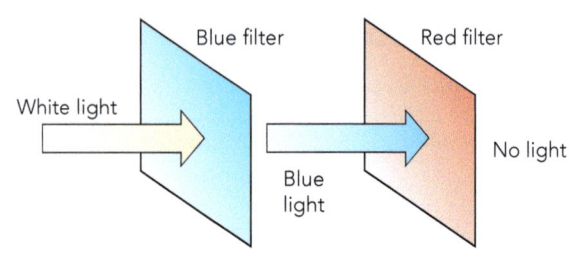

The first filter only lets the blue light through. The second filter would let red light through but there isn't any red light left so no light is transmitted

7 Light

Mixing coloured light

Television and computer monitors can produce a wide range of colours by using three different colours of light called additive primary colours. The primary colours used are red, green and blue. These three colours of light are mixed in the right proportion to create new colours of light.

- When a red and blue light combine they produce the colour magenta.
- Red and green light combine to produce yellow.
- Green and blue combine to make cyan.
- When all three primary colours are added together white light is produced.

Combining colours of light to make new colours is called **additive colour** because you are **adding** colours of light together.

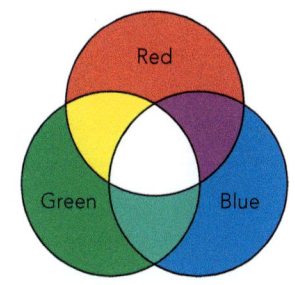

This diagram shows the colours that can be made by combining the three primary colours of light. Other colours can be produced by mixing the lights in different proportion

Practical activity — Mixing lights

Use coloured filters or coloured lamps to test what happens when different coloured lights are mixed. Use a darkened room and shine red and green light onto a sheet of white paper. Try all of the other possible colour combinations.
- You should be able to produce a wide range of colours just by using red, green and blue filters.
- See what happens when you adjust the brightness of one colour by dimming the lamp.

What will happen when you shine different colours of light onto coloured paper?

⚠ **Be careful with the hot lamps**.

Expert tips

Be careful not to mix up what happens when colours of light are mixed (additive colour) and when colours of ink or dyes are mixed (subtractive colour).

Key terms

- **additive colour**
- **colour filters**

Summary questions

1. What coloured light would be produced when:
   a) red light is shone through a red filter?
   b) blue light is shone through a red filter?
   c) green light is shone through a green filter followed by a red filter?

2. a) A piece of paper is white in white light. What colour would the paper appear if only green light was shone upon it?
   b) A second piece of paper is blue in white light. What colour would the paper appear in red light?
   c) A third sheet of paper is green in white light. What colour would this sheet of paper appear in green light?

151

7.8 Sight

Learning outcomes

After this topic you should be able to:
- describe the basic structure of an eye including the function of the major parts
- investigate a range of optical illusions.

Vision is one of the most important senses. We collect more useful information about the world around us by looking than by any other sense.

The structure of the eye

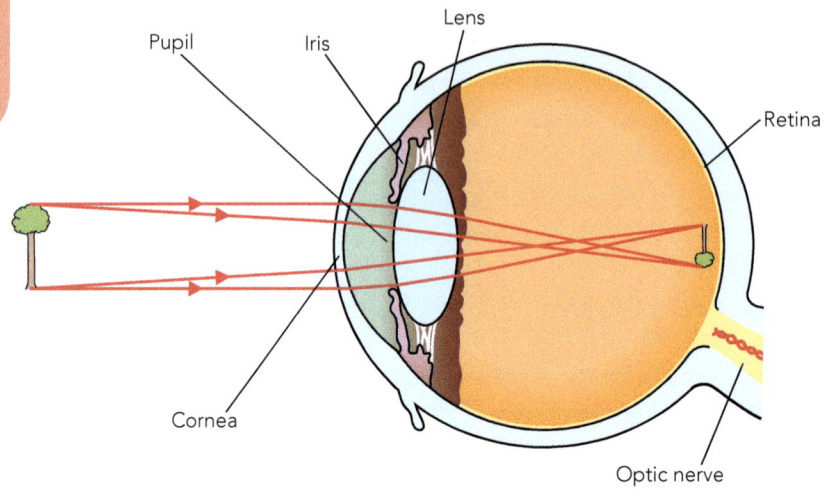

The basic parts of a human eye

Light enters our eyes by passing through the **cornea**; the transparent front surface. The **iris** is the coloured part of the eye. At the centre of the iris is a gap called the **pupil** through which light can pass. The pupil can change size to control the amount of light passing into the eye. In bright light the pupil becomes smaller and in the dark the pupil becomes larger.

The **lens** is behind the pupil and focuses the rays of light that pass through it using refraction. When we are looking at distant objects the lens is stretched thin by small muscles inside the eyeball. When we are looking at nearby objects the muscles relax and the lens is much fatter.

At the back of the eye is a light-sensitive layer of cells that form the **retina**. When light falls onto these cells signals are sent to the brain through a bundle of nerve fibres called the **optic nerve**. Our brains collect all of these signals and interpret what we are seeing.

Imperfect eyes

Our eyes have limitations and as we age these limitations can become worse. The lens can become inflexible and this can limit the range of objects we can focus on. This can make us short-sighted (unable to see distant objects clearly) or long-sighted (unable to see nearby objects clearly).

7 Light

Illusions

This looks like a real object until you think about it carefully. Could it really be made?

Sometimes our brain finds it hard to work out what it is seeing using the information from the retina. It can be confused in different ways, for example the brain decides on colours based on the lighting conditions. It also judges position based on our knowledge of sizes.

Squares A and B are exactly the same shade of grey but our brains see them differently

Practical activity — Seeing is not believing

You have been provided with a range of optical illusions. Investigate the way in which these are deceiving your brain.

Key terms

- cornea
- iris
- lens
- optic nerve
- pupil
- retina

Summary questions

1. Place these stages that explain how we see an object into the correct order.
   A. The light passes through the lens.
   B. Our brain interprets the image telling us what we are looking at.
   C. The light from the object travels to our eyes.
   D. The light forms an image on the retina.
2. a) Why do the cornea and lens in an eye have to be as transparent as possible?
   b) Why does the retina in an eye need to be as dark as possible?

7.9 Lenses and cameras

Learning outcomes

After this topic you should be able to:
- construct a pinhole camera
- compare a camera to an eye.

A camera captures the image of an object in a similar way to the eye. In most cameras the light passes through a lens and creates an image on a surface and the image can be stored.

A camera without a lens

The earliest form of camera was the **pinhole camera**. The pinhole camera did not use a lens. Instead it has a single small hole at the front and a simple screen at the back. Rays of light pass through the 'pin hole' at the front of the camera and reach the screen at the back. If the screen was partially transparent then an image could be seen.

Practical activity Making a pinhole camera

A pinhole camera can be made from a rectangular box and some tracing paper. The box must not have any gaps that allow light in.
- Cut out most of the back surface of the box and replace it with tracing paper. This will be the screen.
- Use a sharp pin to produce a small hole in the front of the box.
- Point the hole towards a bright object like a candle in a darkened room and you will see an image of the object on the screen.

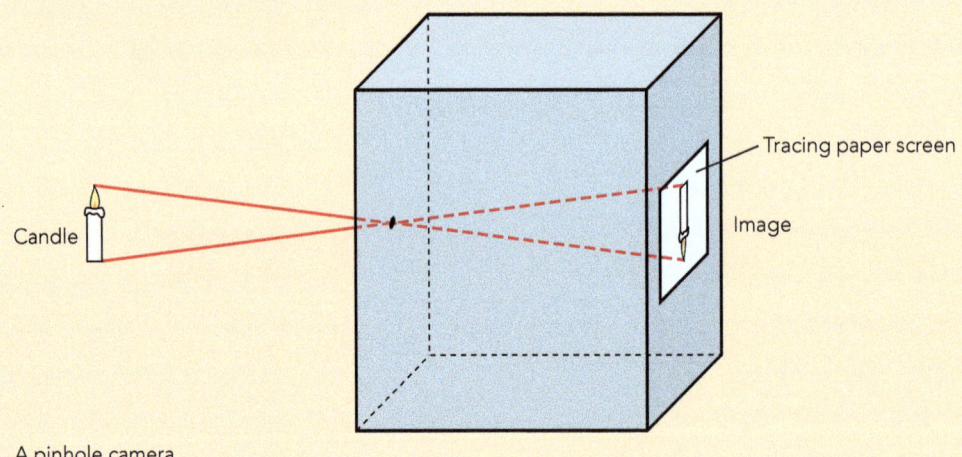

A pinhole camera

What do you notice about the image formed on the screen?

In what way does the image change as the camera is moved towards the object?

⚠ **Be careful with the pin**.

More about lenses

You saw in the previous topic that your eyes have lenses. These lenses use refraction to change the direction of light rays so that they all meet at a certain point. We call this focusing the light to create an **image**.

A converging lens, like the ones in your eyes, brings rays of light together towards a point called the focal point.

7 Light

A camera uses a converging lens to focus light in a similar way to the eye. The lens in a camera is solid glass and so it can't be squashed or stretched to change the focus. Instead the camera has to change the distance between the lens and the film. You may have seen this happen on some cameras as they focus on nearby or distant objects.

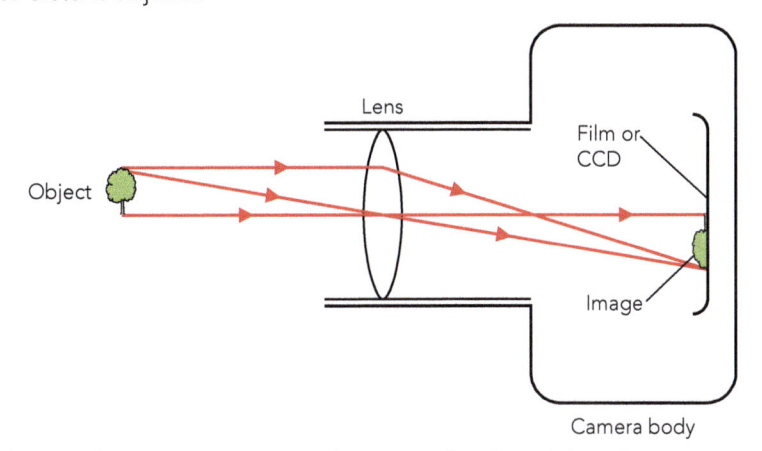

> **Expert tips**
>
> A camera moves the lens to focus an image but the eye changes the shape of the lens.

The lens of the camera moves inwards or outwards to focus light to form an image

Capturing images

Recording the image

Most cameras now use charged couple devices (CCDs) to record images. These are electronic components that detect light levels directly. The image is formed onto millions of tiny detectors all arranged in a grid and the CCDs measure the light level and colour directly. This information can easily be processed by a computer.

This camera has a large lens to collect a lot of light. The lens can be moved in and out to focus at different distances

The camera in this mobile phone is tiny and its lens can't move to adjust the focus. The images it produces will not be as good as those of a larger camera.

> **Key terms**
>
> - image
> - pinhole camera

> **Summary questions**
>
> 1. What advantages do modern cameras have when compared to pinhole cameras? Are there any disadvantages?
> 2. In what ways is a camera similar to a human eye? In what ways is it different?

7.10 Using lenses to magnify

Learning outcomes

After this topic you should be able to:
- describe the tool we can use to magnify images
- construct a simple astronomical telescope.

Single lenses

The simplest optical instruments have only one lens. These include magnifying glasses and spectacles.

Magnifying glasses

A magnifying glass uses a single lens to make objects look larger. We call the apparent increase in size **magnification**.

Objects appear larger through a magnifying glass; they can be studied in more detail easily

Practical activity   Using a magnifying glass

Use a magnifying glass to look at some objects.
- Place the magnifying glass fairly close to the object and then move your eye closer and further away from the lens. What happens to the size of the image you see?
- Try adjusting the distance between the lens and the object while keeping the distance between your eye and the lens the same. What happens to the image?

⚠ Never use a magnifying glass to look at the Sun. It can blind you.

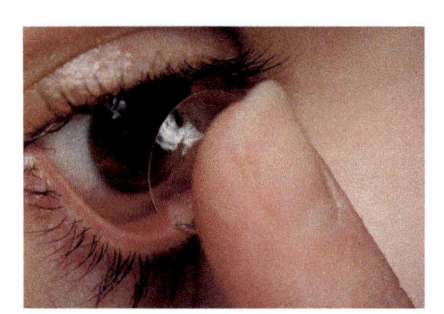

Contact lenses do the same job as spectacles but are placed directly onto the cornea

Spectacles

If your eyesight is not perfect then you might wear spectacles. The lenses in spectacles compensate for the lenses in your eyes which may not be able to focus the light onto your retina. The lenses in spectacles cause refraction on the front and back surface. If you look closely you will see that the two surfaces are curved differently.

Using more than one lens

Sometimes using a single lens is not enough. Combinations of lenses can increase the magnification of an image. To magnify distant objects we use a telescope and for small objects we use microscopes.

Telescopes

Telescopes are used to magnify images of distant objects. Simple astronomical telescopes are used to view the planets and stars. They have two lenses, an eyepiece to look through, and an objective lens to collect the light. Modern telescopes often capture images on a CCD just like a digital camera.

7 Light

Practical activity — Making a telescope

You can construct a telescope with a pair of lenses, some modelling clay and a metre ruler. Place the fatter of the two lenses you have been given 5 cm from the end of the rule and attach it using the modelling clay so that it stands at right angles to the rule. This will be your eyepiece lens. Attach the thinner lens 50 cm further along the rule and make sure it is standing up vertically too. This is the objective lens.

- Look through the eyepiece lens towards the objective lens. You should see that the telescope is magnifying.
- You have built a simple astronomical (space) telescope.

What do you notice about the image you see through this type of telescope.

⚠️ **Never use a telescope to look at the Sun. You may be blinded.**

Microscopes

Microscopes are used to produce magnified images of very small objects such as cells. Microscopes have several lenses including an eyepiece lens and several objective lenses. Together these lenses can magnify an image to over 100 times its original size.

This microscope has a wide range of objective lenses so that different magnifications can be used

Key terms
- **magnification**

Summary questions

1. Which optical instruments would you use to make observations of:

    a) a distant star   **b)** a single human cell   **c)** an insect   **d)** a fingerprint.

2. A microscope is used to measure the size of objects using different magnifications. Use the measured size and the magnification factor to calculate the real size of the objects.

Object	Apparent size	Magnification setting	Real object size
length of a flea	2.5 cm	× 20	
fly's eye	3.0 cm	× 50	
width of a human hair	0.2 cm	× 200	

157

Chapter 7 — End of chapter questions

1 a Match up the words with the best definition. [4]

Key word	Definition
Reflect	A ray of light passes through a material.
Absorb	A ray of light changes direction when it moves from one transparent material to another.
Transmit	The energy from a ray of light is transformed into heat energy warming up an object.
Refract	A ray of light hits a material and 'bounces off'.

b Which of these materials are transparent to visible light?

water
wood
iron
air
glass
gold
diamond [3]

2 A student is investigating how light travels using a rubber tube. When the tube is curved the student can't see through it from one end to the other. When the tube is straightened out the student can see all the way through.

a Draw a diagram showing why the student cannot see all of the way through the curved tube. [1]

b Draw a diagram showing why the student can see all of the way through the straight tube. [1]

3 This diagram shows a ray of light being reflected by a mirror. Only one of the reflected rays is correct.

a State the law of reflection. [1]
b Which of the labelled rays shown is correct? [1]
c What is the name of the line labelled **X**? [1]

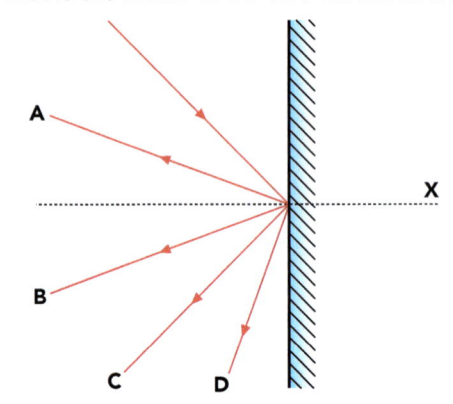

4 We see objects when light enters our eye and an image is formed.

a Which parts of the eye control the amount of light allowed to enter? [2]
b Which part of the eye refracts light rays and focuses a clear image? [1]
c On which part of the eye is the image formed? [1]

5 Which of the following statements about describing refraction as light moved from air into glass are correct?

A The light speeds up.
B The light slows down.
C The ray changes direction towards the normal.
D The ray changes direction away from the normal. [2]

7 Light

6 A group of students is modelling the behaviour of light when it reflects by rolling marbles at a wooden 'mirror' and measuring the angle at which the marbles bounce off. They roll the marbles at set angles and then record the 'angle of reflection'. For each angle, they test the reflection three times.

Angle of incidence/°	Angle of reflection/°			Average angle of reflection/°
	Try 1	Try 2	Try 3	
40	45	43	41	
50	51	51	54	
60	63	55	62	
70	67	74	74	

  a Calculate the average angle of reflection. *[1]*

  b Evaluate how successful the experiment was; do the results match the behaviour of light? *[2]*

7 A student is investigating the effect of filters on white light. She uses a prism to produce a spectrum of white light onto a white screen. She then places different filters in front of the prism one at a time.

  a Complete this list of the seven main colours that form white light.
  Red, _____, yellow, _____, _____, indigo, _____. *[1]*

  b What effect will placing a blue filter in front of the prism have on the spectrum? *[1]*

  c What effect will placing a magenta filter in front of the prism have on the spectrum pattern? *[1]*

  d Why does the filter gradually warm up? *[1]*

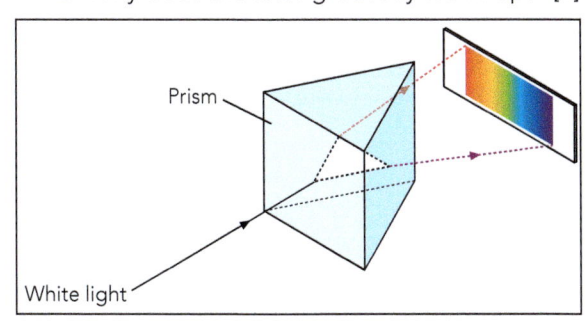

8 Two students are carrying out an experiment to see if different colours of light are refracted by different amounts when they pass from air into a plastic block. They use a white light source and a set of coloured filters. The rays are all passed into the block with an incident angle of 45.0° and the angle of refraction is measured. Their results were:

Light colour	red	green	violet
Angle of refraction/°	42.0	40.5	35.0

  a Describe the way in which the filters can produce coloured light from white light. *[1]*

  b Use the results to make a prediction about the angles of refraction for yellow and indigo light. *[1]*

9 Two students were discussing how mixing paints can produce colours.

  Student A says 'Mixing the paints produce new colours because the different paints give off different colours of light. When you mix the paint together they give off more colours of light and so you get a different overall colour.'

  Student B says 'The paints are absorbing the light and only some of the colours. When you mix them you absorb more of the colours so the paint looks different.'

  a Which student has given the best explanation about mixing paint colours together? *[1]*

  b Why does adding white paint make a colour 'lighter'? Use the words 'absorb' and 'reflect' in your answer. *[1]*

8 Sound

Science *in context!*

Beautiful sounds

Making music

A classical orchestra has a wide range of instruments from violins to cymbals. They are organised in groups based on the way they produce sounds.

Woodwind instruments produce sounds when they are blown. A tiny reed inside the instrument vibrates as the air passes across it. This small vibration is amplified by the shape of the instrument.

Brass instruments also produce vibrations when they are blown. This time the air inside the curved brass tubes vibrates backwards and forwards. Brass instruments are shaped so that the sound becomes louder as it passes through them.

String instruments can produce sound when their strings are made to vibrate by rubbing a bow across them. The hollow shapes make the sounds louder as the whole instrument resonates with the vibration.

Percussion instruments are usually the simplest to play. Banging on a drum will make the drum's skin vibrate. Smashing cymbals together makes the metal vibrate.

Used together the instruments can fill a large hall with musical sounds.

Designing the venue

The design of the music venue is one of the most important aspects of producing good music. Concert halls need to improve the quality of the sounds and allow everybody to hear all of the different instruments.

Hard and flat surfaces will produce echoes and these echoes will ruin the experience. To prevent this, walls are often covered with soft materials that absorb sound and prevent too many echoes.

Many concert halls are in large cities and noise from outside must be prevented from entering. Thick walls and soft insulation can prevent noises from ruining the concert.

Venue designers even have to think about how many people will be in the audience. People are softer than empty seats and will absorb more of the sound.

The bow causes the strings of this violin to vibrate and produce sound

8 Sound

Improving the sound

Most music we listen to has been recorded in a music studio. The sounds of the different instruments and voices are all recorded separately. Sometimes the instruments are played in different rooms or even at different times.

Each sound is analysed by sound engineers. These engineers manipulate the signals to make the music sound as good as it possibly can. The recording engineers decrease the loudness of instruments that were too loud and increase the loudness of instruments that were too quiet to be heard properly. Eventually all of the sounds from the instruments are mixed together to recreate the sound of a full orchestra.

Computers and synthesisers can create a range of sounds that can't be produced by real instruments. Even voices can be changed to make any singing more 'in tune'.

Sounds can be manipulated in many ways. This mixing desk allows the sounds from different instruments to be mixed together for recording

In this chapter you will find out about the properties of sound in terms of the movement of air particles (molecules). You will also learn about the link between loudness and amplitude, as well as the link between pitch and frequency.

Key points

- Sounds are caused by vibrations.
- Sound travels as a wave through materials passing from particle to particle.
- Sound waves cannot pass through empty space (a vacuum) as there are no particles to carry the wave.
- A high-pitched sound has a higher frequency.
- A loud sound has greater amplitude.
- Sound waves travel faster in solids and liquids than they do in gases.
- A cathode ray oscilloscope is used to analyse sound signals.
- We detect sound with our ears and these can be damaged by loud sounds.

8.1 Making sounds

Learning outcomes

After this topic you should be able to:
- describe how sound waves are produced and travel from place to place
- investigate a range of musical instruments and describe how they produce sound.

Vibrations and sound

When objects vibrate they produce sound. The **vibrations** create disturbances, which pass through the air as **sound waves**. The waves are carried by the particles (molecules of gases in the air) passing the vibrations along from one particle to other nearby particles. Each particle in the air vibrates back and forth as the sound wave passes. When the sound waves reach our ears we hear the sound.

We normally hear sound waves after they pass through the air but sound waves can also travel through any other material. We call the material the sound wave is passing through the medium. Sound cannot travel thorough a vacuum (empty space) because there are no particles to pass the energy along.

When a sound wave reaches a boundary like a wall it can reflect off it in a similar way to light reflecting off a mirror. This reflected sound wave is called an **echo**.

Making sounds

Musical instruments

Musical instruments create sound waves when they are used. Different parts of the instruments vibrate when they are hit, blown, plucked or strummed.

Solid surfaces reflect sound waves and produce an echo

Practical activity — Exploring instruments

Use a range of instruments to find out how they produce sound. You will need to find out how the instruments are played and then look out for the parts of the instrument that vibrate.

- For each instrument record what has to be done to produce a musical sound. Using a copy of the table below.
- In what way can the properties of the sound that the instruments make be changed? Can the loudness or pitch be changed?

Instrument	The way we can change	
	Loudness	Pitch

⚠ Take care with the instruments, some are fragile and expensive.

8 Sound

Loudspeakers

Most of the music we hear is now produced by loudspeakers in radios or headphones. These transform electrical signals into sound waves using a paper or plastic cone connected to an electromagnet. As the electrical signal passes through the electromagnet, the electromagnet vibrates and makes the cone vibrate to match the electrical signal.

Practical activity: Controlled vibrations

A signal generator can be used to produce simple electrical signals that can be fed into a large loudspeaker. This allows us to control the sound produced by the loudspeaker and see how the properties of a sound wave can be altered.

Watch a demonstration of the operation of a loudspeaker and a signal generator as the electrical signals are changed to produce sounds with different pitches and loudness.

- What happens to the speed the loudspeaker vibrates as the pitch of the sound increases?
- What happens to the movement of the loudspeaker as the loudness of the sound is increased?

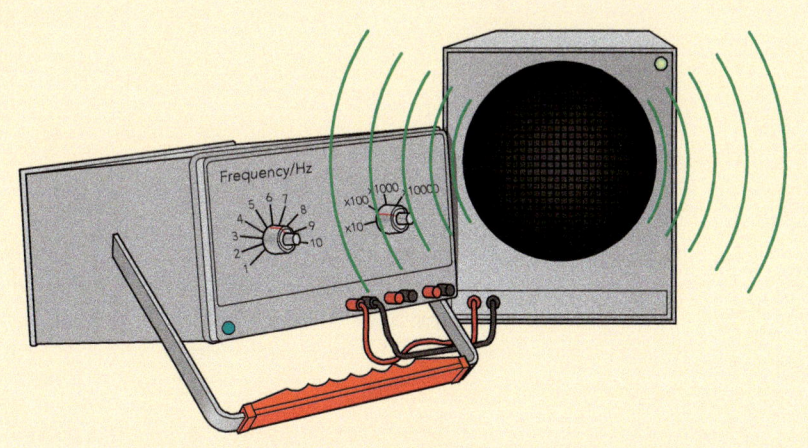

A signal generator and loudspeaker can be used to generate sounds

Key terms

- echo
- sound waves
- vibrations

Summary questions

1. Place each of the following musical instruments into one of three groups – hit, plucked and blown – depending on the way in which they produce sound.

   trumpet, mandolin, piano, guitar, cello, recorder, drum, harmonica, saxophone

   Describe what we can do to increase the loudness of the sounds produced by each instrument.

2. Design an experiment to test whether sound waves follow the same law of reflection as light waves. You will need to think of a way to detect the sound and to make sound travel in more controlled beams. Hint: Long cardboard tubes can help.

163

8.2 Describing sound waves

Learning outcomes

After this topic you should be able to:
- describe the relationships between frequency and pitch
- describe the relationship between loudness and amplitude
- identify patterns in results and recognise anomalous results.

Sound waves have different properties, they can be loud or quiet and they can be of a different pitch.

Frequency and pitch

Practical activity — Exploring simple vibrations

Use a ruler to test how the pitch of a sound wave changes when you adjust the length of the ruler. You should watch out for the changes in how the ruler vibrates and link these to the pitch of the sound produced.

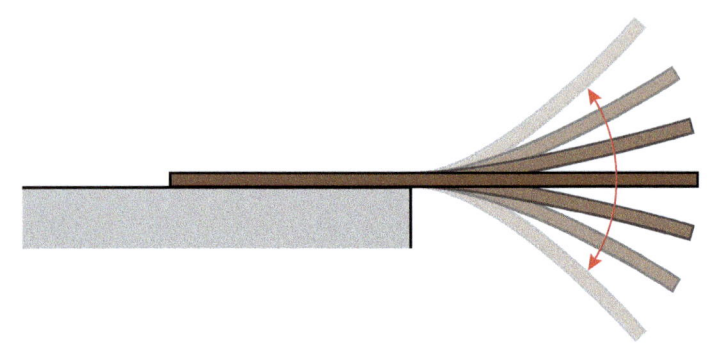

The vibrating ruler generates sound waves

When you hold a ruler over the edge of a desk and push it downwards to make it vibrate, it makes a sound. If you shorten the length of the ruler you should notice that end of the ruler vibrates more rapidly. The sound produced by the shorter ruler is higher pitched.

We call the number of vibrations produced each second the **frequency** of the sound. Frequency is measured in a unit called **hertz** (Hz).

- A frequency of 1 hertz is 1 vibration per second.
- A frequency of 300 hertz is 300 vibrations per second.

Many sounds have frequencies of thousands of vibrations each second so the frequency can be measured in kilohertz where 1 kilohertz = 1000 Hz.

As the frequency of a sound wave increases the pitch we hear increases.

8 Sound

Loudness and amplitude

Sounds can also be loud or quiet. The **amplitude** of a sound wave is a measure of how much energy it carries. High amplitude sounds are louder than lower amplitude sounds. The high amplitude sounds are produced by larger vibrations and carry more energy. The particles carrying louder sounds move further back and forth as they vibrate.

> **Expert tips**
>
> A higher frequency produces a higher pitch.
>
> A higher amplitude produces a louder sound.

Practical activity: Crash

When you drop objects onto the ground they produce sounds. By dropping objects from increasing heights you provide the objects with more energy.

- If you have a sound meter you can measure the loudness of the sound produced when the objects fall.
- Do objects dropping from larger heights produce louder sounds? What is the relationship?
- Is the evidence collected reliable (repeatable)? Are there any anomalous results?
- Can everybody agree on the loudness of the sounds?
- What other factors are affecting the loudness of the sounds produced?

⚠ **Do not drop heavy objects and don't drop anything near your feet.**

> **Key terms**
>
> - amplitude
> - frequency
> - hertz (Hz)

Summary questions

1. Copy and complete these sentences:
   The frequency of a sound wave is the number of _____ each _____. As the frequency increases the pitch of the sound wave _____. The louder a sound is the greater its _____ and the _____ energy it carries.

2. Describe the behaviour of the particles carrying a sound wave when:
   a) the frequency of the sound wave increases
   b) the loudness of the sound wave increases.

3. Copy and complete this table of musical notes and their respective frequencies.

Musical note	C4 (Middle C)	B7	A4	D1
Frequency / Hz	261.6	a)	b)	36.71
Frequency / kHz	c)	4.186	0.440	d)

165

8.3 Analysing sound waves

Learning outcomes

After this topic you should be able to:

- describe the appearance of a sound wave when it is represented on a CRO
- operate a CRO to obtain a trace for different sound waves.

Microphones and the CRO

A microphone transfers sound energy into electrical signals. The electrical signals can then be displayed on the screen of a **cathode ray oscilloscope (CRO)**. The display on the CRO allows the sound signal to be analysed.

Comparing the amplitude of sound waves

A CRO can compare simple sound waves with different amplitudes.

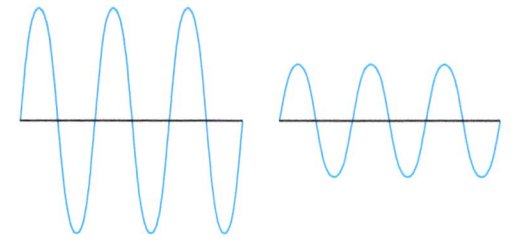

Cathode ray oscilloscope traces for two waves with different amplitudes

The wave to the left was produced by a louder sound than the wave on the right. The wave pattern shown on the left screen has a larger amplitude than the wave pattern on the right screen. The left wave is carrying more energy than the right wave. A larger electrical signal is being produced by the microphone. A louder sound will produce a larger amplitude wave on the CRO screen.

Comparing frequency of sound waves

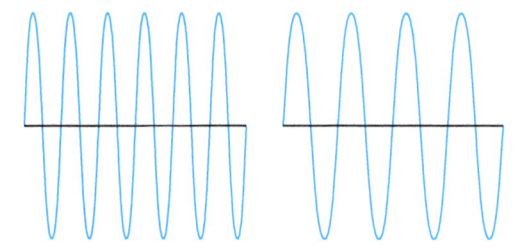

A CRO showing two different frequencies of waves

A sound with more vibrations per second has a higher frequency. The previous diagram shows two waves with the same amplitude but different frequencies.

The trace on the left shows a sound wave with higher frequency than the sound wave on the right. The wave peaks are closer together on the display because there are more waves being produced each second.

8 Sound

Practical activity — Using a cathode ray oscilloscope

Use a CRO to analyse some sounds. Tuning forks produce a single frequency of sound and so the traces they produce on a CRO are quite simple.

You can test a range of pitches and loudness so that you can spot the differences.

Compare the simple sound waves produced by tuning forks to those of a human voice.

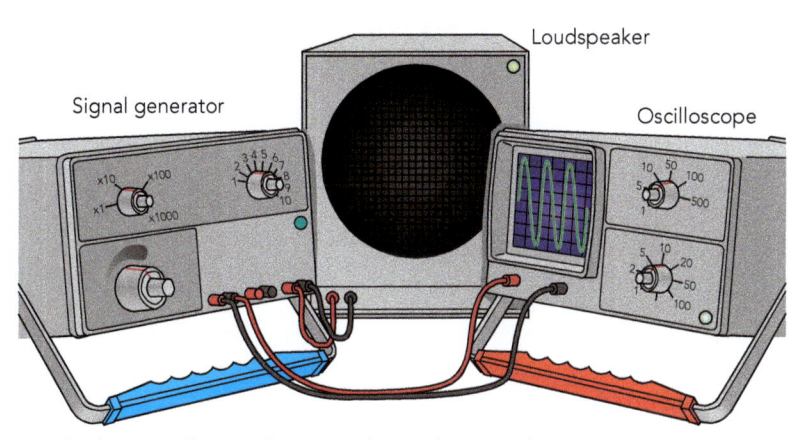

A cathode ray oscilloscope being used to analyse sound waves

Key terms

- cathode ray oscilloscope (CRO)

Summary questions

1. Draw an energy transfer diagram to show how a microphone and CRO transform sound energy.

2. Two sounds (**A** and **B**) are analysed using a CRO. Sound **B** has half the amplitude but twice the frequency of sound **A**. Describe the ways in which their CRO traces would be different.

3. The diagram shows four sound waves displayed on a CRO.

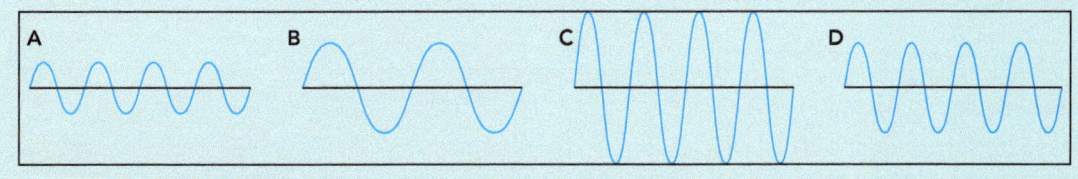

    a) Which two waves have the same frequency?
    b) Which two waves have the same amplitude?
    c) Which of the waves is being produced by the sound with the highest pitch?
    d) Which represents the loudest sound?

167

8.4 The speed of sound

Learning outcomes

After this topic you should be able to:
- calculate the speed of sound
- measure the speed of sound in air by experiment
- calculate the average (mean) of sets of repeat readings.

When a firework rocket explodes you can see the flash of light before you hear the explosion. This is because sound travels through the air much more slowly than light.

The sounds from these firework explosions can take several seconds to reach you

How fast is sound?

When somebody nearby is talking, you don't notice a delay between their lips moving and hearing the sound. This means that sound waves must be moving fairly quickly between you and the person talking. Sound waves take only fractions of a second to travel short distances.

To calculate the speed of sound, we use the speed equation. You will find out more about the use of this calculation in chapter 9.

speed = distance ÷ time

To measure the speed of sound, we need to measure how long it takes for a sound wave to travel a measured distance. Two methods of measuring the speed are described in the following Practical activities. Carry out one of the methods to estimate the speed of sound in air.

Practical activity — Measuring the speed of sound over long distances

If you have a large area such as a sports track you can measure the speed of sound easily.

- Measure out a long distance; a 100 m sprint track is ideal.
- One student stands at one end of the track and another student at the other end.
- The first student needs to produce a loud sound and give a visual signal at the same time.
- The second student starts a stopwatch when they see the signal and stops it when they hear the sound.
- Repeat the test several times and find an average (mean) time for the sound to travel the measured distance.

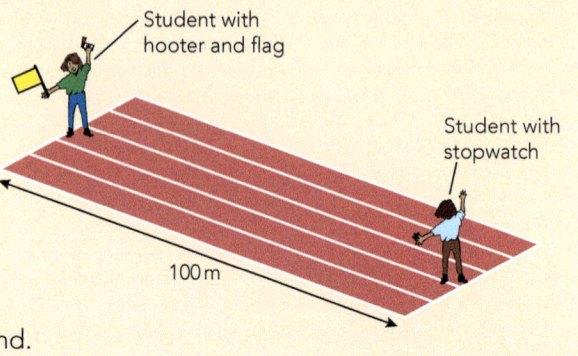

8 Sound

> **Practical activity** — Measuring the speed of sound using echoes
>
> If you have a smaller area you can measure the speed using an echo.
> - Measure the distance between yourself and a large wall using a tape measure.
> - Create a loud sound and measure the time it takes for you to hear the echo. You will need good reactions to do this.
>
> - Repeat the test several times and find an average (mean) time for the sound to travel the measured distance.
> - Use the speed equation to find the speed of sound. Remember that the sound will have travelled twice the distance between you and the wall. It will have travelled there and back again.

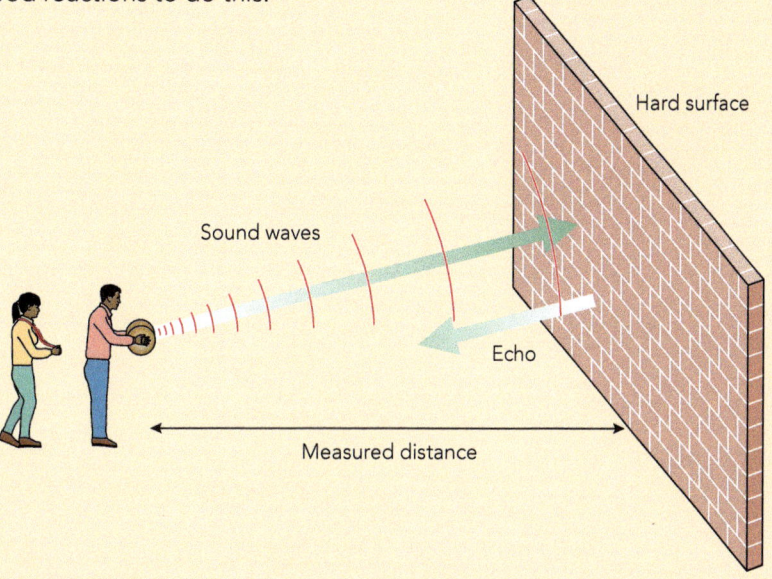

Value for the speed of sound

The speed of sound in air is approximately 340 m/s for air at 20 °C. This value varies depending on the temperature of the air. The higher the temperature of the air the faster the sound travels.

> **Expert tips**
>
> You will learn much more about how to use the speed equation in the next chapter.

> **Summary questions**
>
> 1. Which of these objects travel faster than sound waves through air?
>   - **A** The International Space Station orbiting the Earth at 7700 m/s
>   - **B** A sports car travelling at 15 m/s
>   - **C** A jet travelling at 400 m/s
>
> 2. A student measures how long it takes for sound to travel 60 m using the Practical activity on page 168. The uncorrected time they record on the stopwatch was 0.5 s. The reaction times account for 0.3 s of this time. The remainder is the actual time it took for the sound to travel.
>   - **a)** What is the actual time it took for the sound to reach them?
>   - **b)** What is the speed of sound they measured?

169

8.5 Sound in solids and liquids

Learning outcomes

After this topic you should be able to:
- measure the speed of sound in a solid material
- describe why sound waves travel more quickly in solids and liquids than in gases.

We normally hear sounds after the sound waves have passed though air but sound can also pass through liquids and solids.

Sound in liquids and solids

Sound waves pass through liquids in the same way that they pass through gases such as air. The vibrations are passed from particle to particle.

In a liquid or a solid the particles are much closer together than in a gas. This means that the vibrations can be passed onwards much more quickly and so the sound waves travel more quickly than they would in a gas. Sound waves can travel more quickly in more dense materials. The speed that the wave can travel is also influenced by the type of bonding between the particles.

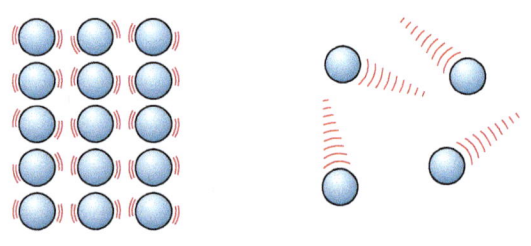

The particles in a solid can pass on sound waves much more quickly than those in a gas

Measuring the speed of sound precisely

To find the speed of sound more accurately, we can use timing instruments which are very precise. They should have a high resolution. To make time measurements of only thousandths of a second requires electronic timers, because human reaction times will be too large.

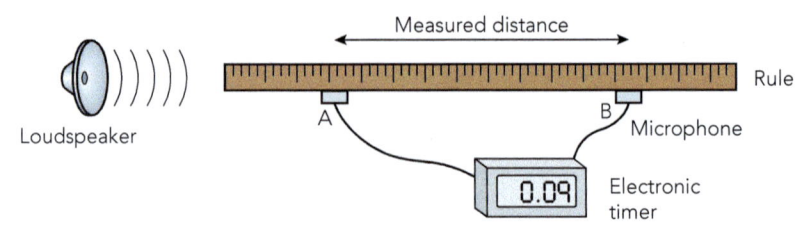

Two microphones are placed a measured distance apart and used to control an electronic stopwatch

The diagram shows how the speed of sound can be accurately measured in a laboratory. A sound is produced by a loudspeaker or another source. Microphone A starts the electronic stopwatch when a sound is detected. Microphone B stops the stopwatch when the sound reaches the microphone. The time and distance measured in the experiment can be entered into the speed equation to find the speed of sound.

Sound waves travel at approximately 340 m/s through the air. If the distance between the two microphones is 1.0 m then the time taken for sound to travel between the two microphones will be 0.003 s.

> **Practical activity** — Measuring the speed of sound in a metal bar
>
> If you have an electronic timing system, you can measure the speed of sound in a metal bar. Place the two microphones a measured distance apart against the bar. The microphones should be connected to a precise timing device that starts and stops the clock when sound is detected.
>
> You can produce a sound wave with a loudspeaker or simply tap the bar at one end.
>
> If you have a range of metal bars you can compare the speed of sound in all of them.
> - Does the density of the material affect the speed of sound?
> - Compare the results you collect to values found by research and explain the possible causes of any differences.
>
> If your results agree with those found by others, we say the results are reproducible. You can have more trust in reproducible results.
>
> ⚠ **Do not attempt to use very loud sounds.**

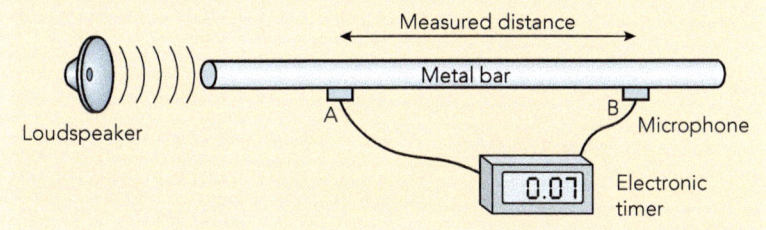

Summary questions

1. A student uses underwater microphones to measure the speed of sound in a swimming pool. The length of the pool is 50 m and the time taken for the sound wave to pass through the water is 0.034 s. What is the speed of sound in this water?

2. Design an experiment to test if the speed of sound in a solid or liquid is affected by the temperature of the material. You will need to highlight any dangers in the experiment.

8.6 Hearing sounds

Learning outcomes

After this topic you should be able to:
- describe the structure of human ears
- design an experiment to test our sense of direction.

We hear sounds when the sound waves reach our ears. Ears are very sensitive organs that convert sound energy into electrical signals that travel to our brains.

The structure of ears

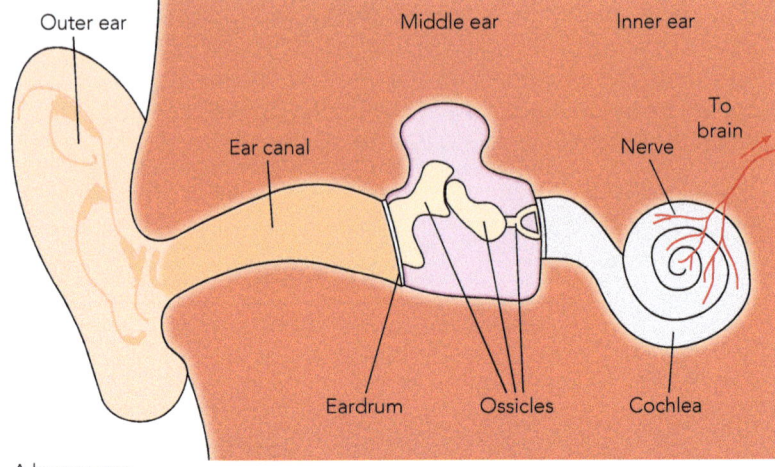

A human ear

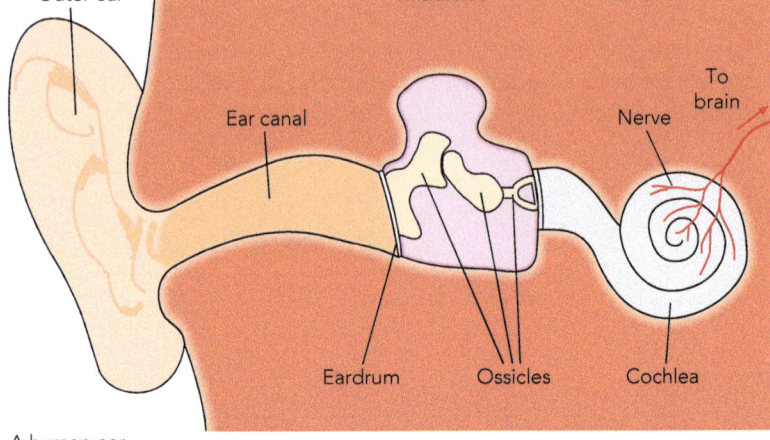

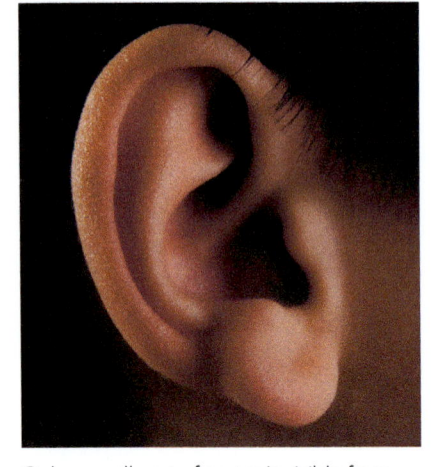

Only a small part of an ear is visible from the outside

The outer ear is called the pinna. It is shaped so that it collects sound energy.

The tube that connects this outer part of the ear to the middle ear is the ear canal.

The **eardrum** in a thin layer of tissue that separates the outer parts of the ear from the internal parts. It transmits the sound onwards and protects the rest of the ear from infection.

Beyond the eardrum there are three small bones called the **ossicles**. These bones work together to pass the energy of the sound wave to the cochlea.

The **cochlea** is a coiled tube filled with a fluid and tiny hair-like structures. When vibrations reach the cochlea the hairs are moved backwards and forwards.

The hairs in the cochlea send electrical signals to the brain along a set of nerves. Our brain interprets these signals as sound.

Ears are also important in our sense of balance. Three tubes called semi-circular canals detect how our head is tilted or if we are rotating. When we spin around, the fluid in these canals spins. If we spin too much we become dizzy because the fluid keeps on moving when we stop.

Pairs of ears

When you hear a sound you can usually tell which direction the sound is coming from. This is because humans have a pair of ears; one on each side of their heads. The two ears detect the sound

8 Sound

waves arriving at slightly different times; there is less than 1000th of a second difference. Our brains can use this timing difference to work out the direction the sound is coming from.

> **Practical activity** — Sound direction sensitivity
>
> Design an activity to test whether our sense of sound direction works accurately.
>
> You will need to wear a blindfold to make sure you can't see where the sound is being produced.
>
> You will need to be able to produce sounds from different directions.
> - What will you do to judge how good a person is at sensing the direction?
> - What measurements can you record?
>
> ⚠️ Be very careful not to move around when you are blindfolded.

This rabbit can point his ears in different directions to listen out for predators approaching

> **Key terms**
> - cochlea
> - eardrum
> - ossicles

> **Summary questions**
>
> 1 Which part of your ear is most likely to be damaged by:
>   a) exposure to loud noises over a long period?
>   b) an extremely loud sudden noise?
> 2 Why can't a person with only one working ear tell which direction a sound is coming from as clearly as a person with both ears working properly?

173

8.7 The dangers of sounds

Learning outcomes

After this topic you should be able to:

- describe the damage that can be caused to hearing by different levels of noise
- plan an investigation to find out how the sound level decreases with distance from the source of the sound
- present results in tables and graphs
- identify relationships in results.

Damaged ears

Many parts of our ears are very small and delicate. They can be damaged by sudden, extremely loud noises such as explosions or very loud music, which can tear the eardrum.

Other loud noises can cause damage to our hearing over longer periods of time. For example, the ossicles (small bones) can wear out and become less sensitive as they rub together. Older people are less sensitive to high frequency sound because of the processes that damage hearing over time.

Measuring the loudness of sounds

Louder sounds carry more energy. We can measure the loudness with a sound meter in a unit called the **decibel (dB)**. The greater the decibel reading the louder the sound is. The decibel system is quite complicated. Doubling the energy of the sound does not double the decibel reading.

The data table shows a range of loudness for different environments or devices. Sounds above 70 dB are usually annoying. Sounds above 100 dB will cause permanent damage if you are exposed for more than an hour. Sounds above 110 dB are painful to hear. Anything louder can rupture your eardrum very quickly.

Noise source	dB
breathing	10
a library or quiet classroom	40
quiet talking	60
dishwasher	80
jackhammer	100
chainsaw	120
jet taking off 25 metres away	150

The loudness of some sample sounds

This passenger jet coming in to land produces an extremely loud sound

8 Sound

> **Practical activity**   Measuring the loudness of sounds
>
> Use a sound meter to measure the loudness of some sample sounds such as the background noise level, the level of normal conversations and some louder noises. Compare your results with the examples in the table.
>
> The further you are away from a sound, the less energy reaches you. Plan an investigation into the effect of distance on the measured sound level.
>
> You will have to think up a method of producing a sound at a fixed level. This could be a constant sound or a noise produced only when you need it.
>
> Measure how far the sound meter is placed away from the source of the sound and compare the changing sound level readings.
>
> Don't forget to take into account the background level of sound and subtract it from your measured results.
>
> - Plot a graph showing the relationship between the sound level and the distance from the sound source.
> - Describe the relationship you have discovered.
>
> ⚠️ **Do not use loud sounds; they can damage your ears or give you a headache.**

Protecting ears from damage

The best way of protecting your ears is to limit the loudness of the noise around you. If that is not possible, ear protection should be worn. Ear protectors insulate your ears from sound. The ear protectors absorb or reflect the sound energy before it can reach your eardrum.

These ear defenders will protect the worker from the damaging sound energy emitted from the equipment he is operating

Key terms
- **decibel (dB)**

Summary questions

1. Copy and complete:
   The loudness of a sound wave is measured in _____. The loudness of a sound _____ as the distance to the source increases.

2. Explain why the measured loudness of a sound decreases with distance from the source.

3. Design an experiment to test the effectiveness of ear protection. The experiment must be able to measure the sound level outside and inside the protection being used. Predict which types of material will be the best at providing sound insulation.

175

8.8 Beyond our range of hearing

Learning outcomes

After this topic you should be able to:
- describe the uses of ultrasound
- identify the range of human hearing in terms of frequency.

Our ears can only detect frequencies up to 20 000 Hz but sound waves can be produced with much higher frequencies. These sound waves are called **ultrasound**.

Ultrasound

Ultrasonic waves can be used in medical examinations.
- A transducer sends sound signals into the body.
- The signals reflect off the boundaries between different types of tissue (e.g. muscle and bone).
- The transducer receives the echoes.
- A computer uses the timings of the echoes to calculate the positions of the tissue boundaries and then creates an image of the surfaces.

A similar method can be used to detect flaws in metal objects such as pipes. A crack will cause ultrasonic echoes that can be detected.

Species	Hearing range / Hz
human	20–20 000
dog	67–45 000
cat	45–64 000
owl	200–12 000
bat	2000–110 000
dolphin	75–150 000
elephant	16–12 000
horse	55–33 500

The ranges of frequencies that can be detected by animals

Bats can fly in total darkness due to their ability to use echo location to 'see' obstacles

Ultrasound scans are harmless and so can safely be used for prenatal examinations

Ultrasonic animals

Animals are able to hear different frequency ranges to humans. Some are able to hear much higher frequencies than humans can.

Dolphins and bats can use ultrasound very effectively. Bats can produce very high frequency pulses of sound that they send outwards. The sound waves reflect off obstacles and the bat hears the echo, detecting the object so that it doesn't fly into it. The sound waves also reflect off small insects and the bats can find and catch the insects even in total darkness. This is an example of echo location.

8 Sound

Dolphins can communicate and detect their surroundings using high-pitched squeaks

Dolphins use echo location techniques underwater to find fish and avoid obstacles deep underwater where there is very little light. Dolphins can also communicate effectively through these high frequency pulses.

Practical activity — Testing the limit of human hearing

Your teacher will use a signal generator and loudspeaker to produce higher and higher frequencies of sound.

See what the limit of your hearing is. You should notice that the sound waves seem to become quieter at very high frequencies. This is because our ears are very inefficient at detecting these waves even when they have the same amplitude as the lower frequency sound waves.

Key terms

- ultrasound

Summary questions

1. Use the data table of animal hearing ranges to decide which animals can hear the following sounds:
   a) 50 Hz
   b) 100 000 Hz
   c) 10 000 Hz

2. Is there a correlation between the size of an animal's ears and the highest frequency it can detect? Research data comparing ear size and the frequency range an animal can hear to test the theory.

Chapter 8 End of chapter questions

1 a What happens to the pitch of a sound as its frequency increases? [1]

b What happens to the loudness of a sound as its amplitude decreases? [1]

2 Match up these devices to the correct definitions:
   A Microphone
   B Loudspeaker
   C Oscilloscope
   1 a device that displays the shape of electrical signals on a screen
   2 a device that transforms sound energy into electrical signals
   3 a device that transforms electrical energy into sound energy [3]

3 a Which of these oscilloscope traces represents the sound with the highest frequency? [1]

b Which trace represents the sound with the lowest amplitude? [1]

c Which two traces show waves with the same pitch? [1]

d Which two traces show waves with the same loudness? [1]

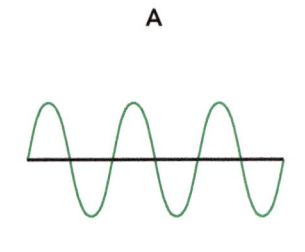

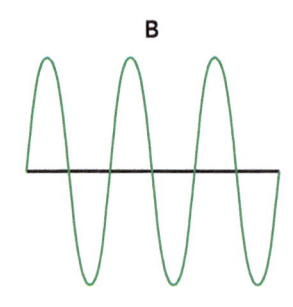

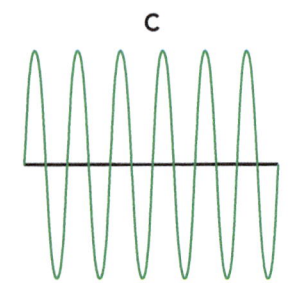

4 Place these stages describing how we hear sounds into the correct order. They are not already in the correct order.
   1 The sound waves enter our ears.
   2 The source of the sound vibrates creating sound waves.
   3 The sound waves pass through the parts of our ear and stimulate nerves.
   4 Sound waves pass through the air.
   5 The nerves send electrical signals to our brains. [5]

5 A student measures some of the properties of sound waves and records the information in a table as shown. The student has not used appropriate headings.

Sound wave	Waves each second	dB
X	25 000	14
Y	10 000	45
Z	5 000	70

a Copy and complete the table correcting the headings. [2]

b Which of the waves has the highest frequency? [1]

c Which wave has the lowest pitch? [1]

d Which sound is the loudest? [1]

e Which sound could not be heard by a human? [1]

178

8 Sound

6 Research scientists have measured the speed of sound in water at different depths in the ocean for a new submarine sonar system. As the depth of the water increases the water becomes denser due to the increase in pressure.

Depth in the ocean / m	Speed / m/s
0	1489
500	1498
1000	1506
1500	1515
2000	1523
2500	1532
3000	1540

Data generated from the Unesco equation using the method of Wong & Zhu 1995, Speed of Sound in Sea-Water

a Plot a graph showing the relationship between the depth and the speed of sound in the liquid. [2]

b Describe the relationship between the speed of sound and the depth in the ocean. [2]

c Use ideas about density to explain the results of the experiment. [2]

7 A group of students investigates how sound levels vary with distance from a loudspeaker. The graph of their results is shown below.

a Which of the results is anomalous? [1]

b Describe the pattern in the loudness of the sound. [2]

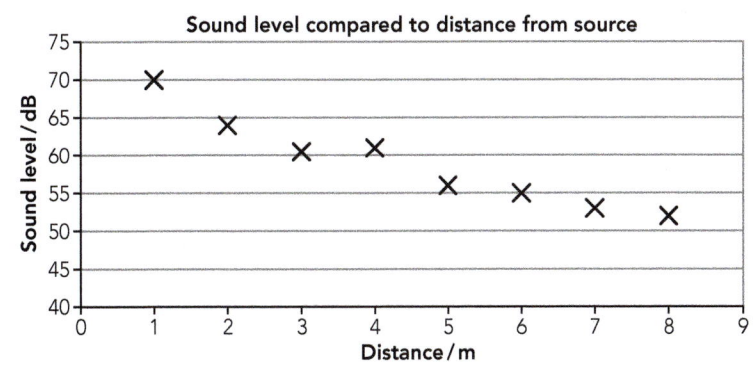

8 This diagram shows the waveform of a sound on an oscilloscope. The *x*-axis has a scale of 0.1 seconds per division.

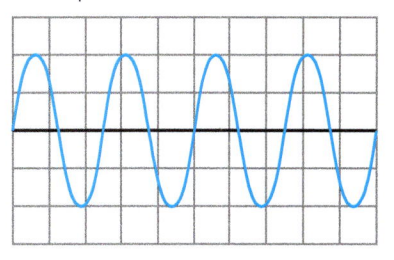

a How many complete waves are shown in the waveform? [1]

b How long does it take to produce one complete wave? [1]

c How many waves would be produced each second? [1]

d What is the frequency of the wave? [1]

179

9 Forces and magnets

Science in context!

From super fast to super small

Magnets can be enormous or incredibly tiny and so they have a very wide range of uses in industry. Simple uses include lifting metallic objects in scrapyards or keeping doors closed. But magnets can also be found in unexpected locations.

The surface of a hard disk is coated in magnetic materials

Magnetic storage

Magnetic materials are used in tiny electronic devices. The hard disks inside a computer have a magnetic coating covering them. The disks are spun at very high speed, 7200 revolutions per minute. As the disks spin a tiny electromagnet inside the disk-drive can magnetise or demagnetise parts of the surface. This produces a pattern of magnetism that is a record of the data to be stored. This pattern can be read or re-written over and over again thousands of times. Disks like this can store billions of 'bits' of information. The internet relies on massive storage where thousands of these disks work together.

Mechanical hard disks such as these are now being replaced by solid state electronics. These solid state disks are more reliable as they have no moving parts but they are more expensive than the magnetic disks.

Magnetically levitating trains

Most trains run on rails. The train's large metal wheels roll along the steel tracks fairly easily but energy is wasted because of the friction between the wheel and the track. As trains become faster and faster the effect of this friction increases. These trains can also be noisy as friction produces a large amount of sound energy. The rough tracks can also make the train vibrate as it moves.

Maglev (magnetically levitating) trains remove this friction completely. These trains float above their tracks – only touching the ground when they stop in stations. Maglev trains use powerful electromagnets that make them float above the track so that there is no friction due to the ground. The magnets are also used to push the trains forwards at incredibly high speeds.

Because the train is not actually touching the track there is very little vibration as the train moves along. This means that the trains travel smoothly and also make very little noise. This makes them ideal for use in urban areas.

This train in Shanghai uses magnetic levitation – it travels smoothly at over 430 km/h

Maglev trains and tracks are much more expensive to build and operate than conventional trains. This means that there are only a few systems currently operating. However, some countries continue to develop the technology with the goal of making the fastest train possible.

9 Forces and magnets

Big magnets – small particles

Particle physicists use some of the largest and most powerful machines on Earth to investigate the smallest particles. These sub-atomic particles are smashed together at incredibly high speeds in an attempt to produce conditions similar to the beginning of the Universe. Scientists hope to discover much more about how the Universe works from the huge amount of information they gather.

The sub-atomic particles need to be accelerated in perfect circles and giant electromagnets are needed to steer the beams with powerful magnetic fields. The particle beams reach speeds close to the speed of light as they travel.

Large particle accelerators cost billions of dollars to construct and operate and so teams of scientists are funded by governments from around the world.

In this chapter you will find out about how to measure the speed of moving objects and how information about movement can be displayed. You will also discover how magnets, including electromagnets, can be used.

Strong electromagnets are used to steer particle beams in this particle accelerator in Grenoble, France

Key points

- The speed of an object is the distance it travels in a particular time.
- Speed can be measured in metres per second or kilometres per hour.
- Average speed = distance travelled ÷ time taken
- Electronic timing systems improve the accuracy of speed measurements.
- Distance–time graphs can be used to represent the movement of objects.
- Unbalanced forces cause acceleration.
- Magnets produce forces that act on magnetic materials.
- There are only a few magnetic materials, including iron and steel.
- Opposite poles of a magnet attract each other while similar poles repel.
- Magnets are surrounded by magnetic fields.
- Electrical currents produce magnetic fields in electromagnets.
- Electromagnets can be controlled more easily than magnets. They can be turned on or off and their strength can be changed.

9.1 Speed

Learning outcomes

After this topic you should be able to:

- use the speed equation to calculate the speed of a range of objects
- measure the average speed of an object
- investigate the effect of the slope of a ramp on the speed of an object
- make predictions using scientific knowledge and understanding.

In chapter 8, Sound, the speed of sound was calculated to be 340 m/s. This means that sound travels a distance of 340 metres each second. The speed tells us the distance an object will travel in a given time. The greater the speed of an object, the further it will travel during each second.

This jet fighter is travelling at the speed of sound: 340 m/s

Speed calculations

During a journey an object can travel at different speeds. The **average speed** for the journey can be calculated using the total distance travelled and the duration of the journey.

To calculate the average speed of an object the following equation can be used:

$$\text{Average speed} = \frac{\text{distance travelled}}{\text{time taken}}$$

Different sets of units for the speed, the distance and the time are used depending on the situation. The most common units are shown in the table.

Distance unit	Time unit	Speed unit
metres (m)	seconds (s)	metres per second (m/s)
kilometres (km)	hours (h)	kilometres per hour (km/h)

The most common units for measuring speed

Example calculations

Example 1
A runner travels a distance of 400 m in 80 s.

- Average speed = $\frac{\text{distance travelled}}{\text{time taken}} = \frac{400}{80} = 5.0$ m/s

Example 2
A train travels a distance of 40 km in 2 h. The average speed of the train is found using the equation:

- Average speed = $\frac{\text{distance travelled}}{\text{time taken}} = \frac{40 \text{ km}}{2 \text{ h}} = 20$ km/h

9 Forces and magnets

Practical activity — A simple speed investigation

Use a ramp to investigate the speed of a toy car, small ball or marble.

Make a shallow ramp for your object to roll down.

Mark out two lines at the bottom of the ramp. The first line must be at the base of the ramp. The second line must be a measured distance away from the first line. A distance of 50 cm or more is best.

Measure the distance between these lines accurately.

Let your car or ball roll down the ramp and time how long it takes for the car to travel between the lines.

Repeat your timing measurements and find the average time it takes for the object to cover the distance.

Use the speed equation to calculate the average speed of the car or ball.
- Watch the movement of your object carefully. Is it moving at a constant speed between the lines?
- Investigate if the steepness of the slope has an effect on the average speed of your object.
- Predict what you think will happen, explaining your reasoning.
- What effect will your reaction time have on the accuracy of your results?

⚠ **Do not use large objects.**

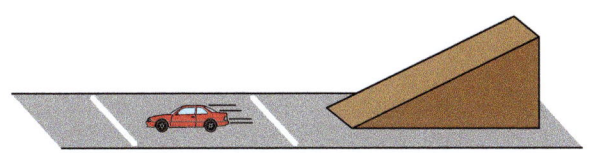

Measuring the speed of an object with a stop clock

Expert tips

Be careful to use the correct units for speed, based on the units in the question.

Key terms

- average speed

Summary questions

1. Complete this table to calculate the speeds of the objects:

Object	Distance travelled	Time taken	Average speed
bus	60 km	2 h	
athlete	400 m	50 s	
passenger plane	2000 km	8.5 h	
racehorse	1800 m	120 s	

2. The table of data shows some of the world records for the 800 m race.

   a) Calculate the average speed for each of the runners.

   b) Plot a graph to show how the average speed has increased from 1972 to 2012.

Runner	Year	Time / s
Dave Wottle	1972	104.3
Alberto Juantorena	1976	103.5
Sebastian Coe	1977	102.4
Wilson Kipketer	1997	101.1
David Rudisha	2012	100.9

9.2 More about the speed equation

Learning outcomes

After this topic you should be able to:

- use the speed equation to calculate the distance travelled by objects
- use the speed equation to calculate the time taken for objects to travel certain distances.

Rearranging the speed equation

Sometimes the speed of an object and the time it was travelling for are known. These two facts would allow the distance the object has travelled to be calculated. Similarly the journey time can be calculated when the speed of an object and the distance the object has travelled are known.

Finding the distance travelled

To find the distance travelled by a moving object the speed equation can be used. This time the equation is rearranged into a slightly different form:

$$\text{distance travelled} = \text{average speed} \times \text{time taken}$$

This car can travel at 340 m/s. In 3 s it would cover a distance of 1020 m

Example 1
A racehorse travels at an average speed of 12 m/s for 30 s. What distance does it cover?

- Distance travelled = average speed × time taken
- Distance travelled = 12 m/s × 30 s = 360 m

Example 2
A tram travels at an average speed of 15 km/h for 30 minutes. What distance does it cover?

- Distance travelled = 15 km/h × 0.5 h = 7.5 km

Finding the time taken

To find the time it takes for an object to cover a distance when travelling at a constant speed, this arrangement of the speed equation can be used:

$$\text{Time taken} = \frac{\text{distance travelled}}{\text{average speed}}$$

9 Forces and magnets

Example 3
What is the time it takes for a motorboat to travel 1000 m if the boat has a steady speed of 20 m/s?

- Time taken $= \dfrac{\text{distance travelled}}{\text{average speed}}$

- Time taken $= \dfrac{1000\,\text{m}}{20\,\text{m/s}} = 50\,\text{s}$

The winner of this horserace will be the horse with the highest average speed for the whole race

Summary questions

1. Complete this table to show the missing values for time taken or speed:

Object	Speed	Distance	Time
rocket	20 000 km/h		30 h
eagle	17 m/s	4000 m	
snail	5 cm/s	100 cm	

2. A car travels 50 km/h for 2 h. Then the car travels at 30 km/h for 1 h and finally it travels at 40 km/h for 2 h.
    a) What is the total distance travelled by the car?
    b) What is the average speed the car travelled for the whole journey?

3. A helicopter flies at 50 m/s. What is this speed in kilometres per hour?

9.3 Measuring speed electronically

Learning outcomes

After this topic you should be able to:

- measure the speed of an object using electronic timing gates
- explain why electronic timers can produce more accurate timing measurements.

Improving our measurement of speed

To measure the speed of an object accurately both the distance travelled and the time taken must be measured accurately.

Our reaction times can be as much as half a second when starting or stopping a stopwatch. This will make the time measurement inaccurate. This timing problem is even greater when attempting to measure small periods of time. To solve the problem, electronic timing systems can be used.

Light gates

A **light gate** is an electronic device that can trigger a timer when an object moves past it. A beam of light passes between a transmitter and a receiver. When an object moves through this beam the time taken to pass through is measured.

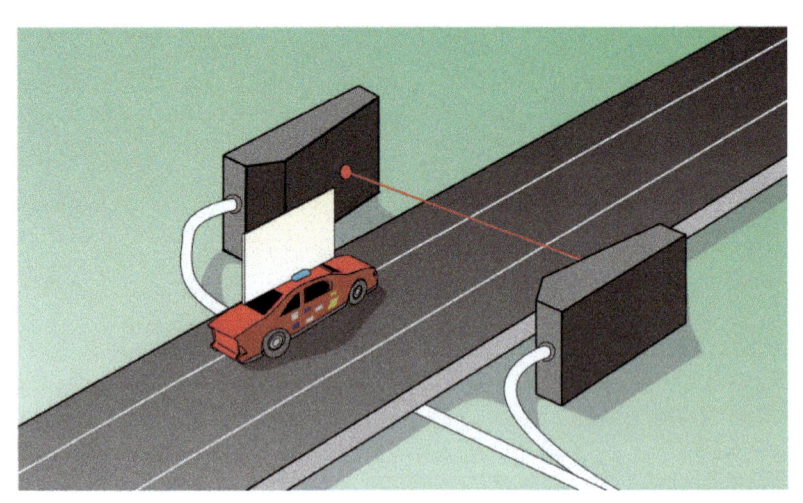

Expert tips

Using electronic timers removes the errors in measurement caused by reaction times.

This improves accuracy.

A toy car passes through the light gate breaking the beam

To measure the speed of a toy car:
- Measure the length of a piece of rectangular card. You must record the length of the card as accurately as possible.
- Attach the card to the top of the car as shown in the diagram. Make sure that the card is vertical.
- Make the car pass through the beam.
- As the card on the car breaks the beam an electronic stopwatch is started.
- When the card has passed completely through the beam the stopwatch is stopped.
- Use the time recorded and the length of the card (the distance travelled) to calculate the speed of the car as it was passing through the light gate.

This method can be adapted to measure the speed of other small objects as long as the object passes through the beam of light.

Example

length of card = 10 cm
time taken = 0.2 s
$$\text{speed} = \frac{10 \text{ cm}}{0.2 \text{ s}}$$
$$= 50 \text{ cm/s}$$

9 Forces and magnets

> **Practical activity** — Measuring speed with a light gate
>
> Use a light gate with an electronic timer or computer attached to measure the speed of an object as it passes through the gate. Use the method described opposite.
>
> Attempt to measure the speed of the object using a simple stopwatch first, using the techniques from topic 9.1.
>
> Repeat the experiment several times to see how much the electronic timing varies.
>
> Compare the results produced by the electronic system to the manual timing method.
>
> ⚠ Make sure that objects cannot roll off desks or tables.

Measuring speed using waves

The speed of an object can also be measured by reflecting ultrasound waves off the object as it moves. An ultrasonic sensor sends out an ultrasonic pulse that reflects off the object and travels back to the transmitter. The transmitter can then calculate the position of the object. More ultrasound pulses are sent and the movement of the object is measured over a period of time. This time and distance information allows the speed of the object to be monitored.

Even more accurate measurements of speed can be made using reflections of radio waves from an object.

> **Expert tips**
>
> Electronic timers improve the accuracy of speed measurements.

> **Key terms**
>
> - light gate

Summary questions

1. What advantages do electronic timing systems have when compared to manual timing systems?

2. A group of students measure the time it takes for a ball to fall to the floor from a height of 1.0 m using a hand-operated stopwatch. They repeat the experiment five times giving the results in the table below.
   a) Why are the drop times different to each other?
   b) What is the average value for the drop time?
   c) Why should the students use the average value in their calculation of average speed?

   | Drop time / s | 0.45 | 0.39 | 0.46 | 0.52 | 0.50 |

3. An ultrasonic transmitter times how long it takes for echoes to arrive from a moving object. The sound waves travel at 340 m/s.
   a) The first pulse sent produces an echo 0.001 s after the signal was sent. How far away was the object?
   b) The second pulse produces an echo 0.003 s after the signal was sent. How far away is the object now?
   c) The two pulses were sent 0.5 s apart from each other. Use the answers from parts **a** and **b** to calculate the speed.

9.4 Showing movement with graphs

Learning outcomes

After this topic you should be able to:
- compare the relative speeds of objects using a distance–time graph
- interpret a distance–time graph to describe the movement of objects in detail.

Distance–time graphs

Distance–time graphs allow us to understand the movement of objects more easily. They show us a picture of how far an object is from a starting point and how this distance changes over a period of time.

When using a distance–time graph:
- The horizontal axis represents time.
- The vertical axis represents the distance from the starting point.

Simple journeys: travelling at a steady speed

The simplest types of journeys are those where the speed of an object remains constant for the whole journey.

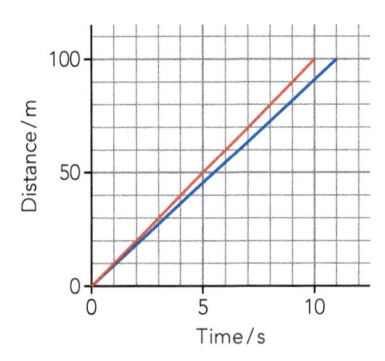

Two sprinters moving at different speeds

This distance–time graph shows the journeys of two different sprinters in a race. The sprinters both run a total distance of 100 m but they are running at slightly different speeds.

The red line represents the movement of the first sprinter. From the graph the speed of the sprinter can be found:

The red sprinter travelled 100 m in 10 s.

His speed was $\frac{100 \text{ m}}{10 \text{ s}} = 10 \text{ m/s}$

The blue line represents the movement of the second sprinter. From the graph:

The blue sprinter travelled 100 m in 11 s.

His speed was $\frac{100 \text{ m}}{11 \text{ s}} = 9.1 \text{ m/s}$

The slope of the red line is steeper than the slope of the blue line.

The steeper the slope of a line on a distance–time graph, the faster the object is moving.

If the slope of the line on the distance–time graph is horizontal (flat), then the object is not moving. Its distance from the start is not changing.

9 Forces and magnets

More complicated journeys: changing speed

During a journey an object may change speed several times. The changes of speed can be seen clearly as changes in the slope of the line on the graph for that journey.

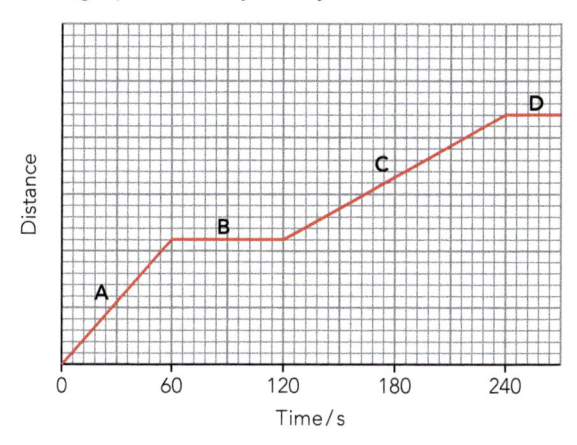

The journey of a subway train

> **Expert tips**
>
> Examine graphs carefully – you can find information about the distance travelled and the time taken for different parts of the journey.

This distance–time graph shows the journey of a subway train between three stations.

Journey part	Description of the movement of the train	How the graph represents this movement
A 0–60 s	During the first 60 s the train is moving at a steady speed.	The line on the graph slopes upwards showing that the distance travelled is increasing.
B 60–120 s	The train stops in a station for 60 s.	From 60 to 120 s the line on the graph is horizontal. The distance is not changing and so the train is not moving.
C 120–240 s	The train moves at a steady speed again. This speed is slower than for part A of the journey.	The slope of the line on the graph is upwards but has a shallower slope than for part A. This means the train is travelling more slowly.
D 240 s	Finally, the train stops at another station.	The line on the graph is horizontal again and so the train must have stopped.

> **Key terms**
>
> - **distance–time graph**

> **Summary questions**
>
> 1. a) What does the horizontal axis on a distance–time graph represent?
>   b) What does the vertical axis represent?
>   c) In what way does the graph represent an object that is moving fastest?
> 2. This is the distance–time graph for a short car journey. Describe the movement of the car in each of the sections A–B, B–C, C–D and D–E.

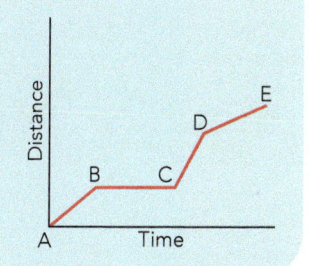

189

9.5 Forces and movement

Learning outcomes

After this topic you should be able to:
- explain what resultant forces can do to an object
- describe the motion of objects as they fall through the air
- investigate the motion of objects as they fall.

Acceleration

In Stage 7 it was shown that forces acting on objects can:
- speed the object up,
- slow the object down or
- change the direction of travel

if the forces are unbalanced.

All three of these changes in movement are called **acceleration**.

Force, mass and acceleration

The greater the resultant force acting on an object, the greater the acceleration will be.

For example: a 1 kg mass will be accelerated more by a resultant force of 50 N than by a force of 10 N.

The acceleration of an object also depends on the mass of the object. The greater the mass of the object, the more difficult it is to accelerate.

For example: a 2 kg mass will accelerate less than a 1 kg mass when the same size resultant force is acting on it.

Falling and forces

When a ball is dropped from a great height the weight of the ball pulls it downwards. At the moment it is dropped, its weight is the only force acting on the ball. So there is an unbalanced force acting on the ball, and it accelerates downwards.

As soon as the ball begins to move downwards, a second force begins to act. This force is air resistance (drag), caused as the ball pushes through the air.

The drag produces an upwards force acting on the ball. The resultant force on the ball is still acting downwards but is decreased as the drag cancels out some of the weight. The ball now accelerates less because the resultant force acting on the ball is getting smaller. The ball still moves downwards but it is speeding up less and less.

As the ball speeds up, the air resistance becomes larger while the weight stays the same size. Eventually the air resistance is the same size as the weight of the ball and the forces are balanced. The balanced forces mean that the ball stops accelerating so it stays at a steady speed. The steady speed of a falling object is called the **terminal velocity**.

The skydiver will accelerate downwards due to the force of gravity until the air resistance matches his weight. When the forces reach the same size the skydiver will have reached terminal velocity

9 Forces and magnets

Practical activity   Do objects accelerate as they fall?

Prediction: If an object is accelerating when it falls, the object's average speed should be greater when it falls from a greater height and travels for a greater time.

Test this prediction by measuring the average speed of an object when it is dropped from increasing heights. You should drop a small object from a gradually increasing height and measure the time it takes to reach the ground.

If you have light gates, these can be used to increase the accuracy of your measurements.

If you are using a stopwatch, you will need to repeat the experiment and calculate the average (mean) times.

Copy the table below and use it to record your results.

Height / cm	Time of fall / s			Average speed / cm

- Is the prediction correct?
- Extend the activity to find out if heavier objects take longer to fall than lighter objects.

⚠️ **Do not drop objects from dangerous heights. Check your safety precautions with your teacher.**

Expert tips

Acceleration means a change in speed or direction. This includes speeding up and slowing down.

Key terms
- acceleration
- terminal velocity

Summary questions

1. a) Calculate the resultant force acting on these three objects.
   b) Which of the objects will accelerate most?

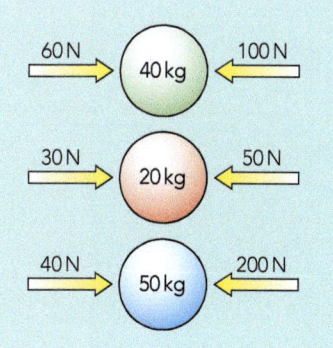

   60 N → 40 kg ← 100 N
   30 N → 20 kg ← 50 N
   40 N → 50 kg ← 200 N

2. Why do parachutists slow down when they open their parachutes? Explain the deceleration using the idea of resultant force.

191

9.6 Magnets

Learning outcomes

After this topic you should be able to:
- describe the effects that magnets have on each other
- carry out an investigation to find out if materials are magnetic or non-magnetic.

Magnetic forces

Bar **magnets** are made from rectangular bars of steel. Steel is a magnetic material. Magnetic materials produce forces that act on other magnetic objects without making direct contact.

One bar magnet will produce a force on another bar magnet when they are placed near each other. This force may be attractive or repulsive depending on the position of the magnets.

North and south poles

The ends of a bar magnet are called the north pole and the south pole. In a simple bar magnet these poles are at opposite ends of the bar. They are often marked with different colours or letters.

Practical activity — Magnetic effects

Test the interaction between magnets. Use simple bar magnets and test how the magnets affect each other when different combinations of poles are placed very closely together.

- Copy and complete the results table for the experiment.

Test	Effect on each other
north pole near north pole	
south pole near south pole	
north pole near south pole	
south pole near north pole	

Magnetic rules

The interactions between magnets can be summarised by these rules:

- Opposite poles attract each other – south poles attract north poles.
- Like poles repel each other – south poles repel south poles. North poles repel north poles.
- The closer the magnets are to each other, the stronger the force is between the magnets.

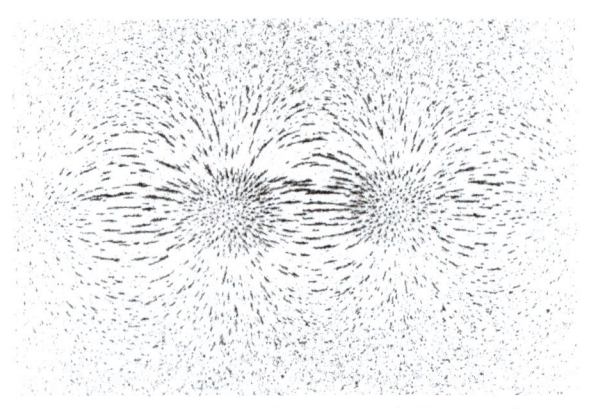

Iron filings are used to map the magnetic field lines and show that opposite poles attract

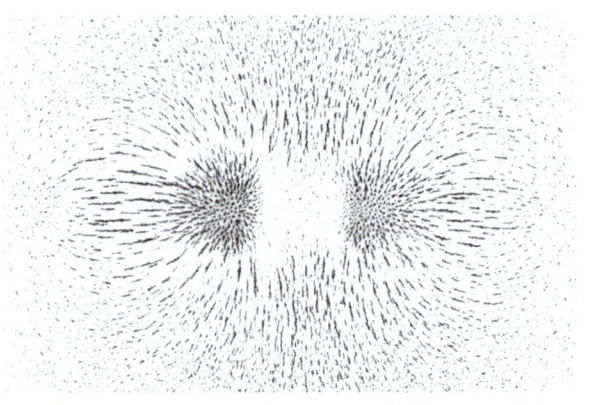

Iron filings are used to map the magnetic field lines and show that like poles repel

9 Forces and magnets

Magnetic materials

Practical activity — Is it magnetic?

Use a bar magnet to test if a range of materials are magnetic. Simply test if the materials are attracted towards a magnet.

Place the materials on a desk and attempt to pick them up using a bar magnet.
- Record the results of the test in a table.
- Which materials were magnetic?
- Are some materials attracted more strongly than others?
- Describe a way to measure the strength of the attraction.

The steel in these clips is a magnetic material. They are attracted to this horseshoe magnet

Only a few materials are magnetic (affected by the forces produced by magnets). Iron, nickel and cobalt are all **magnetic** elements. Some alloys, such as steel, or compounds containing these elements are also magnetic. Magnetic materials can be used to create permanent magnets.

Expert tips

Only a few metals are magnetic – not all of them.

Key terms

- **magnet**
- **magnetic**

Summary questions

1. Copy and complete:
   A south pole of a magnet will be attracted to the _____ pole of another magnet.
   A north pole of a magnet will be repelled by the _____ pole of another magnet.

2. Which two of these metals are magnetic?
   iron, aluminium, gold, steel, lead, calcium

3. A student finds a bar magnet that has nothing to show which end is the north pole and which is the south pole. Explain a method that the student could use to find out which pole is which.

9.7 Making and testing magnets

Learning outcomes

After this topic you should be able to:

- use one magnet to produce another
- test the strength of a permanent magnet.

Magnetite (a form of iron oxide) is a naturally occuring magnetic mineral found in the Earth's crust. Small pieces of magnetite were used thousands of years ago to form the first compasses. These pieces of magnetite were called lodestones. Lodestones are not very strong magnets. We can make much stronger ones from pure iron or steel.

Making magnets

Magnets can be made using other magnets or by using large electric currents. The simplest way to produce a new magnet is to move a strong magnet along a piece of iron or steel in one direction as shown in the diagram. After many strokes the new piece of metal becomes **magnetised**.

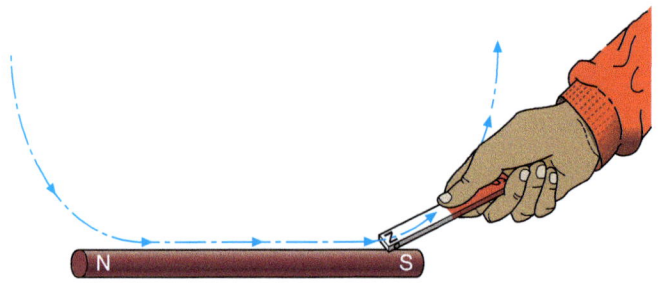

One magnet can be used to make another

Magnetite is a naturally occuring magnetic material

Practical activity — Making a magnet

Use the technique described above to magnetise a large iron nail.

Test the nail to show that it has become a magnet.

- Describe a way that you can tell which end of your nail has become the north pole.
- Is the magnet you have made stronger than the original magnet? Use the second practical activity to find out.

Testing magnets

The stronger a magnet is the greater the force it will be able to produce on a magnetic material or another magnet. This means that stronger magnets can lift larger objects and affect them from a greater distance.

9 Forces and magnets

Practical activity — Testing the strength of a magnet

A simple way to test the strength of a magnet is to pick up steel paper clips with it. The more clips it can hold the stronger the magnet is. Test a range of magnets to find out which is the strongest.

Connect twenty steel paper clips into a chain and lay the chain flat on a desk.

Use the magnet to slowly lift one end of the chain.

Count how many paperclips are lifted off the desk before the paperclips fall off the magnet.

Repeat the test five times and calculate the average number of paperclips lifted by each magnet.

If a magnet can lift all of the chain then you may need to add more paperclips to the end.

- Evaluate the precision and reliability (repeatability) of your measurements.
- Describe a way that the precision of this experiment can be improved. If you have time, try your ideas out.

Magnets can be shaped into U or horseshoe shapes to bring the poles closer together. This makes the magnet much stronger

Expert tips

Don't drop magnets. They become weaker or may even lose all of their magnetism.

Key terms

- **magnetised**

Summary questions

1. Can the poles of a magnet be forced to change from north to south? Design an experiment to try to convert the poles of the magnet you created in the first practical activity. Describe a way to test whether the magnet is becoming weaker or changing.

2. A student has designed a way of measuring the strength of a magnet as shown in the diagram.
Explain what will happen when a magnet is placed above the iron block. Explain why this could be used to compare the strength of different magnets.

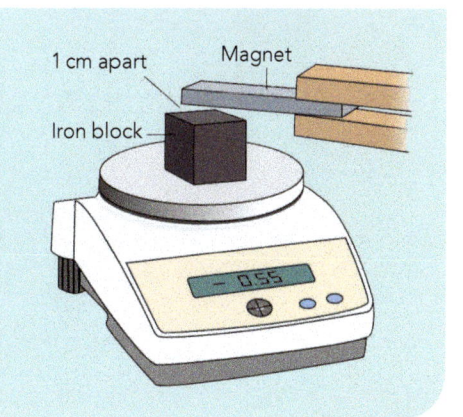

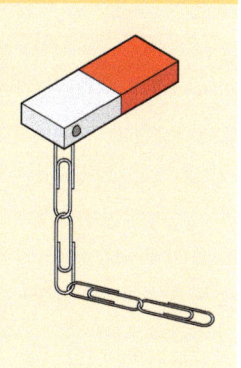

9.8 Magnetic fields

Learning outcomes

After this topic you should be able to:
- find the shape of a magnetic field using iron filings
- describe the shape of the Earth's magnetic field
- explain how compasses work.

Magnets are surrounded by **magnetic fields**. These fields are regions in which magnetic forces act and so magnetic materials placed inside the field will be affected by it.

The shape of a magnetic field

Magnetic fields are invisible but we can detect their shapes by looking at how the fields affect magnetic materials.

Practical activity	Using iron filings to find the shape of a magnetic field

You can find the shape of a magnetic field by sprinkling iron filings near a magnet. The iron filings will line up with the field and show its shape.

Place a bar magnet underneath a large sheet of paper.

You should place books the same thickness as the magnet on either side so that the paper lies flat.

Sprinkle iron filings from a few centimetres above the paper so that the filings fall on top of the magnet.

The iron filings will align themselves to the magnetic field from the magnet.

- Sketch the shape of the magnetic field and compare it to the shape shown below.
- Repeat the experiment using two bar magnets placed so that their opposite poles are close to each other. Sketch the shape of the field.
- Repeat the experiment again with like poles near to each other and observe the shape of the magnetic field.

⚠️ **Iron filings can damage your eyes – wear eye protection.**

Drawing magnetic fields

The magnetic field around a bar magnet can be drawn as a set of **magnetic field lines** as shown in the diagram opposite. These lines show the direction of the force that would act on a north pole placed inside the magnetic field.

The force would be away from the north pole of the bar magnet. That is why we always draw the magnetic field lines coming out from the north pole of the magnet.

We draw the magnetic field lines going in to the south pole.

When magnets are placed close to each other their magnetic fields interact and this will change the shape of the magnetic field.

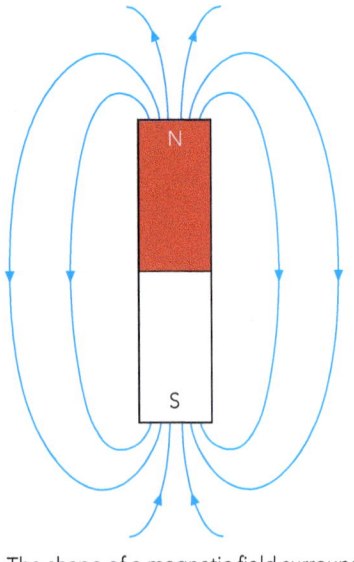

The shape of a magnetic field surrounding a bar magnet

9 Forces and magnets

The Earth's magnetic field

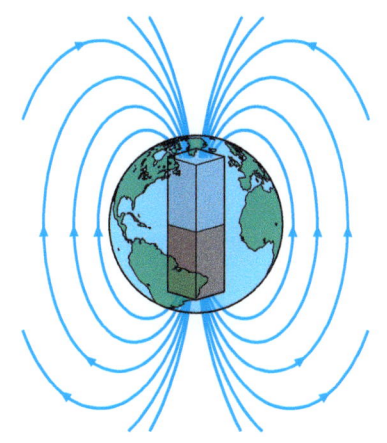

A magnetic field surrounds the Earth

The north pole of a compass will always point in the direction of the magnetic field

The Earth is surrounded by a magnetic field. This field is similar in shape to the field produced by a bar magnet. Magnets inside the Earth's magnetic field will be affected by it and be attracted or repelled by the magnetic poles. A compass uses the effect of the Earth's magnetic field to show direction:

- The Earth's geographic north pole is actually a magnetic south pole. The north magnetic pole of a compass will point towards the Earth's geographic north pole.
- The Earth's geographic south pole is a magnetic north pole. The south magnetic pole of a compass will point towards it.

The Earth's magnetic poles are not in exactly the same position as the geographic north and south poles. The Earth's magnetic poles are also slowly moving due to changes in the Earth's core. (Remember from Stage 7 that the Earth's core is made from the magnetic elements iron and nickel.)

A compass can also be used to show the shape of a magnetic field produced by a magnet. As the compass is moved through the magnetic field, the north pole will point in the direction of the field lines.

Expert tips

The magnetic field lines come out from the north pole of a magnet and go in to the south pole.

Key terms

- **magnetic field**
- **magnetic field line**

Summary questions

1. Copy and complete:
   All magnets are surrounded by a _____.
   This is a region where other _____ materials will feel a force acting.
   A compass is affected by the magnetic field produced by the _____. The north seeking pole will point towards the _____.

2. Which end of this magnet shown on the right is a north pole?
   Explain your answer.

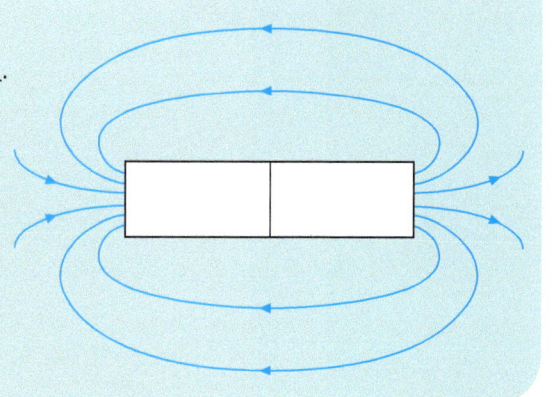

197

9.9 Electromagnets

Learning outcomes

After this topic you should be able to:

- describe the construction of an electromagnet
- investigate the factors that affect the strength of an electromagnet
- discuss explanations for results using scientific knowledge and understanding and communicate these clearly to others.

Electric currents and magnetic fields

Magnetic fields are also produced by electric currents in a wire. This effect can be used to make **electromagnets**. Unlike permanent magnets, electromagnets can be turned on and off by turning the electric current on and off.

The strength of an electromagnet can be increased by:

- Increasing the size of the electric current. The larger the current the stronger the magnet.
- Looping the wire into a coil. The more loops of wire the stronger the magnetic field.
- Using an iron core. An iron core concentrates the magnetic field so that it is stronger at the end of the core.

If we use a large current, many turns of wire and an iron core, very strong magnets can be produced.

A simple electromagnet

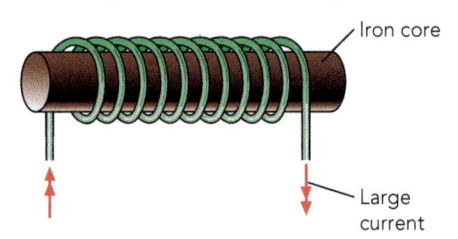

Constructing an electromagnet

This diagram shows a simple electromagnet. The current in the coil produces a strong magnetic field coming from the iron core. The shape of the magnetic field is the same as the shape of the field around a bar magnet. One end of the core will be a north pole and the other end will be a south pole.

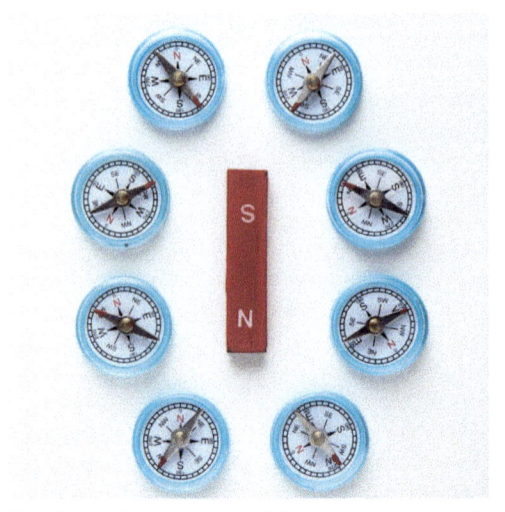

The shape of the magnetic field around a magnet is shown by these compasses

9 Forces and magnets

Practical activity — Investigating the strength of electromagnets

Make a simple electromagnet by wrapping turns of insulated wire around an iron bar. The ends of the wire can be connected to a battery pack or low voltage power supply. Test that the electromagnet works by picking up a small magnetic object with it.

Investigate if changing the number of turns of wire in the coil affects the strength of the electromagnet.

Use a method similar to the one you used in topic 9.7 or design your own test.

- Discuss the relationship between the number of turns of wire and the strength of the electromagnet.
- Does doubling the number of turns double the strength of the magnet?

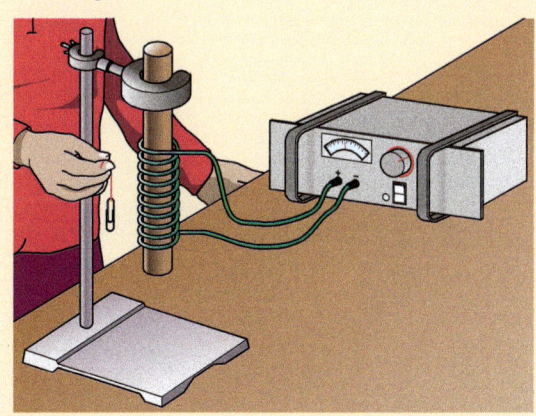

Testing an electromagnet

⚠ **The wire can become hot; only use small electric currents.**

Key terms

- electromagnet

Summary questions

1. Complete this table to show the difference between a weak and a strong electromagnet. Select the correct word from the options in each box.

	Size of electric current	Number of turns of wire	Iron core
Strong electromagnet	large/small	many/few	yes/no
Weak electromagnet	large/small	many/few	yes/no

2. What advantages and disadvantages do electromagnets have when compared to permanent magnets?

9.10 Electromagnetic devices

Learning outcomes

After this topic you should be able to:
- describe how an electric bell operates
- describe how an electric motor operates.

Some of the most useful energy transformations are the transformations from electrical energy to other forms of energy. Electromagnets allow us to perform these transformations in a number of ways. Using electromagnets we can transform electrical energy into sound or kinetic energy.

Electric bells

An **electric bell** uses the forces produced by an electromagnet to produce movement and sound.

Practical activity — Operating an electric bell

Observe how an electric bell operates using electromagnets.

Press the button to switch on the circuit and ring the bell.

Watch the arm carefully as it moves backwards and forwards.

- What happens when the size of the electric current provided to the bell is increased?

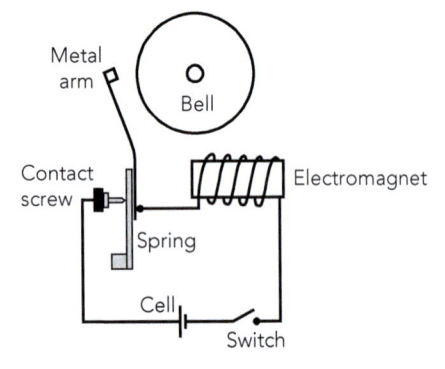

Electrical bell circuit diagram

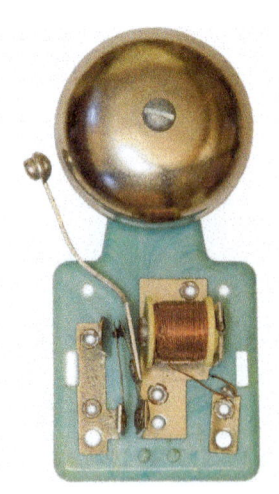

The arm on an electric bell forms part of an 'electrical circuit'

The electric bell uses a metal arm to strike a bell repeatedly.
- When there is no current the arm is held away from the bell by a spring. The circuit is connected and current flows.
- When the current flows, the arm is pulled towards the electromagnet and towards the bell and produces a sound.
- When the arm touches the bell the circuit is broken – the electromagnet switches off.
- The arm is pulled away from the bell by the spring.
- The circuit is reconnected and so the electromagnet turns back on.
- This process repeats and the bell continues to ring until it is turned off at the switch.

9 Forces and magnets

Spinning electric motors

A motor uses permanent magnets and electromagnets to transform electricity into movement

Electric motors are devices that transform electrical energy into movement energy. This is how they operate:
- Permanent magnets are used to produce a magnetic field.
- A coil of wire is placed inside this field and a current is switched on.
- The current in the coil makes the coil become a magnet.
- The two magnetic fields interact and produce forces.
- The magnetic coil is repelled by the permanent magnets and begins to rotate.

Electric motors are used in a large number of devices from the starter motors in cars to tiny vibrating motors in mobile phones.

Practical activity — Electric motors

Observe how a model electric motor operates.
- What happens when the size of the electric current provided to the motor is increased?

Expert tips

Nearly every time electrical energy is transformed into movement or sound electromagnets are used.

Key terms

- electric bell
- electric motor

Summary questions

1 Draw a flowchart to show the sequence of events that takes place as an electric bell operates.
2 Plan an investigation into the factors that affect the lifting power of a simple electrical motor. You must list the possible factors and design a method to show how changing them affects the lifting power of the motor.

Chapter 9 — End of chapter questions

1 Calculate the average speeds of the following objects:
   a A car that travels 100 km in 4 hours. [1]
   b A motorcycle that travels 500 m in 20 seconds. [1]
   c A helicopter that travels 30 km in 30 minutes. [1]

2 Which of these are descriptions of acceleration?
   A A car speeding up
   B A motorcycle travelling at a steady speed
   C A motorboat slowing down
   D An ice skater changing direction [3]

3 a Which of these objects travels the greatest distance?
     A A zebra running at 12 m/s for 30 s
     B A lion running at 8 m/s for 40 s [1]
   b Which of these takes the longest time to complete their journey?
     A A truck driving 40 km with an average speed of 50 km/h
     B A man walking a distance of 4000 m at an average speed of 2 m/s. [1]

4 This distance–time graph shows the movement of three aircraft. The aircraft stop when they have completed their separate journeys.

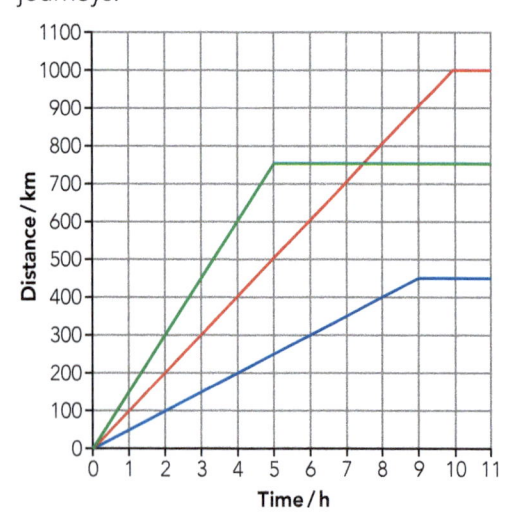

   a Which of the aircraft travels the greatest distance? [1]
   b Which of the aircraft travels fastest during its journey? [2]

5 Draw a distance–time graph to represent this journey:
   A motorcycle stationary at a set of traffic lights.
   When the lights change the motorcycle moves off at a steady speed of 5 m/s.
   After 30 s the motorcycle stops at another set of traffic lights.
   The lights change after 15 s and the motorcycle moves off at a steady speed of 8 m/s.
   The motorcycle reaches its destination 20 s later. [4]

6 a What factors affect the size of the acceleration on an object? [2]
   b Why do falling objects reach a terminal velocity if they fall from a great height? [1]

7 Complete this description about the behaviour of magnets:
   a The _____ pole of a magnet will repel the north pole of another magnet. [1]
   b The _____ pole of a magnet will attract the south pole of another magnet. [1]
   c The south pole of a magnet will attract the _____ pole of another magnet. [1]

8 Which of these energy transformations represents the energy changes that take place in:
   a a motor
   b a loudspeaker
   c an electric bell. [3]

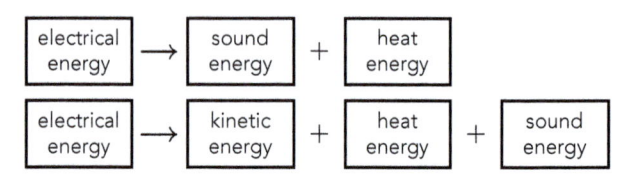

   electrical energy → sound energy + heat energy

   electrical energy → kinetic energy + heat energy + sound energy

202

9 Forces and magnets

9 A student places six compasses around a bar magnet as shown in the diagram. Copy and complete the diagram by showing the direction each compass needle points. The first one has been drawn in for you. [2]

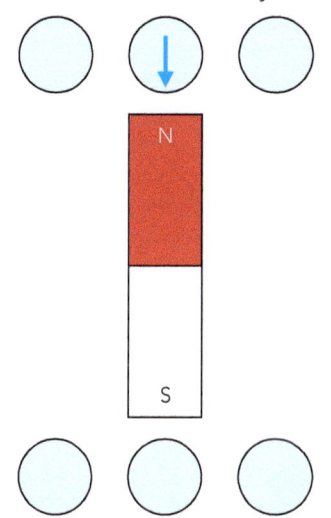

10 A student predicted that both poles of a magnet must be the same strength. The student carried out an investigation to test this prediction. They measured the weight each pole could support as shown in the diagram. The results are in the table.

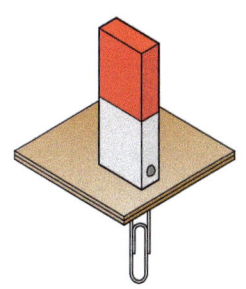

   a Identify and remove the two anomalous results. [2]
   b Calculate the average mass each of the poles could support (excluding the anomalous results). [2]
   c Are both poles the same strength? [1]

Pole	Mass supported / g					Average
	Test 1	Test 2	Test 3	Test 4	Test 5	
north	10	17	17	18	20	
south	17	19	15	19	25	

11 Which of these will increase the strength of an electromagnet?
   A Increasing the current in the electromagnet
   B Reversing the direction of the current
   C Replacing the iron core with an aluminium core
   D Increasing the number of turns of wire in the magnet
   E Switching the electromagnet on and off rapidly [2]

12 A group of students was investigating which factor would have the greatest effect on increasing the strength of an electromagnet. They measured the strength of the electromagnet by testing how large a mass it could lift. They investigated two different factors: increasing the current and increasing the number of loops of wire. They recorded their results in three tables, as shown below.

Current 0.5 A				
Number of loops of wire	10	15	20	25
Mass lifted / g	1.1	1.3	1.5	1.7

Current 1.0 A				
Number of loops of wire	10	15	20	25
Mass lifted / g	2.2	2.6	3.0	3.4

Current 1.5 A				
Number of loops of wire	10	15	20	25
Mass lifted / g	3.3	3.9	4.5	5.1

   a Why should the students use an iron core during all of the experiments? [1]
   b Which of these conclusions is correct?
      A Doubling the current doubled the strength of the electromagnet.
      B Doubling the number of loops of wire doubled the strength of the electromagnet. [1]

Glossary

A

Absorb To take in the energy of light without allowing it to pass through. Objects warm up when they absorb light energy.

Acceleration A change in speed or direction of movement. Acceleration is caused by resultant forces.

Additive colour Changes to the colour of light when different colours of light are mixed.

Aerobic respiration The process by which cells break down glucose to release energy using oxygen. Carbon dioxide and water are produced as waste products.

Alimentary canal Also known as the digestive system.

Amino acids The small molecules which join together to form proteins.

Amniotic fluid The fluid which surrounds and cushions the developing ovum through pregnancy.

Amplitude A measure of the amount of energy carried by a wave. The greater the amplitude the louder the sound.

Angle of incidence The angle between the incident ray of light and the normal.

Angle of reflection The angle between a reflected ray of light and the normal.

Angle of refraction The angle between a refracted ray and the normal.

Arteries Blood vessels that carry blood away from the heart and have a pulse.

Atheroma A deposit of fat on the wall of an artery.

Atom The smallest part of a chemical element.

Average speed Average speed = distance travelled ÷ time taken.

B

Benedict's test A test for sugars. Blue Benedict's solution will change to green then yellow, orange and red when sugar is present.

C

Caffeine The drug contained in coffee.

Calorimeter Apparatus for measuring the energy content of food.

Capillaries Very tiny thin-walled blood vessels that link the arteries and capillaries which are where substances are exchanged between the blood and the cells.

Carbohydrase An enzyme which speeds up the breakdown of complex carbohydrates to simple sugars.

Carbohydrate Type of food which is full of energy easily used by the body, e.g. starch, sugars, bread, rice.

Carbonates Compounds that react with dilute acids, giving off carbon dioxide gas.

Catalyst A substance which speeds up chemical reactions but is not used up in the process.

Cathode ray oscilloscope (CRO) A device that can represent waves on a screen for analysis.

Cervix The narrow opening from the uterus to the vagina.

Chemical formula An abbreviation used to show how many of each type of atom there are in a molecule, e.g. H_2O.

Chlorides Salts made from hydrochloric acid (or by reacting an element with chlorine gas).

Chlorophyll The green colour found in chloroplasts in the leaves of plants which traps energy from the Sun.

Chloroplasts Small green structures found in some plant cells which contain the green colour chlorophyll. This is where photosynthesis takes place.

Cilia Small hair-like parts of cells. In the respiratory system they move dirt away from the lungs.

Cochlea A curled tube that detects sounds and produces electrical signals that are sent to the brain.

Colour filters Sheets of glass or plastic that transmit only certain colours of light, other colours are absorbed.

Combustion The reaction in which substances burn by reacting with air or oxygen gas.

Compound A substance made up of two or more different types of atom.

Contraceptive pill Drugs which stop a woman ovulating and control her fertility.

Cornea The transparent protective layer at the front of an eye.

Coronary arteries The arteries that supply the heart muscle with oxygenated blood.

Corrosion The 'eating away' of a material by a chemical reaction, e.g. often with the oxygen, water or acids in the environment.

Cretinism Mental retardation and slow growth caused by a lack of iodine in the diet.

D

Decibel (dB) A measure of the loudness of a sound.

Decompose The breaking down of a chemical compound.

Deficiency diseases Diseases which result from the lack of certain vitamins or minerals in the diet, e.g. scurvy.

Deoxygenated blood Blood which has been around the body and is low in oxygen but high in carbon dioxide.

Diffusion The automatic spreading out of substances caused by the random motion of the particles in gases and liquids.

Digestion The process by which large food molecules are broken down into smaller molecules which can be taken in and used by the body.

Dispersion The separating out of the colours in white light during refraction.

Distance–time graph A graph showing how the position of an object changes over time.

E

Eardrum A layer of tissue that separates the outer and inner parts of the ear.

Glossary

Echo The reflection of sound waves.
Egestion The removal of undigested material from the gut through the anus.
Ejaculation The release of semen from the penis during sexual excitement.
Electric bell A device that transforms electrical current into sound energy using electromagnets.
Electric motor A device that transforms electrical energy into kinetic energy using electromagnets.
Electrolysis The breaking down of a chemical compound by electricity.
Electromagnet A magnet that produces a magnetic field only when there is an electric current in it.
Electroplating Protecting the surface of a metal by coating it with a thin layer of another metal applied by electrolysis.
Element A substance made up of only one type of atom. Alternatively, a substance that cannot be broken down into simpler substances.
Embryo The very early stages of development after the egg is fertilised until about 12 weeks.
Enzyme A biological catalyst which speeds up reactions in the cells.
Essential amino acids Amino acids which you have to eat as part of your diet as your body cannot make them.
Exhale To breathe out.

F

Faeces The mixture of undigested material. Dead skin cells and micro-organisms passed out to the end of the digestive system.
Fat Food very high in energy, e.g. butter, cream.
Fertilisation The joining of the male and female gametes.
Fertiliser Substance spread on the soil to increase the mineral content.
Fertility drugs Drugs which can help some infertile women to have children.
Fetus The developing baby in the uterus.
Fibre An indigestible material in plants which we cannot digest which helps to keep food moving through the gut.
Flame test The heating of an unknown compound in a Bunsen flame in order to identify the metal present in the compound by its characteristic coloured flame.
Frequency The number of vibrations each second.

G

Galvanising Protecting iron from rusting by coating with a thin layer of zinc.
Gamete The special sex cells which join during sexual reproduction.
Gas A substance that has, on average, large spaces between its fast-moving particles. A gas has a very low density, takes the shape of its container and can flow.
Gas exchange The movement of oxygen from the air in the lungs to the blood and of carbon dioxide from the blood to the air in the lungs.
Gas pressure The force per unit area exerted by a gas.
General equation A summary word equation that applies to a series of reactions that have reactants and products that are similar.
Growth chart Graph which shows the average expected growth of children over time.

H

Hertz (Hz) The unit of frequency. One hertz is one vibration per second.
HIV/AIDS An STD caused by the human immunodeficiency virus which cannot be cured although it can be treated.
Hormones Chemicals which carry messages around the body from the cells in one area to the cells in another area, e.g. sex hormones which control puberty and the menstrual cycle.
Hydroxides Basic compounds that contain the OH grouping.

I

Image The 'picture' of an object you can see in a mirror or through a lens, the picture forms from the rays of light coming from an object.
Implantation When a fertilised egg settles into the built-up lining of the uterus.
Inhale To breathe in.
Iodine test A test for starches. Yellow iodine solution changes to blue-black in the presence of starch.
Iris The coloured part of the front of the eye.

K

Kilojoule A unit of energy.

L

Law of reflection A rule about how a light ray reflects from any surface. The angle of reflection is always the same size as the angle of incidence.
Lens The part of the eye that focuses rays of light using refraction. It can change thickness to change focus.
Light gate An electronic timing system to improve the accuracy of speed measurements.
Light source An object that releases visible light. These are usually very hot objects or ones in which chemical reactions are taking place.
Lipase An enzyme which speeds up the breakdown of lipids to fatty acids and glycerol.
Lipids The scientific name for fats.
Liquid A substance that can flow, takes the shape of its container and is made up of randomly moving particles that are very close together.

Glossary

M

Magnet An object which produces forces that act on other magnetic objects without making direct contact.

Magnetic A material that experiences a force when placed near a magnet.

Magnetic field The region of space around a magnet in which a magnetic material will experience a force.

Magnetic field line A line which shows the shape of a magnetic field and direction of the force acting on a north magnetic pole in that field.

Magnetised Turned into a magnet.

Magnification The apparent increase in size of an object when it is viewed through a lens.

Menstrual cycle The monthly changes which result in the release of a fertile egg in the reproductive organs of human females.

Metalloid An element that has some metallic properties and some non-metallic properties.

Mineral Substance needed in the diet in very small amounts for health, e.g. iron.

Mineral ions Chemicals found in the soil and absorbed by the roots of plants, e.g. nitrates, phosphates.

Mitochondria The organelles in cells where aerobic respiration takes place.

Molecule A group of two or more atoms bonded together.

N

Neutralisation The reaction between an acid and base to produce a salt plus water.

Nicotine The addictive chemical in cigarette smoke.

Normal A line at right angles to a surface. Angles of reflection and refraction are measured between the normal and the ray.

O

Obesity A state of being so overweight that your health is at risk.

Optic nerve A bundle of nerves that carries signals from the eye to the brain.

Ossicles Small bones inside the ear that transmit vibrations.

Ova See *Ovum*.

Ovary The female reproductive organ which contains eggs.

Oviduct The tube which leads from the ovary to the uterus.

Ovulation The release of an egg from the ovary approximately every 28 days.

Ovum The female gamete in animals.

Oxidation The reaction of a substance with oxygen resulting in the formation of oxides.

Oxides Compounds made when elements burn in air or oxygen gas.

Oxygenated blood Blood which has passed through the lungs and is rich in oxygen but low in carbon dioxide.

P

Particle theory The theory that all matter is made up of particles, which describes the arrangement and motion (movement) of these particles.

Penis The male organ that becomes erect and places the sperm inside the body of the female.

Periodic Table A table showing all the chemical elements, lined up in groups of similar elements.

Peristalsis The waves of muscular squeezing which move food through the digestive system.

Pharmaceutical drugs Drugs which treat or cure illnesses.

Phloem The food transport tissue of plants made of living cells. Transports down and all around from the leaves.

Photosynthesis The process by which plants make food using carbon dioxide, water and energy from the Sun. Oxygen is formed as a waste product.

Pinhole camera A very simple camera that does not use a lens.

Placenta The special organ which contains blood from both the mother and the fetus and which supplies the growing foetus with what it needs.

Plasma Liquid that carries all blood cells.

Platelet Small piece of cell that is carried in the blood and makes clots and scabs.

Precipitation The reaction in which an insoluble solid is formed when two solutions are mixed and react together.

Pregnant Expecting a baby.

Products The substances formed when a chemical reaction takes place.

Protease An enzyme which speeds up the breakdown of proteins to amino acids.

Protein Food used in the body for growth and repair, e.g. meat, milk, eggs.

Puberty The stage of development when the body becomes sexually mature.

Pupil The hole in the iris that allows light to pass through. It can change diameter to allow more or less light through.

R

Reactants The substances we start with before a chemical reaction takes place.

Red blood cell Carries oxygen around the body.

Reflect When a ray of light 'bounces off' an object, continuing in a different direction.

Refraction When light changes direction as it moves from one transparent material to another.

Glossary

Respiratory system Your lungs and the tubes connecting them to your nose and mouth. The system used for gas exchange.
Retina The back surface of the eye. It detects light and sends electrical signals to the brain.
Root hair A microscopic hair which grows out from the roots and greatly increases the surface area for absorbing water.
Root hair cells The cells from which root hairs grow.
Rusting The reaction of iron with oxygen, from the air, and water to form a flaky orange solid known as rust.

S

Sacrificial protection Where iron is prevented from rusting by contact with a more reactive metal, such as zinc or magnesium.
Saliva The liquid made in the mouth which makes food easier to swallow and starts to digest it.
Salt A compound formed when all or some of the hydrogen in an acid is replaced by a metal, e.g. magnesium sulfate.
Saturated solution A solution in which no more solid (solute) will dissolve.
Scrotum The bag of skin that holds the testes outside the body.
Section A thin slice of plant or animal tissue prepared for viewing under a microscope.
Semen Liquid that contains sperm.
Semi-metal An element that has some metallic properties and some non-metallic properties.
Sexual reproduction The form of reproduction which involves two parents and special sex cells or gametes.
Sexually transmitted diseases (STDs) Infectious diseases which are passed on through sexual contact.
Solid A substance that has a fixed shape and volume, made up of regularly arranged, touching particles that vibrate in fixed positions.
Sound waves Energy passed from particle to particle as they vibrate.
Spectrum A continuous range of colours produced when white light is dispersed.
Sperm The male gamete in animals.
Sperm duct The tube that carries sperm from the testes to the penis.
Stainless steel An alloy of steel that does not rust; made by alloying iron with nickel and chromium.
Stent Metal mesh inserted into an artery to hold it open and allow blood to flow.
Stomata Small holes in the surfaces of leaves which allow carbon dioxide, oxygen and water vapour to move in and out of the leaf.
Subtractive colour Changes to the colour of an object because of absorption of colours by a surface.
Sulfates Salts made from sulfuric acid.

T

Tar One of the main cancer-causing chemicals in cigarette smoke.
Tarnished Describes a metal surface that has lost its shiny appearance due to reactions with substances in the air.
Terminal velocity The steady speed that a falling object may reach.
Testes (singular **testis**) The male sexual organ that makes the sperm and the male sex hormone testosterone.
Transmit To allow light energy to pass through. Glass transmits light energy.

U

Ultrasound Sound with a frequency above the limit of human hearing. Over 20 000 Hz.
Umbilical cord This carries blood between the fetus and the placenta.
Uterus The female reproductive organ where the baby develops.

V

Vagina The tube which leaves from the uterus to the outside world.
Vascular bundles The bundles found in the roots and stems of plants containing the xylem and the phloem.
Veins Blood vessels that carry blood back to the heart and do not have a pulse.
Vibrations Repeated movements back and forth.
Villi Finger-like projections on the lining of the small intestine which increase the surface area for the absorption of digested food.
Vitamin Substance needed in the diet in very small amounts for health, e.g. vitamin C.

W

White blood cell Defends the body against disease.

X

Xylem The water and mineral transport system of plants made of dead cells. Transports up from the roots.

Index

Note: Key (glossary) terms are in **bold** type.

A

Absorb, light 140–141, 150
Absorption
    Digestion 19, 22–23
    plants 28–29
Acceleration, forces and mass 190–191
Addictive behaviour 69
Additive colour 151
Adolescence 64–65
Aerobic respiration 44–45
Alcohol 69
    Fetus 61, 66
Alimentary canal 18–19
Alkali metals 102
Alveoli 42
Amino acids 8
Amniotic fluid 60
Amplitude 164–165, 166
Angle of incidence 142–143
Angle of reflection 142–143
Angle of refraction 144–145
Arteries 26–27, 32–35, 39
Atheroma 9, 39
Atoms 74–75, 82–83
Average speed 182–185

B

Balanced diets 2–5
    see also Cooking
Behaviour, disease 71
Behaviour-affecting drugs 68–69
Benedict's test 6
Birth 61
Blood 36–37
Blood circulation 26, 32–39
Blood pressure 35
Blood vessels 26–27, 32–35
Breathing 40–43

C

Caffeine 68–69
Calorimeters 5
Cameras 154–155
Capillaries 32–33
Carbohydrases 21
Carbohydrates 4, 6–7
Carbon 103
    Combustion 124
Carbon dioxide 44
    Gas exchange 42
    making 128–129

Photosynthesis 12–13, 16
Carbonates 128–129
Catalysts 20
Cathode ray oscilloscope (CRO) 166–167
Cervix 53
Chemical formulae 75, 84–85
Chemical symbols 84–85
Chlorides 120–121
Chlorophyll 15
Chloroplasts 12–13
Cilia 40, 47
Circulation, blood 26, 32–39
Cochlea 172
Colour 148–151
    Additive colour 151
    reflection 148
    Subtractive colour 149
Colour filters 150–151
Combustion 119, 124–125
Compounds 74–75, 88–93
    Elements 88–93, 104–105
    vs mixtures and **Elements** 90–93
Contraceptive pill 66
Cooking 118–119
    see also Balanced diets
Cornea 152
Coronary arteries 34–35, 39
Corrosion 108–115
Cretinism 70

D

Decibel (dB) 174–175
Decompose 104–105
Deficiency diseases 10
Deoxygenated blood 34–35
Diffusion 75, 80–81
Digestion 4, 18–23
    absorption 22–23
    digestive system 18–19
    Enzymes 20–21
    waste 23
Disease 50–51
    behaviour 71
    growth/development 70–71
    impact 70–71
    reproduction 70
Dispersion 146–147
Distance–time graphs 188–189
Drugs
    behaviour-affecting 68–69
    growth 66–67
    Pharmaceutical drugs 66–67
    reproduction 66–67

E

Eardrum 172
Ears 172–173, 174, 175
Echo 162
    echo location 176–177
    sound speed measuring 169
Egestion 23
Ejaculation 58
Electric bells 200
Electric motors 201
Electrolysis 104–105
Electromagnetic waves 137
Electromagnets 198–201
    devices 200–201
    electric bells 200
    electric currents 198–199
    electric motors 201
    Magnetic fields 198–199
    particle accelerators 180–181
Electroplating 112
Elements 97–99
    Compounds 88–93, 104–105
    vs **Compounds** and mixtures 90–93
    defining 82–83
    exceptional 102–103
    historical ideas 74–75
    Periodic Table 86–87
Embryo 59
Energy
    Aerobic respiration 44–45
    Carbohydrates 6–7
    Fats 7, 8
    food 4–5
    Photosynthesis 12–13, 16
Enzymes 20–21
Essential amino acids 8
Exhale 40
Eye structure 152

F

Faeces 23
Fats 4, 8–9
Female reproductive system 52–55
Fertilisation 56, 58–59
Fertiliser 29
Fertility 54–55
Fertility drugs 66
Fetus 52, 60–61, 66–67
Fibre 4, 11
Flame tests 119, 130–131
Forces, mass and **Acceleration** 190–191
Frequency 164–165, 166

Index

G
Galvanising 112–113
Gametes 52
Gas 76–77
   Diffusion 80–81
Gas exchange 42–43
Gas pressure 75, 78–79
General equation 107, 120
Goitre 2
Graphs, **Distance–time graphs** 188–189
Growth 62–63
   disease 70–71
   drugs 66–67
Growth charts 62–63

H
Heart
   fitness and problems 38–39
   historical ideas 26
   structure and circulation 32–35
Hertz (Hz) 164–165
HIV/AIDS 69, 70, 71
Hormones 53, 54
Hydrogen 96, 106–107
Hydroxides 126–127

I
Illusions 153
Images
   cameras 154–155
   light 142–143
Implantation 59
Inhale 40
Iodine 2
Iodine test 6, 14
Iris 152

K
Kilojoules 4

L
Law of reflection 142–143
Lens 152, 154–157
   Magnification 156–157
Light 136–159
   behaviour 140–141
   Dispersion 146–147
   historical ideas 136–137
   producing/detecting 138–139
   reflection 140, 142–143
   Refraction 144–145
   shadows 140–141
   Spectrum 146–147
Light gate 186–187
Light sources 138–139

Lipases 21
Lipids (fats) 4, 8–9
Liquids 76–77
   Diffusion 80–81
   sound in 170–171

M
Maglev (magnetically levitating) trains 180
Magnetic 192–193
Magnetic field line 196–197
Magnetic fields 196–199
Magnetic storage 180
Magnetised 194
Magnets 180–181, 192–201
   making 194
   testing 194–195
Magnification 156–157
Male reproductive system 56–57
Mass, forces and **Acceleration** 190
Menstrual cycle 54–55
Mercury 103
Metal **Hydroxides** 126–127
Metalloids 98–99
Metals
   alkali metals 102
   Flame tests 130–131
   reactions with water 132–133
   Semi-metals 98–99
   Tarnished 115
Metals/non-metals
   Periodic Table 98–99
   properties 100–101
Microphones 166
Microscopes 157
Mineral ions, soil 29
Minerals 4, 10
Mitochondria 44–45
Mixtures, vs **Compounds** and **Elements** 90–93
Molecules 75, 82–83, 85
Motors 201
Music 160–163

N
Neutralisation 122–123
Nicotine 46–47
Nitrates 120
Non-metals/metals
   Periodic Table 98–99
   properties 100–101
Normal 142

O
Obesity 7
Optic nerve 152

Ossicles 172
Ova see **Ovum**
Ovary 53
Oviduct 53, 54–55
Ovulation 54–55
Ovum 53, 56, 58–59
Oxidation
   Combustion 124–125
   Rusting 110–111
Oxides 119, 124–125
Oxygen
   Combustion 124–125
   Photosynthesis 12–13, 16
Oxygenated blood 34–35

P
Paint colours 149
Particle accelerators 180–181
Particle theory 76–77
Penis 56–57
Periodic Table 75, 86–87
   metals/non-metals 98–99
Periods, **Menstrual cycle** 54–55
Peristalsis 18
Pharmaceutical drugs, growth/reproduction 66–67
Phloem 30–31
Photosynthesis 12–17
Pinhole cameras 154–155
Pitch, sound 161–165
Placenta 60–61
Plants
   food making 12–13
   leaf factory 12–13
   Photosynthesis 12–17
   transport systems 30–31
Plasma 36–37
Platelets 37
Precipitation 126–127
Pregnancy 59–61
Products 90–91
Proteases 21
Protein 2, 4, 8
Puberty 54, 62, 64–65
Pupil 152

R
Rainbows 146–147
Reactants 90–91
Red blood cells 36–37
Reflection
   colour 148
   light 140, 142–143

Index

Refraction 144–145
Reproduction
   disease 70
   drugs 66–67
Reproductive systems
   female 52–55
   male 56–57
Respiration
   Aerobic respiration 44–45
   cells 44–45
Respiratory system 40–43
Retina 152
Root hair cells 28
Root hairs 28
Rusting 108–113

S
Sacrificial protection 113
Saliva 18
Salts 120–123
   carbonates 128
   chlorine from common salt 105
   common salt 90, 105
   defining 119
   General equation 107, 120
   Rusting 111
   Sulfates 120, 122–123
Saturated solutions 120–121
Schistosomiasis 51
Scrotum 56–57
Section 31
Semen 56–57
Semi-metals 98–99
Sexual reproduction 52
Sexually transmitted diseases (STDs) 70
Shadows, light 140–141
Sight 152–153

Smoking 46–47, 50
Solids 76–77
   sound in 170–171
Sound 160–179
   Amplitude 164–165, 166
   dangers 173–174
   direction 172–173
   Frequency 164–165, 166
   hearing 172–173, 176–177
   in **Liquids** and **Solids** 170–171
   loudness 165, 174–175
   making 162–163
   music 160–161
   pitch 161–165
   speed measuring 168–169, 170–171
   Ultrasound 176–177
   Vibrations 162–163
Sound waves 162–167
Spectacles 156
Spectrum 146–147
Speed 182–189
   Average speed 182–185
   Distance–time graphs 188–189
   measuring 168–169, 170–171, 182–189
   sound 168–169, 170–171
   speed equation 182–185
Sperm 56–57, 58–59
Sperm duct 57
Stainless steel 113
Starches
   Carbohydrates 6–7
   digesting 21
   testing for 14
States of matter 76–77
Stents 39
Stomata 12–13

Subtractive colour 149
Sulfates 120, 122–123
Symbols 84–85

T
Tar 46–47
Tarnished 115
Telescopes 156–157
Terminal velocity 190–191
Testes (Testis) 56–57
Thalidomide 67
Trains, Maglev (magnetically levitating) trains 180
Transmit 150
   light 140–141
Transport systems
   humans 26–27, 32–33
   plants 30–31

U
Ultrasound 176–177
Umbilical cord 60
Uterus 53, 54–55

V
Vagina 53
Vascular bundles 31
Veins 26–27, 32–35
Vibrations 162–163
Villi 22–23
Vitamins 4, 10

W
Water, reactions with 132–133
White blood cells 36–37

X
Xylem 30–31

Photo acknowledgements

Alamy: Medical-on-line, p2 (top); Art Directors & TRIP, p26 (left); World History Archive, p26 (top right); Dinodia Photos, p32; Medical-on-Line, p66 (right); Boitano Photography, p67; Medical-on-Line, p70 (right); Phil Degginger, p85 (Beryllium, Silicon); Westend61 GmbH, p143; Phil Degginger, p193; **Centers for Disease Control and Prevention:** Department of Health and Human Services/National Center for Health Statistics, p63; **Corbis:** Andres Martínez Casares/epa, p23; Shawn Baldwin, p118 (right); **Fotolia:** p10; p62; p113 (bottom); p115 (right); p138; p146; p156 (top); p176 (left); **Getty Images:** Barcroft Media, p5 (top left); itsabreeze photography, p147 (top); **Ian Couchman:** p30; **iStockphoto:** p5 (right); p6 (top); p11; p12; p14; p15; p17; p26 (bottom right); p28 (top); p37; p40; p68; p77; p85 (Boron); p92; p96 (left); p98; p103 (top); p108; p109; p112; p113 (top); p114; p115 (left); p118 (left); p119; p123; p144; p147 (bottom); p149; p150; p153 (left); p155; p156 (bottom); p157; p160 (left); p161; p162; p168; p172; p173; p174; p175; p176 (right); p177; p180; p181; p182; p185; p190; p194; p195; p197; p201; **Lawrie Ryan:** p86; **Martyn Chillmaid:** p85 (Chlorine); p93; p120; **Panos Picture:** Chris Sattiberger, p2 (bottom left); **Press Association:** Matt Crossick/Empics Entertainment, p160 (right); **Rex Features:** Pacific Press Service, p5 (top right); Sipa Press, p184; **Rightlivelihood Award reps www.rightlivelihood.org:** p51; **Science Photo Library:** Dr M. A. Ansary, p2 (bottom right); David Munns, p4; Andrew Lambert Photography, p6 (bottom); p8 (bottom); BSIP VEM, p9 (right); Martyn F. Chillmaid, p20; Eye of Science, p22; Dan Guravich, p28 (bottom); Nigel Cattlin, p29; Dr Jeremy Burgess, p31 (top); Herve Conge, ISM, p31 (bottom); National Cancer Institute, p36; Simon Fraser, p39; Dr David Furness, p44; David Mack, p46; Steve Gschmeissner, p47; Corbin O'Grady, p50; Dr Yorgas Nikos, p53; Thierry Berrod, Mona Lisa Production, p59; Edelmann, p60 (top); Neil Bromhall, p60 (bottom); p70 (left); p74 (left); Sheila Terry, p74 (right); p75; Martyn F. Chillmaid, p78; Andrew McClenaghan, p80; Charles D. Winters, p85 (Phosphorus); US Navy, p96 (right); p97 (left); Gregory Tobias, p97 (right); Andrew Lambert, p103; p107; Martyn F. Chillmaid, p121; p124; Andrew Lambert, p126; p127; David Taylor, p130 (top left, top right, middle left); Andrew Lambert, p130 (middle right, bottom); p136 (left); Sheila Terry, p136 (right); Emilio Segre Visual Archives/American Institute Of Physics, p137; Los Alamos National Laboratory, p139; Giphotostock, p198; **Shutterstock:** p8 (top); p9 (left); p18; p45; p52; p64; p65; p66 (left); p71; p103 (bottom); p200; **Wikipedia:** p153 (right).